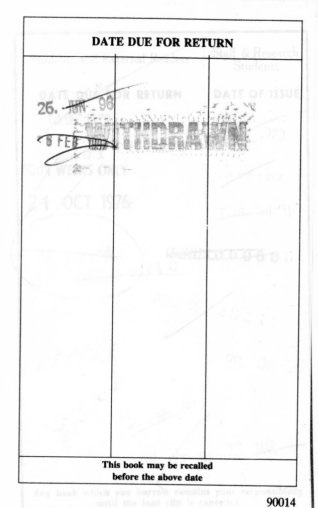

BARBAROUS
KNOWLEDGE

BOOKS BY DANIEL HOFFMAN

•

The City of Satisfactions
Form and Fable in American Fiction
A Little Geste
The Poetry of Stephen Crane
An Armada of Thirty Whales
Paul Bunyan, Last of the Frontier Demigods
American Poetry and Poetics (Editor)

•

Barbarous Knowledge

Myth in the Poetry of Yeats, Graves, and Muir

DANIEL HOFFMAN

New York
OXFORD UNIVERSITY PRESS
1967

CONTENTS

•

INTRODUCTION

•

While writing these chapters on Yeats, Graves, and Muir,
I have been well aware of a disparity in the magnitude of
my three subjects. Graves and Muir are poets of consider-
able achievement, the unity of whose work still needs
clarification; I have therefore attempted rather a full survey of their respective careers. But to do the same for
Yeats would surely be supererogatory. Indeed, it may be
wondered what need there is for yet another reading of
Yeats. The editors of the most recent collection of essays
on his work, issued at the end of the Yeats centenary year,
have observed that, 'On the one hand, his greatness is almost everywhere acknowledged; on the other, his place
in modern literature is often considered marginal, oblique.
One sometimes detects, in critical opinion, the hope that
Yeats may turn out to have been a special case . . . an
Irish case.' [1]

What has made Yeats seem marginal, special, Irish? His
repudiations of the dominant intellectual tradition of his
time, the commitment of his thought to such irrational
sources as magic and superstition, folklore, and myth, have
served to make Yeats seem to many readers a major talent
in an irrelevant context. This impression has been strength-
ened by Yeats's polemical advocacy of unfamiliar Irish
antiquities as well as contemporary Irish affairs as the sub-

[1] Denis Donoghue and J.R. Mulryne, *An Honoured Guest: New
Essays on W.B. Yeats* (London, 1965), p. v.

vii

jects of his poems and plays. Stylistically, too, he has not been in the triumphant party of twentieth-century verse; for while he resembles the symbolists in his occult search for spiritual values, he repudiated their abandonment of rational syntax and with great determination forged his style on traditional models, however much he altered those models. Calling himself a 'last Romantic,' he seems more a last Elizabethan in both his grandeur and his seemingly easy commerce with the ballad meters of folk tradition.

In each of these respects Yeats's thought and craft differ radically from those of Pound, Eliot, Stevens, and their followers. Yet it is certainly inaccurate to conclude that he stands alone in our century in either his enthusiasms or his repudiations. Robert Graves and Edwin Muir are in no sense Yeats's followers, yet they resemble him in their need to root imagination in an *a priori* structure of experience, a frame of archetypes or myth which each poet worked out for himself independently of the solutions found by the others. All three share an identification with the primitive and folk cultures of the outlands of Britain —Celtic Ireland, Wales, the Orkney Islands—which offered them alternative casts of feeling and contrasting associations to those of the modern industrial culture they abhorred. In all three, Romantic primitivism was expressed through reliance upon myths, which they either found in their inheritance or constructed from their readings to conform to the shape of their experience. And all, reflecting the Pre-Raphaelite aesthetic of their youth, began as ballad poets. In that ancient and communal poetic form they found a sense of solidarity with a community and a means of experiencing and expressing archetypal, often atavistic, emotion. Graves and Muir, like Yeats, conserve conventional syntax during a time of widespread experi-

ment, and consequently all write apart from the dominant style of modernism.

I have taken up the work of each in turn, beginning
with his roots in ballad tradition and working toward his
construction of myth. Then I discuss the other poems
which each poet's myth has made possible. I hope not to
have yoked these poets by violence together; respecting
the individual achievement of each author and of each
poem, I have tried not to subjugate their work to a structure of analysis as arbitrary as are some of their own
myths.

My interest in the grounds Yeats shares with Graves
and Muir has led me to consider in what ways he made
the local legends of a remote country into the substance of
great literature. Not only ballad tradition but folk beliefs
in the supernatural and the body of myths and legends
from the Irish Heroic Age contributed subjects to his
poems and plays. His firsthand observation, when a youth,
of the folklore beliefs in the West of Ireland comprised
his initial experience of the spiritual reality denied by the
deterministic philosophy of the day. He later fused this
knowledge with what he had learned from hermetic and
Platonic traditions. Yet, with the exception of several
articles by Colonel R. K. Alspach, critics have little heeded
Yeats's tenacity in holding and remolding the folk beliefs
with which he started out. Much though he remade his
style and changed his attitudes toward life, he did not re-
pudiate this first area of his experience and research. Instead he found ways to change his use of it to conform
with the evolution of his art and of his thought. I have
chosen the long central section of his poem 'The Tower'
to show how Yeats brought into his mature art a
cluster of conceptions and characters—beliefs and images

of the peasant poets who held them—which had gathered meanings and intensity as he enriched them over almost forty years.

Early in his career Yeats identified balladry and epic with the needs of his country's literature. My other chapters on his work take him at his word. Yeats's are the most distinguished literary ballads in the language. In the form of folk poetry most imitated by his Pre-Raphaelite elders he found the structural principle of contrast amidst simplicity, and the syntactical movement of vigorous speech in seeming song, which exactly fitted his celebrations of love, of courage, and of spiritual transcendence. Committing himself also to an epic theme, among the myths and legends from Ireland's Heroic Age he discovered (as had others before him) the tales of a putatively national hero, Cuchulain. After an early, unsuccessful attempt to write a short narrative poem on Cuchulain, Yeats took his adventures for the subject of five verse plays. Written between 1903 and 1939, these trace the hero's spiritual biography and his temporal struggles. In stagecraft and in verse form his plays differ widely, one being based on Jacobean tragedy, another on farce, and three, in varying degrees, on the Japanese Noh play to which Yeats was introduced by Ezra Pound. Yet in the development of character and action there is an impressive consistency among these works. They comprise a Romantic rendering of an epic character. As T. S. Eliot said, Yeats 'did not master this legend until he made it a vehicle for his own creation of character. . . . In becoming more Irish, not in subject-matter but in expression, he became at the same time universal.'[1]

I should not wish the reader to imagine that my Yeats

[1] *On Poetry and Poets* (New York, 1957), p. 301.

chapters offer yet another rehearsal of *A Vision*. I am aware of having gone against the grain of much recent scholarship—indeed perhaps against the poet's own emphasis—in paying such scant heed to that extraordinary synopticon of his symbols and his thought. For one thing, *A Vision* has been elucidated by interpreters abler than myself; for another, it does not, for all its inclusiveness, subsume the inherited structure of myth that Yeats found in Irish antiquity and bent to the needs of his own work while retaining its essential values and outlines. Some commentators, interpreting Yeats's poems and plays, have too mechanically applied the rigid arrangement of his theories in *A Vision;* I have run the opposite risk of resisting recourse to what he called its 'harsh geometry' to provide a gloss upon his texts. Instead I have tried to elucidate the texts themselves, concentrating, as in the heroic plays, upon the carefully wrought interrelationships of characters, scenes, and conceptions. These usually reveal a self-sufficient pattern, a completed meaning.

During Robert Graves's long career as poet, polemicist, historical novelist, and mythographer, he has himself steadfastly been the first to explain to his readers what his poems are about. Both his poems and his explanations of intention have changed over the years; and further, in publishing his own *Collected Poems* a couple of times in each decade since 1925, Graves has from volume to volume altered the corpus of surviving verse. Critical opinion came rather late to try to do justice to this prolific and obdurate author, and by that time—since the publication in 1948 of *The White Goddess*—Graves had laid down some ground rules for the reading of his career which most of his critics have all but unquestioningly followed. In addition to the useful brief surveys by Martin Seymour-

Smith and by J. M. Cohen there is Douglas Day's book, *Swifter than Reason*. Concerned to heed Graves's guidance on the phases of his career and the poet's estimate of the worth of his own work, Mr. Day finds five stages in Graves's poetic development. My concern has been with what seem to be the two main aspects of his work, and to show that they are complementary facets of a unified achievement. Graves's chief themes are the supremacy of intuition over rationality and the submission of the poet to his Muse. *The White Goddess* ostensibly provides 'an historic grammar' for the poetic treatment of the latter theme, but it in fact also dramatizes the Romantic conviction of the poet's need to experience a life of feeling rather than of thought. Graves is an extreme case of the 'dissociation of sensibility' which Eliot tried to heal. Before Graves marshaled his own intellectual armor to prove what he believes in, he had written some of the most durable verse of the century on the themes of psychomachia, the conflicts of appearance and essence, of intellection and passion, of body and spirit. His early work, written to exorcise the traumas of war, reflects an aesthetic constructed with the help of the psychoanalytic theories of the pioneer Freudian W. H. R. Rivers. Over twenty years later, in *The White Goddess*, Graves exorcised this vocabulary, substituting that of myth to express and universalize his theme. While *The White Goddess* is contrived from an astonishing range of knowledge, the effect of its rigid doctrine upon Graves's poetry seems to me to have been, after an initial liberation of imaginative energy, a narrowing of subject and a repetitiveness of treatment. Yet among what he has written on this theme are some of the most memorable love poems of our time. His prose statement remains a masterpiece as peculiar to, and as typical of, its time as is Burton's *Anat-*

omy of Melancholy. Graves's *White Goddess* is perhaps the most extreme statement of Romantic primitivism we are likely to have.

While Edwin Muir's work has been surveyed in a short biography by Peter H. Butter and in appreciative articles by R. P. Blackmur, Michael Hamburger, and Kathleen Raine, among others, there still seems need to trace the shape of his career. His verse, like that of Graves and Yeats, depends upon a structure of myth, but unlike theirs, his myth is at no point fully revealed to him. He discovers the parts of it patiently in poem after poem. His childhood in a remote folk community on the Orkney Islands was followed by disastrous experiences in the modern industrial slums of Glasgow—sufferings as bleak and hopeless as Graves's in World War I. An archetypal myth, based upon the image of man's fall and his search for the recovery of lost innocence, becomes in time Muir's own redemption from the seeming chaos of modern life. Curiously, he begins with all the ancient beliefs available to him which Yeats and Graves had in later life to excavate by toil and study; but Muir abjures these given structures for a myth of his own which reflects his Christian humanism as well as his sense that modern Scotland is one with ancient Troy, and that he, a contemporary man, relives the fable foretold in the Old Testament.

ACKNOWLEDGMENTS

The author of such a study as this one is fortunate indeed if, as was true for me, he has had many 'Hearers and hearteners of the work.' This book was made possible by a research fellowship from the American Council of Learned Societies and a sabbatical leave from Swarthmore College in 1961–62, which enabled me to spend that year in London and Dublin where much of the necessary research was done. Early drafts of several of the resulting chapters comprised the George Elliston Lectures in Poetry at the University of Cincinnati in January 1964; my thanks to Professor and Mrs. William R. Clark of that university extend also to many other members of their hospitable community. My third and fourth chapters, in earlier form, were read at the Sixth International School of Yeats Studies at Sligo, Ireland, in August 1965. Chapter Two was given as one of the Eberhart Faber Memorial Lectures at Princeton University in October of that year, in a series commemorating the centenary of Yeats's birth. The interested response of colleagues and students on these occasions has been very helpful to me.

A special debt of thanks is owed to Mrs. W. B. Yeats for her great kindness in making available to me many of the manuscripts, notebooks, and other writings of W. B. Yeats. Mr. Michael B. Yeats has given my study further welcome encouragement. To Willa Muir I am grateful for opportunities to discuss Edwin Muir's life and writings.

Many friends and colleagues have aided my work in various ways; some of my debts are mentioned in the course of the following chapters. Others who have been generous with helpful suggestions, with access to sources, and most of all with encouragement, include the late R. P. Blackmur, Seamus Delargey, Denis Donoghue, Richard Ellmann, Michael Hamburger, Mrs. Joseph Hone, Liam Miller, Helen Hennessey Vendler, and Thomas Wall. I am particularly grateful to Whitney Blake, editor at the Oxford University Press. Mary Ollmann has saved me from many errors. This work could not have been as complete without the concern of all those who offered their help; its shortcomings of course are my own responsibility.

Students in my courses and seminars in modern poetry at Swarthmore College have been a captive but by no means compliant audience for the trying out of some of the approaches and analyses in the ensuing pages. Among many others, I wish to mention Ruth Gilman, whose determination to write an honors thesis on Edwin Muir in 1959 led me to the work of a fine poet I had hitherto neglected; and Stephen Gessner and his cast for *On Baile's Strand*, whose performance in 1964 validated our conviction, as readers in a course, that Yeats's heroic plays can be dramatically effective.

I am grateful for helpful courtesies to the staffs of the libraries at Swarthmore College; the Universities of Pennsylvania; Villanova University; the Royal Borough of Kensington; the British Museum; the Irish Folklore Commission; the National Library of Ireland; the Royal Hibernian Society; Trinity College; and University College, Dublin.

Unless other acknowledgment is given, the following editions are the sources for the verse quotations in this study: *The Collected Poems of W. B. Yeats* (New York, Macmillan, 1956); *The Collected Plays of W. B. Yeats* (New York, Macmillan, 1952); for Robert Graves, *Collected Poems* (New York, Doubleday, 1961); and for Edwin Muir, *Collected Poems* (New York, Oxford, 1965).

For permission to make quotations from work protected by copyright acknowledgment is made:

To Mr. Michael B. Yeats, A. P. Watt & Son, Macmillan & Co., Ltd., and The Macmillan Company (New York), for quotations from the following works by W. B. Yeats: *The Collected Poems of W. B. Yeats; The Collected Plays of W. B. Yeats; The Autobiography of William Butler Yeats; Essays and Introductions; Mythologies; A Vision; The Letters of W. B. Yeats*, edited by Allen Wade. Excerpts from the early periodical writings of W. B. Yeats are used with the permission of Columbia University Press, which is to be the publisher of John B. P. Frayne's forthcoming edition of this material.

To Collins-Knowlton-Wing, Inc., to A. P. Watt & Son, to Doubleday & Co., Inc., and to Cassell & Co., Ltd., for permission to quote from the following works by Robert Graves: *Collected Poems* (1961), copyright © 1958, 1961 by International Authors N. V.; *Good-Bye to All That*, copyright 1929, © 1957 by International Authors N. V.; *Poems (1914–1926)*; *The Poems of Robert Graves* (Anchor Books, 1958); *Man Does, Woman Is*; *Oxford Addresses on Poetry*; to Cassell & Co., Ltd., for permission to quote from *The Crowning Privilege* by Robert Graves; to Faber & Faber Ltd. and A. P. Watt & Son for permission to quote from *The White Goddess* by Robert Graves; and to Penguin Books for permission to quote from Robert Graves's translation of *The Golden Ass*.

To Mrs. Willa Muir and The Hogarth Press, Ltd., for permission to quote from *An Autobiography* by Edwin Muir; to the foregoing and to The Viking Press, Inc., for permission to quote from *Transition* by Edwin Muir; to Oxford University Press, Inc., and Faber & Faber Ltd. for permission to quote from *Collected Poems* by Edwin Muir, copyright © 1960 by Willa Muir.

To Alfred A. Knopf, Inc. for permission to quote from *Kings, Lords & Commons* by Frank O'Connor; and to Routledge & Kegan Paul Ltd. for permission to quote from *Conflict and Dream* by W. H. R. Rivers.

I am indebted also to the editors of *The Sewanee Review*, *Shenandoah*, and *The Yale Review*, in which chapters from this book have appeared.

The greatest of my debts, which I acknowledge with most pleasure but can least adequately requite, is to my wife Elizabeth and to Kate and Macfarlane, who for five years and in three countries forebore the chaos of my research, travels, irascibility, and proofreading, because capable of believing the myth that, someday, my labors on this book would be ended.

DANIEL HOFFMAN

Swarthmore, Pennsylvania
March 1966

BARBAROUS
KNOWLEDGE

: I :

LAST ROMANTICS

On the first page of her *Collected Poems*, Miss Marianne Moore sends a steeple-jack to the top of a church spire. There he will gild

> the solid-
> pointed star, which on a steeple
> stands for hope.

From this precarious perch he looks down on the town and on the sea—the world of man and of nature, the changing and the unchanging. What else can this steeple-jack feel but that 'it is a privilege to see so / much confusion'?

Miss Moore's response to the seeming chaos of contemporary life is to take delight in its variety. The representative of her democratic sensibility is not inside the church, but atop it, where he gilds the image of a star that men have put there. He's not a hero but a humble craftsman plying his risky trade of balancing on high. This is one fine poet's way of responding to our world, and assuredly it is a delightful way. But other poets, her contemporaries and ours, have been compelled to look at 'so much confusion' from a different stance.

3

Nobody would propose to himself to 'hammer my thoughts into unity,' as Yeats did, unless he was obsessed by the disunity of his own mind. Nor would a poet be likely to insist, as does Robert Graves, that 'There is one story and one story only,' unless driven to a monistic response to life in the world of appearances where, he admonishes us, 'you say you live.' No more can Edwin Muir take a steeple-jack's delight in such confusion:

> Chaos is new,
> And has no past or future. Praise the few
> Who built in chaos our bastion and our home.

Theirs is the great dilemma of modernity to which artists of the past century have responded in many ways. Whitman overcame chaos by merging his own identity with the entire created universe. William Carlos Williams, on a lesser scale, kept this possibility alive. Ezra Pound reconstituted diction and syntax to denote the true movement of feeling, and so redeemed the style of modern poetry from an exhausted language; but the form of his thought and the constituents of his thought itself—his jumble of idiosyncratic history, eclectic myths, and crackpot economics—are mastered by or imitate the chaos to which they fail to give coherence. On the other hand Wallace Stevens, like the French symbolists, deified imagination and created an autonomous world, 'the supreme fiction,' in which, as is not the case outside it, what is created can be perfectly made. T. S. Eliot, unlike Pound, mastered the chaotic flux of modern life by concentration upon the still point around which all our turnings turn. Unlike Stevens, he could find stability within the order of Christian orthodoxy and the cultural institutions that support it. This solution made possible one of the most impressive poetic achievements of the past half-century, but it is not a solution whose basis many of his contemporaries have found it possible to share. W. H. Auden early used political and psychological theories as the secular substitutes for the religious thought toward which he was turning, and in recent years he has found existential Christianity a haven. But for a variety of historical reasons, Christianity, to most poets as to many men, has no longer seemed an adequate source of either understanding or imaginative energy since the attacks upon its historicity made by Darwin, Spencer, Huxley, and after them, indirectly by Frazer, Freud, and Jung.

Scientific materialism was felt toward the end of the nineteenth century in a most exacerbated way, even more inhibiting to spiritual experience than had been the rationalism of the Enlightenment. But if the natural and social scientists seemed to deny the absolute authority of Christian doctrine or the truth of mystical experience, these iconoclasts proved saviors in disguise for the de-faithed poets of the turn of the century and since. All whom I have mentioned write necessarily in the shadow of the golden bough, but for Yeats, Graves, and Muir the discoveries of the Cambridge anthropologists and of other similar researchers into pagan antiquity were to have special importance. Further, Yeats, working in the scientifically discredited traditions of hermetic magic, Neo-Platonism, and spiritism, would find, through these and his studies of folklore and myth, an aesthetic doctrine similar to Jung's conceptions of the archetypes. Muir and Graves would bring into their poetry and poetic theories more directly the conceptions of modern psychology; each was psychoanalyzed early in his career, the first by a Jungian analyst, the latter by one of Freud's major disciples.

'The fundamental reason for the mythological barrenness of the eighteenth century,' writes Douglas Bush, 'was the dominance of rationalism and realism, and the fundamental impulse of the mythological renascence was contained in the romantic protest against a mechanical world and mechanical verse stripped, as it seemed, of imagination and emotion, of beauty and mystery.' [1] A century later the universe seemed still more mechanistic, and everywhere in the English-speaking world save in the Celtic outlands mythology had receded still further from common experience. The myths to which the first Romantics turned were those of Greece and Rome, but by Yeats's time these had been all but voided of imaginative energy by a hundred years of elaboration. Such mythic scenes as had inspired an ode by Keats had become the commonplace designs on wallpaper. Myth once more could bring emotion, truth, and mystery into literature, but it must be myth made new. Although no mythologist or poet could avoid his classical heritage, or would want to, Yeats and Graves had a given advantage of working also from within an unfamiliar though analogous mythical tradition, that of Celtic pagandom. Edwin Muir's advantage was to have been born into a society where that pantheon was still remembered with awe.

It has been maintained by one eminent writer that

A poet in our time is a semi-barbarian in a civilised community. He lives in the days that are past. His ideas, thoughts, feelings, associations, are all with barbarous manners, obsolete customs, and exploded superstitions. The march of his intellect is like that of a crab, backward. The brighter the light diffused around him by the progress of reason, the thicker is the darkness of antiquated barba-

[1] *Mythology and the Romantic Tradition in English Poetry* (Cambridge, Mass., 1937), p. 526.

rism in which he buries himself like a mole, to throw up
the barren hillocks of his Cimmerian labors.

This acerb conceit against the poetry of myth is by
Thomas Love Peacock, writing in 1820 of the first, not the
last, Romantics. No wonder Shelley wrote his *Defence of
Poetry* as a rejoinder. It would seem, from the concerns of
the three poets before us, that Peacock's aim was true. And
yet, although poets a hundred years later still appear as
'semi-barbarian in a civilised community,' working not by
the light of reason but under the barbarous manners and
exploded superstitions of the past, these very characteristics
mark them as poets of the contemporary world. Now that
science and rationalism are indeed the reigning beacons of
the material world, the cost to the imagination of such
guidance has been the loss of sacred objects, sacred emotions, sacred mysteries. Whatever the barbarism of the past,
the 'progress of reason' seems to lead relentlessly toward
the rule of materialism. To these poets the qualities of modern life appeared alien. Since they regarded themselves not
as English but as Irish, Welsh, and Scots, the scientific rationalism and materialism of their times seemed to typify
the dominant Englishness of contemporary Britain. From
his home on the Celtic fringes of the islands, each poet
drew imaginative sustenance for the myth by which he redeemed the soul from its subjugation to a mechanistic
world.

II

When Edwin Muir was alive his poems seemed closer to
the Victorian verse most poets were trying to avoid writing. In the past ten years or so an increasing number of
readers have found the rewards that await them behind the

sometimes old-fashioned surface of his language. His characteristic gesture appears in this posthumously published
lyric, called 'The Poet':

> And in bewilderment
> My tongue shall tell
> What mind had never meant
> Nor memory stored.
> In such bewilderment
> Love's parable
> Into the world was sent
> To stammer its word.
>
> What I shall never know
> I must make known.
> Where traveller never went
> Is my domain.
> Dear disembodiment
> Through which is shown
> The shapes that come and go
> And turn again.
>
> Heaven-sent perplexity—
> If thought should thieve
> One word of the mystery
> All would be wrong.
> Most faithful fantasy
> That can believe
> Its immortality
> And make a song.

What makes this so poignant is the note of bewilderment
in certainty, of assurance in perplexity. Muir does not
speak from a platform of revealed dogma, as Yeats so often
seems to; nor is he given to Graves's vatic possession of exclusive truths. Muir speaks 'in bewilderment,' 'stammers'

the word of the transfiguration of love. Almost hidden in this little poem are some of the images that recur in many of his others: the poet as a seeker and a wanderer, finding an unanticipated place of revelation—a place which proves to be situated on the mainroads of common experience, repeated in each of our lives, available to all. The love which Muir invokes is not at all the desperate immolation of Graves, but something close to Christian compassion. It includes both a touching and faithful tenderness for his wife and a general compassion for mankind. But like Graves he can say, 'If thought should thieve / One word of the mystery / All would be wrong.' The truth Muir seeks in bewilderment and discovers through 'Heaven-sent perplexity' is not an intellectual construct, nor is it rationally discernible. This 'Most faithful fantasy' is an intuitive apprehension of the unity of life, the unity within one's own life of its beginning and its end, the identity of one's own life with the general experience of the race.

Discovering that unity, Muir renders it in a myth of his own devising. The materials from which he devised it are native, Biblical, and classical. As a later chapter will show, Muir's archetypal experiences emerge from his childhood on the remote Orkney islands, and take historical shape in the tale of Troy as well as in the contemporary lives of men. Scotland is Muir's homeland, and while in his poems he sees himself both out of time and as reliving the Trojan and Biblical fables, he lives also his individual story, as a Scot in twentieth-century Europe. Muir is among the last poets to whom the medieval sense of Christendom as a unified culture has been possible. Yet he has seen more directly than most the chaos of our time—its political dangers as well as its spiritual dissolution; for, as director of the British Council in Prague, he saw the Communist *coup d'état* in

Czechoslovakia and the ensuing subjugation of a people whose tough integrity he had known and admired.

No less than for Yeats or Graves, the transcendence of circumstance which Edwin Muir finds to be man's salvation cannot be discovered by the conscious will or mind. It is the pattern which gradually becomes revealed to him throughout his life as he lives it. The first edition of Muir's autobiography was titled *The Story and the Fable*, the story being the particular vicissitudes of one man's life, the fable his recognition of the eternal rhythms underlying apparent random change. Although the materials of this fable are evident in myth, they may come to the individual in dreams. In the 1920's Muir was treated for severe neurosis —as was Robert Graves, then suffering from another blight of the modern world, a soldier's combat fatigue. In quite different ways the experience of psychoanalysis contributed to the imaginative comprehension of life by both of these poets and helped to make their fulfillments possible.

I I I

Edwin Muir's characteristic gesture is the patient exploration of his own experience, to discover his fable in his story. Robert Graves's unmistakable gesture is evident in the concluding lines of his poem 'The Second-Fated':

> Fortune enrolled me among the second-fated
> Who have read their own obituaries in *The Times* . . .

Although this poem was written in 1958 the experience occurred in World War I, when Captain Graves was reported dead of wounds. He did not know it then, but this suffering in war was to mark his life forever after. Now,

forty years later, he sees himself as having descended into
the underworld of the dead—and come back, with supernatural knowledge and the gift of song. But in Graves's
case the Orphic lyre is pitched in a wry key:

> Fortune enrolled me among the second-fated
> Who have read their own obituaries in *The Times*,
> Have heard 'Where, death, thy sting? Where, grave, thy
>   victory?'
> Intoned with unction over their still clay,
> Have seen two parallel red-ink lines drawn
> Under their manic-depressive bank accounts,
> And are therefore strictly forbidden to walk in grave-yards
> Lest they scandalise the sexton and his bride.
>
> We, to be plain with you, taking advantage
> Of a brief demise, visited first the Pit,
> A library of shades, completed characters;
> And next the silver-bright Hyperborean Queendom,
> Basking under the sceptre of Guess Whom?
> Where pure souls matrilineally foregather.
> We were then shot through by merciful lunar shafts
> Until hearts tingled, heads sang, and praises flowed;
> And learned to scorn your factitious universe
> Ruled by death which we had flouted;
> Acknowledging only that from the Dove's egg hatched
> Before aught was, but wind—unpredictable
> As our second birth would be, or our second love:
> A moon-warmed world of discontinuance.

What is one to make of 'Hyperborean Queendom,' 'the
sceptre of Guess Whom'? Where do 'pure souls matri-
lineally foregather'? Even the reader uninitiated to Graves's
particular view of myth might recognize that 'merciful
lunar shafts' suggests the arrows or javelins of the moon
goddess, be her name Diana, Astarte, Ishtar, or one

still less familiar. Surely 'hearts tingled' and 'heads sang' particularly at the rending of Orpheus by the drunken maenads, who flung his head, still singing, into the river Hebrus, from which his scattered body was gathered by the Muses and buried near Olympus. If these suggestions really are inferences useful to our reading of the poem, let us recall Orpheus' double character as both an analogue of Dionysus, the sacrificed incarnate god, and the founder of a religious sect of purificatory and expiatory rites and mysteries. Orpheus is especially appropriate to Graves not only because of these traditions, relevant as they will prove to be, but also through the peculiar circumstances of his suffering and subsequent deification; for Orpheus' fate resulted from his unswerving fealty beyond death to his lover. Eurydice is usually thought of as merely a mortal woman who was loved by a cultic hero. But to Graves it is Eurydice, not Orpheus, who is the central force in his retelling of the story and the object of his veneration. For the White Goddess manifests herself to each poet in the momentary form of the woman whom he is fated to serve. Fated to serve, and second-fated to celebrate, at whatever dire cost to himself.

'The Second-Fated' brings into this knot of mythic meanings yet another theme of Graves's work, the inadequacy of reason to disclose the ultimate truths of life. The poet, granted that special wisdom which is the Muse's only reward for his voluntary sufferings, has 'learned to scorn your factitious universe / Ruled by death which we had flouted.' Not until after Graves had defined for himself the tradition of the White Goddess did this theme coalesce with the worship of the Muse in his poems. From the beginning, however, Graves has been a celebrant of 'Love Without Hope,' the title of a poem written in 1925.

Although the mythical references in 'The Second-Fated' are of Greek provenience, Graves discovered the myth of the White Goddess in both Mediterranean and Celtic sources. In fact, some of his sources are very much the same as Yeats's, and what Graves chooses from Greek religion and from Celtic pagandom is similar to Yeats's choice from the same bodies of myth and romance. At some points they extract analogous myths from the same materials.

This is not surprising, for one might expect Graves to draw upon the Irish past. After all, his father, Albert Percival Graves, was a D. Litt. from Trinity College, Dublin, and a fluent translator of much of the Irish poetry in which Yeats was getting literary people to take an interest toward the turn of the century. Yet it was exactly because of his father's professional identification with Irish letters that Robert Graves at first spurned these materials so close at hand, although he felt deeply the need of such a Celtic heritage with its emphasis upon magic, poetic power, and sacred mysteries. Instead he looked to Wales, where, as he has said, he found a spiritual home: one in which the legendary bases of poetry were almost identical with those in Ireland, yet had been pre-empted by no important poet since Daffyd ap Gwyllam in the fourteenth century and, more importantly perhaps, by no member of his family before him.

Graves's service with a Welsh regiment in the First World War became a crucial event in his imaginative life, as we have seen, and had much to do with his later immersion in the sources of *The Mabinogion*. His involvement with modernity may be said to begin—and to end—with his soldiering in the Royal Welch Fusiliers. In his verse as in his autobiography and discursive prose he relives again and again that trauma and its consequences. When modern

Europe passed from the seeming stability of the Edwardian era—to Graves this meant a Victorian household with a rather pompous Papa, an Edwardian school where old boys bullied and young boys fagged in a hierarchy of caste that seemed destined to outlast the Empire—when all this was succeeded by the dehumanization of trench warfare, then the individual was thrown back upon his atavistic resources for his very survival, for courage, for a rebirth of feeling after the numbness of pain. He is alone on the bedrock of his own humanity, whatever that may prove to be, for 'civilization' has unwound its garments and disclosed the bones. Since the war, Graves has in a sense had nothing further to do with society. He retired from modernity to the most backward corner of Europe, Majorca, where the folk-life was still at a stage like that of the Orkneys when Muir was born. There Graves wrote much poetry, polemical criticism, and historical fiction, and perfected his researches into a form of primitive religion which he maintains to be the source and true subject of all that is permanently valuable in poetry.

As was true before him of Yeats, Robert Graves was driven to construct a systematic myth of his own, one as arcane and extraordinary as that in Yeats's book *A Vision*. Both poets are extremely eclectic thinkers, and from the standpoint of contemporary scholarship their intellectual constructs seem irresponsible, although from their standpoint contemporary scholarship merely borrows scientificism to proclaim relative truths as absolutes. Both poets adopted the deterministic rationalism of the age they shun, and use it to confect an individual synthesis of the past, partly on intuitive grounds but with almost complete coherence according to their own premises. They needed the assurance behind their imaginations of having come to

terms intellectually with their situation. Like Blake, each
had to make for himself the usable tradition that his culture had failed fully to provide. What is proposed in
Graves's *The White Goddess* does not, like Yeats's system,
come disguised as a philosophy of history, but it does demand a revision of our understanding of the past. For
Graves, the primal emotions of love, fear, and worship are
the vital centers of human experience. He finds the divine
nexus of life in the mythic figure of the Muse, derived from
the earliest matriarchal religion. In his best-known poem he
claims 'There is one story and one story only'—her propitiation, her exactions, her celebrant's ecstasy and doom. She
must appear to the poet as a personal muse: woman as mystery, ecstasy, the source of life, fruition, and death.
Graves's mythographic arguments are a mare's nest to
untangle. While he proclaims a monomyth at the same time
that he proposes ritual origins and reads myths as history,
his theory is yet more plausible than may at first appear. As
a psychological exploration of the creative impulse it is invaluable. Without his ever having proposed a doctrine
analogous to Yeats's psychology of masks, Graves too has
split his personality into fragmented opposites. He is both
Methodical Thinker and Romantic Primitivist, as in his
verse he is both a formalist and an ecstatic. It is the interplay of these personae in his writings which makes them at
once so baffling and so compelling.

Graves, too, is a modern poet who refuses to belong to
the modernist movement. Although he welcomed the work
of Cummings and John Crowe Ransom, and was for years
associated intimately with another ex-Fugitive poet, Laura
Riding, it is the classicism of the Fugitives, and their and
Cummings's emotional honesty to which he was drawn, not
the technical experimentation of modernists like Eliot, or

Pound (whose work he particularly detests). Indeed, Graves scorns as academic any poetry which is more concerned with style (be it traditional or experimental) than with saying the honest truth. His own style assimilates wit to reverence, a prose-textured line to lyric emotion, a kind of un-music to the occasions of song. His ironic tone accords with his sense that all pleasure is haunted and that man's fate is to love gratefully one whose disdain he is foredoomed to suffer. In his poetry, as in *The White Goddess* and *The Greek Myths*, his reason and his sensibility are in fruitful conflict.

I V

For Yeats, this is the text I choose for theme:

> We were the last romantics—chose for theme
> Traditional sanctity and loveliness;
> Whatever's written in what poets name
> The book of the people; whatever most can bless
> The mind of man or elevate a rhyme;
> But all is changed, that high horse riderless,
> Though mounted in that saddle Homer rode
> Where the swan drifts upon a darkening flood.

In this last stanza of 'Coole Park and Ballylee, 1931,' Yeats pays graceful tribute to his friend and patroness Lady Gregory, recalling the plays and stories they had written, the folktales collected, together. These lines of tribute hold a cluster of his governing themes. It is not surprising that the stanza, like his themes—and like his mind—should hold in taut balance several pairs of images opposed in their implications but here so harmonized by verbal patterning and syntactical control as to be wrought into unity.

Our view of the Romantics does not generally bring to

mind, as *their* theme, 'traditional sanctity and loveliness.' We think of Wordsworth's discovery of innate powers and blessings in his own mind, and his radical search for purity of diction based on common speech. Or again of Coleridge's explorations of the 'caverns measureless to man,' of trackless seas on which the fated Mariner suffered. Their early social energies were revolutionary and would have torn down traditional sanctities. Equally revolutionary were Shelley and Blake, but their Platonism and symbolic contrarieties do bring us closer to Yeats. Yet how reconcile Platonism with 'Whatever's written in what poets name / The book of the people'? And again, in Yeats's stanza 'the book of the people' is syntactically equated with 'whatever most can bless / The mind of man . . .' as though the wisdom of the fireside tale conferred a knowledge as valuable as Plato's of transcendent things. Further, the line goes on, '. . . or elevate a rhyme,'—as though *that* were of equal value to whatever most could bless the human mind.

But, Yeats continues, 'all is changed, that high horse riderless.' This returns us to the tone of the lamentation in the first line, 'We were the *last* romantics . . .' and completes the poem with the double image of Pegasus riderless although Homer rode him 'Where the swan drifts upon a darkening flood.'

Since Yeats's poems are, to use one of his favorite terms, so woven of the same threads,[1] it is helpful to trace a thread from one poem to another and sometimes through his prose writings. The swan upon the darkening flood must allude to that passage in 'Nineteen Hundred and Nineteen' written ten years earlier,

> Some moralist or mythological poet
> Compares the solitary soul to a swan . . .

[1] Richard Ellmann discusses this analogy in *The Identity of Yeats* (New York, 1954), pp. 20 ff.

The comparison occurs in a familiar passage from *Prometheus Unbound,*

> My soul is an enchanted boat
> Which like a sleeping swan doth float . . .

And so the ghost of Shelley in the final line revives the burden of 'last romantics' in the first line of the stanza. Nor is it inappropriate to remember that it was as a swan that Jove covered Leda, and from their union was born Helen of Troy whose beauty brought into being all of Homer's song. And Yeats's song, like Homer's, is epic by design. The parallel may seem inexact, but we shall see that in a very literal sense Yeats considered his themes analogous to those of the blind poet, finding the ancient religion and heroic tales of Ireland identical with those of Greece, and hoping to express the character of his country as Homer had done for his. Yeats did desire to ride in that empty saddle where Homer rode.

There is both poignancy and heroic abandon in this role. To follow the passage of the soul upon the darkening flood—the sea, of course, is a traditional image of both birth and death, as the floating bird is symbolic of a questing voyager—we must, with Yeats, discover what unites man's highest blessings with his humblest ways. And one final contradiction, if it is a contradiction: he who would read the people's book says so in a poem written to an aristocratic patroness, celebrating the loveliness of her great house and the cultural life her hospitality made possible there. What makes inevitable for Yeats the reconciliation of these contraries is the fact that that great house was Irish. In Ireland, so Yeats would persuade us, the unification of culture was still possible, as was the unity of mind. He could believe, and make us accept his belief in, both, but only by a heroic intellectual endeavor a part of which the next few chapters will retrace.

For Yeats—for all three poets, as for most modern artists, indeed for modern man—contemporary reality is a field of painful action, of sufferings whose meanings are not given. Modernity means social disintegration, undirected movement away from traditional sanctities and ancestral solace. Christianity once had held the natural, social, and moral worlds together in a unity against which man's vicissitudes were measured. The withering of religious assurance left it to the individual imagination to reconstitute those unities of growth, of feeling, of culture, of being, which history would seem to deny it. Yeats's attempt is, of course, best understood in the context of the symbolist movement, a broad effort to recapture the primacy of the spiritual and imaginative powers latent in our lives.

By its very nature such an enterprise was bound to turn toward intellectual traditions that had been driven underground by two and a half materialistic centuries. Neo-Platonic philosophy had been dethroned by the mathematical certainties of Descartes; alchemy had been discredited as a legitimate inquiry by chemistry since Lavoisier; and since Tycho Brahe and the telescope, astrology had been driven into the back rooms of charlatanry and the tents of gypsy fortune-tellers. Magic, with its twenty centuries of practice, was disowned. It was these outlandish nonsciences that the symbolists cultivated. What bound them together was a common conviction of correspondences between the properties of elements, between matter and spirit, between the movements of the heavens and the fortunes of men. Holding spirit to be the paramount property of life, and assuming a corollary belief in the transmigration of souls, the real power a wise man seeks is not the manipulation of transitory things but the control of spirit, emanating through time and across the boundaries of being.

Symbolist art from Blake to Redon, Maeterlinck, and Mallarmé is explicable in terms of such an anti-intellectual intellectual history. But while Yeats's interests in magic, alchemy, astrology, and the writings of Thomas Taylor and Plotinus place him in this recognizable tradition, he had another and unusual string upon his Irish harp. To be a young man in the 1880's and 1890's was, in Ireland, to move in the midst of an unexampled interest in both the legendary literature of the remote Irish past and the recovery from the peasantry of folktales and beliefs that had been handed down unchanged since before the coming of Saint Patrick. These materials offered heroic myths, local wonders, and mysteries of the supernatural. Here was a vocabulary unlike the jaded terms of the outworn conventional belief, and a spiritual heritage based on doctrines of correspondence which were similar (or could be thought to be so) to those of the Hermetic scholarly tradition. For Irish literature the mingling of these strains was an inescapable destiny. For half a century, Irish antiquarians had been translating their medieval manuscripts into verse and prose. Yeats early came on the work of Sir Samuel Ferguson, a jurist, archaeologist, translator from the Gaelic and an energetic though not very talented poet in the outworn style of Pope's *Iliad*. Similar work had been put into prose during Yeats's boyhood by Standish O'Grady, whose versions of the Irish heroic tales presented Cuchulain as a Celtic Achilles. Later, Lady Gregory would collate these with many other translations and retell the tales in the lilting peasant speech that is her hallmark in books to which

Yeats wrote prefaces; her versions are the immediate sources of his plays about Cuchulain.

When Yeats began to write, the local-color movement, that world-wide phenomenon of mid-nineteenth-century Romanticism, was taking a particular form in Ireland. The movement was in part a reaction against Enlightenment critical conceptions of literature as based upon general laws; local-color writing celebrated the individualities of particular places, and gloried in whatever dialectal speech or surviving antiquities of custom or belief could be offered to prove the uniqueness of life in a given locality. Such a course, while risking quaintness, could put into a writer's hands ancient traditions as yet untouched by the mechanical forces of change since the Industrial Revolution. But in Ireland the impetus toward the literary uses of such material was not only from Romantic nostalgia. From the beginning, the local-color movement had an overt political significance. John O'Leary, a broad-spirited and humane leader of the Fenian movement and Yeats's early mentor, had counseled, as part of his campaign to forge among his countrymen a sense of spiritual nationality, the study of 'what the learned call folklore.' He urged his hearers and readers to 'write down, even in the baldest form, but as accurately as you can,' the fairy stories known to them. Moving from folklore to mythological history, O'Leary went on to speak of Irish poetry—Thomas Davis, James Clarence Mangan, the poets of the mid-century Young Ireland nationalistic movement, but he had the courage to admit, 'It is one of among the many misfortunes of Ireland that she has never yet produced a great poet.' [1] One young man who followed O'Leary's advice became the foremost folk-

[1] *What Every Irishman Should Know* (Cork, 1886), pp. 4–7.

lorist of his country, and the president of the Irish Republic, Douglas Hyde. Another joined the study of folklore with poetic genius. Seven years after O'Leary's lecture, Yeats took up the same theme:

> I affirm that we are a young nation with unexhausted material lying within us in our still unexpressed national character . . . and behind us in our multitude of legends. Look at our literature and you will see that we are still in our epic or ballad period. All that is greatest in that literature is based upon legend—upon those tales which are made by no one man, but by the nation itself through a slow process of modification and adaptation, to express its loves and hates. . . . Our best writers, De Vere, Ferguson, Allingham, Mangan, Davis, O'Grady, are all either epic writers or ballad writers, and all base their greatest works . . . upon legends and upon the fortunes of the nation.[1]

Legend, epic, and ballad from the first represented to Yeats the Matter of Ireland. A great career had its beginnings in this conviction, for Yeats himself became the poet for whose advent John O'Leary had called, who would base his work upon the legends of the nation, taking theme and form suggested by the ballads and epics of the past. Yeats, like Douglas Hyde, set himself to the study of country folklore, in which, as we shall see, he found ancient and plebeian validation of his own belief in the reality of the soul.

But in the same year as his lecture 'Nationality and Literature,' Yeats wrote a poem that gives another version of his intentions. Neither ballad nor epic, it was addressed 'To Ireland in the Coming Times.' Now he would be counted a 'true brother' of those who 'sang to sweeten Ireland's

---

[1] 'Nationality and Literature,' *United Ireland* (Dublin), 27 May 1893, p. 2.

wrong.' But he insists that his invocation of the Rosicrucian
symbol of the Rose is as much a part of Ireland's spiritual
heritage as are the other strains he is about to mention:

> Nor may I less be counted one
> With Davis, Mangan, Ferguson . . .

because, he says, 'My rhymes more than their rhyming tell'
of 'elemental creatures' which, when the body sleeps, bring
him eternal truths from 'unmeasured mind.' Yeats ends this
apostrophe to an imagined future Ireland with the cry,

> Ah, faeries, dancing under the moon,
> A Druid land, a Druid tune!

Only Yeats's lulling tetrameter couplets hold together the
mystical Rose, the 'rhyming' of Ireland's earlier patriot
poets, theosophic elementals, dancing faeries, and Druids.
These would seem to be five discrete categories of spiritual,
historical, and literary experiences. But it is by no mere
caprice that Yeats makes these not only comparable but interchangeable symbols. Already he has put his imagination
in touch with, and in fealty to, 'unmeasured mind,' what
the seventeenth-century Neo-Platonist Henry More
called, in a term Yeats would make his own, the *Anima
Mundi*.

It would take Yeats half a lifetime to hammer these
thoughts into unity. He made a mythic system of his
knowledge in *A Vision*, that willful construction forcing
into one large pattern the world's history, the divided personality, and the progress of the soul. No doubt those
exegetes are right who advise that this is primarily an aesthetic and a psychological testament, not a philosophy of
history.[1] Because *A Vision* attempts to project a mythic

---

[1] This point is made with particular strength by Helen Hennessey,
Vendler in *Yeats's Vision and the Later Plays* (Cambridge, Mass., 1963).

structure upon history, however, it does not contain one major element of mythical—and thus ahistorical—thought which is prominent in his art from his beginnings to the end. *A Vision* tells us nothing of Irish folklore or legend, although Yeats continued to write on themes from these mythologies until the last day of his life. The penultimate poem in *Last Poems* is based on a book of Irish folklore by Oscar Wilde's mother that Yeats had reviewed forty years before, underlining the relevant passage,[1] and his final play is *The Death of Cuchulain*. These works have little to do with the machinery of *A Vision*, although that intellectual framework can be invoked to interpret them. I propose, however, to trace the development of certain of Yeats's poems and plays that are based on his immersion in and manipulation of the Matter of Ireland. In his eclectic fashion he would fuse his later researches into magic and spiritism together with his own experience of folk belief, and join to these his readings in Irish epic literature and mythographic studies of Irish pagandom. In time he would make an artistically successful fusion of the elements that seemed so arbitrarily yoked together in 'To Ireland in the Coming Times.' His grounding in native myth and folklore is of first significance in understanding the way he handles character and theme, while his lifelong preoccupation with ballad form and with epic action seems likewise based upon his early attitude toward those Irish materials he determined to make his own.

[1] The poem is 'The Black Tower.' Yeats's use in it of Lady Wilde's *Ancient Cures, Charms & Usages of Ireland* is discussed by Jon Stallworthy in *Between the Lines* (Oxford, 1963), pp. 228-9.

One: William Butler Yeats

: 2 :

'*I am of Ireland*': YEATS THE BALLAD POET

Yeats was by destiny a ballad poet. Between the four ballads in *Crossways* and the score in *Last Poems* fifty years later he mastered a craft and a form, and he used its resources to express a range of emotions in speech at once passionate, musical, and direct. He could write

> 'O but I saw a solemn sight,'
> *Said the rambling, shambling, travelling man*

as well as

> Come gather round me, players all:
> Come praise Nineteen-Sixteen

and

> What shall I do for pretty girls
> Now my old bawd is dead?

These are the three most important themes—transfiguration, heroism, and love—which Yeats took from Irish folklore and from balladry. He fused them together in ways unmistakably his own.

But why would Yeats select the ballad as a form to cultivate with special pertinacity? One might think the sonnet a more attractive choice to a young poet in the 1880's, who would have the examples of Wordsworth, Keats, and Shelley as well as those of the eminent Renaissance and Victorian poets before him. Yet, apart from 'Leda and the Swan,' Yeats has little to do with the sonnet form. The ballad, however, had also a literary ancestry going back to both the early Romantics and the Renaissance, and among the Pre-Raphaelites of Yeats's youth the form had distinguished contemporary practitioners. And there were still more compelling reasons for Yeats's life-long engagement with balladry—reasons having to do with his nationalism, his search for spiritual certitude, and his poetics. In each of these concerns, ballad tradition offered him special advantages.

Further, for Yeats the writing of ballads was inextricable from his conception of the character of the ballad poet. This in turn derived from the artistic and spiritual traditions which the peasant ballad poet, as Yeats imagined him, conserved and helped to create. For Yeats's image of the ballad poet is that of a true spokesman of the spiritual inheritance of his people. Thus the ballad form implies the life of the poet who uses it, and his character in turn conserves the supernatural folklore of the peasantry. The ballad poet is a bard revered by the commoners and nourished by the nobility, a personage of consequence in his society. Indeed, his prestige and power betoken a society in which peasant, poet, and noble are united in the contemplation of the same thoughts and sing them in the same songs. And, as Yeats wrote in *Irish Fairy and Folk Tales*, 'Poetry in Ireland has always been mysteriously connected with magic.' The ballad poet's powers are indeed magical, granted by the spirits of the gods and the dead.

The form of the ballads, as well as their content and

character, offered special qualities to Yeats, once he understood the genius of that form. Balladry provided a combination of narrative with lyrical emotion: not only a stanzaic form, a way of telling a tale in verse, but a syntax passionate, direct, and musical. Yeats's earliest ballads, as we shall see, are based upon poor models and do not embody a functional mastery of the form. It took Yeats years to achieve that mastery; not until his own sensibility had outgrown the evasions of his youthful verse could he profit from the simple power or the ribald energies of some of the best of the ballads in folk tradition.

II

The childhood of a poet will, if he is lucky, fill his memory with a thesaurus of experience and impressions from which in maturity he may draw succor as well as symbols. Yeats was fortunate to have passed much of his impressionable boyhood in the West of Ireland among country people as yet untouched by the economic or intellectual dislocations which had elsewhere swept away that old agrarian order since the Industrial Revolution. The folk beliefs of the Irish countrymen conserved a mythology older than Christianity. The boy who heard their tales of faery from his mother and from old servants, and then wandered among the thatched cottages and out on the strands and mountains near Ballisodare and Rosses Point, studded with cairns and dolmens, remembered for a lifetime their folk beliefs as among his earliest experiences of the existence of a spiritual world. He had himself been touched by beliefs and experiences as old as the memory of man. Anti-rationalist though he was, Yeats yet felt compelled to study and to systematize the evidence that disproved the reign of scientific materialism. And so he projected a scholarly analysis of Irish fairy lore, and published several articles based upon his many years of folklore collecting.[1] In one of these he says,

> None among people visiting Ireland, and few among the people living in Ireland, except peasants, understand that that the peasants believe in their ancient gods, and that to them, as to their forebears, everything is inhabited and mysterious. The gods gather in raths or forts, and about the twisted thorn trees, and appear in many shapes, now little and grotesque, now tall, fairhaired and noble, and seem busy and real in the world, like the people in the markets or at the crossroads. The peasants remember their old names, the *sheagh sidhe*, though they fear mostly to call them by any name lest they be angry, unless it be by some vague words, 'the gentry,' or 'the royal gentry,' or 'the army,' or 'the spirits,' or 'the others,' as the Greek peasant calls his Nereids; and they believe after twelve Christian centuries, that the most and best of their dead are among them.[2]

This is the lore that Yeats associates with the peasants and with the peasant poets whose ballads he imitated and whose character he in time interpreted in the *personae* of his poems. For Yeats must participate in that unity of spirit which was once a national property but today is the special knowledge of only two classes in society. The peasant, still living in the midst of the Sidhe, crosses easily the borders

[1] This he promised in the preface to the 1902 edition of *The Celtic Twilight*, but the book was never published. Several fugitive pieces from which I quote in these chapters, published between 1898 and 1902, would, I think, have been parts of this study, abandoned after Maud Gonne's marriage in 1904. Then, wrote Yeats, 'I have no happiness in dreaming of Brycelinde. . . Nor lands that seem too dim to be burdens on the heart' ('Under the Moon'). Maud Gonne had collaborated in his studies of Celtic myth. Yeats later used some of this folklore material from the 1890's in his notes and essays in Lady Gregory's *Visions and Beliefs*.

[2] 'The Prisoners of the Gods,' *Nineteenth Century* (Jan. 1898), p. 91.

between this world and the next. And the occult philosopher, the student of magic, theosophy, and astrology, can also summon up the spirits, and cross through the Gates of Death, and return into our life.

Because Yeats presents us with so many arcane mysteries and speaks of his having achieved a 'mysterious wisdom won by toil,' his exegetes have naturally enough taken the Neo-Platonist and student of occultism to be the true Yeats. They have dismissed the dreamy Pre-Raphaelite who actually did listen to the legends and beliefs of cottagers and fishermen, and have thought Yeats's long apprenticeship to the study of Irish legend and folklore merely a sentimental dalliance in the Celtic Twilight, irrelevant to the emergence of his grand design. Yet at the end of his life Yeats chose for publication under the title *Mythologies* his early folklore sketches, his *Stories of Red Hanrahan* (based on the life of a ballad poet), and his occult fiction, as though to reassert their underlying relevance and unity.

These interests in folk religion and occultism separated Yeats from the middle-class culture of his time. In a brilliant little book, *The Romantic Image*, Frank Kermode offers Yeats to exemplify the alienation from life of the symbolist artist. And one of Yeats's chief successors as a poet in Ireland, Patrick Kavanaugh, has proclaimed that Yeats's true spiritual home was not Ireland at all but the Rhymers' Club in London, that group of doomed and decadent poets of the 1890's so poignantly described in his *Autobiographies*.[1] Professor T. R. Henn is perhaps closest to the mark in the title of his magisterial book on Yeats, *The Lonely Tower*.

Yeats's imaginative relationship to his culture was a dou-

[1] Kavanaugh, 'William Butler Yeats,' *Kilkenny Magazine* (Spring 1962), No. 6, pp. 25-8.

ble one, both as insider and as outsider. Indeed he typifies
the symbolist's alienation from society, yet sees himself as
more truly representing the traditions of the society from
which he separates himself than does the predominant middle class that has lost contact with both the high tradition
and the low. 'I declare this tower is my symbol,' he wrote
in 'Blood and the Moon,' inhabiting his tower at Ballylee
with the ghosts of Swift and Goldsmith, Berkeley and Burke.
Yet their

> . . . bloody, arrogant power
> Rose out of the race
> Uttering, mastering it,
> Rose like these walls from these
> Storm-beaten cottages—

Unity of culture seems impossible in a time 'Half dead at
the top.' But unity of spirit can be achieved as well by men
who live in 'storm-beaten cottages' as by those in the
tower, and much better than by any who drift in the undirected, masterless society of our time. If we attend to the
unity of spiritual experience we find that Yeats insists upon
the identity of his purposes with those of the lowliest people in the land, just as he wrote ballads he hoped would be
sung at crossroads in ignorance of his authorship, but published them in limited editions on fine rag paper. He would
be at once a member of an elite and have communion with
the people. For symbolist poet and peasant, though they
might speak a different vocabulary, shared the same beliefs.
And as a ballad writer he could make them sing like songs.

From William Morris and Rossetti to Masefield and
Alfred Noyes, the conception of a ballad-singing populace
and the ballad poet they would honor seemed a Pre-
Raphaelite fantasy. No doubt Yeats heard it at first from

Morris himself during the years after 1887 when he often visited Morris's atelier in Hammersmith, where his sisters were learning to weave tapestries and run a hand-press. Unlike his English contemporaries, however, whose experience of balladry was wholly literary and antiquarian, Yeats could recognize in this chapter of the Pre-Raphaelite gospel a description of actual contemporary life he had known.

One place where he had known that life was in the village of Ballisodare, just south of Sligo, where his great-uncle William Middleton had a home ('Avena House') and his grandfather Pollexfen owned the flour mill which is still the only industry in the community. There he met Paddy Flynn, his chief informant for the folklore in *The Celtic Twilight*, who claimed Ballisodare to be ' "the most gentle" —whereby he meant faery—"place in the whole of County Sligo." ' [1] The village is in the parish of Father Hart, a local Saint Francis about whom Yeats wrote a ballad in 1888.[2] Nearby lie buried the Firbolgs, those giants who waged war upon the Fomorians, inhabitants of Ireland before the coming of the Tuatha De Danaan, that race of gods now known as the fairies (so Yeats tells us in a note to 'The Wanderings of Oisin'). And in Ballisodare Yeats had heard a washerwoman sing a snatch of song which he wrote down and expanded into the earliest poem to bring him wide fame, 'Down by the Salley Gardens.' [3] In Ballisodare, too, he heard another woman sing and trans-

[1] *Mythologies* (New York, 1959), p. 5.
[2] 'The Ballad of Father O'Hart,' first published in *Irish Minstrelsy*, ed. H. Halliday Sparling (London, 1888), reprinted by Yeats in his *Fairy and Folk Tales of the Irish Peasantry* (London and N.Y., 1888) and subsequently in *Crossways*. The ballad is discussed below. Father Hart is a character also in Yeats's play *The Land of Heart's Desire*.
[3] The folksong origin of this poem is discussed by C. Mooney, P. S. O'Heggerty, and Austin Clarke in *The Irish Book Lover*, April 1950 and February and November 1951.

late for him from the Irish (he had no Irish at all) another old ballad of a fairy abduction which he remade into a ballad of his own. In this village above the salmon falls where the Unshin River drops toward the sea, and the huge peak of Knocknarea, crowned by Queen Maeve's cairn, looms across the bay, balladry is still a living tradition. Ninety years after Yeats's boyhood, men like those whose lined and ruddy faces Jack B. Yeats had so often drawn with verve and delight still gather to sing such songs as this:

> You may sing and speak about Easter Week
>   And the heroes of 'Ninety-Eight,
> Those Fenian men that roamed the glen
>   For victory or defeat,
> Those boys who died on scaffold high,
>   They were outlawed on the moor,
> And side by side they fought and died
>   In the valleys of Knockanower.

Their themes were loving and fighting, ever the two staves of balladry. Such songs were made by men not unlike the singers, men whose gift of rhyming described heroic action in heartfelt doggerel, synthesizing into the one stanza a reckless death and a glimpse of the somber, brooding countryside. Their songs hailed Sir Roger Casement, the heroes of 1916, Emmet and Wolfe Tone, and the lad from Garryowen shot by the Royal Ulster Constabulary only a few years ago, when the I.R.A. raided the barracks at Fermanagh nearby. All to them were heroes of the one stamp, of the one will.

Poetry—at least this kind of poetry—is a masculine occupation, a skill communally admired, a prowess. This is a conception of a poet's role in his society entirely different from what Yeats found among the Rhymers in London, those elegant and isolated aesthetes dying of drink and drugs, of loneliness and insatiate spiritual longings in the great hubbub of a modern city which didn't know or care of their existence.

Ernest Dowson and Lionel Johnson had no concern with ballads, but they were not the only community of poets to whom Yeats felt allegiance. Not only did all the Pre-Raphaelites have a go at ballads; the form was much favored by such other contemporaries as Katharine Tynan, John Todhunter, T. W. Rolleston, AE, and Douglas Hyde.

> Nor may I less be counted one
> With Davis, Mangan, Ferguson,

—all minor writers, true, but they were Irish and all wrote on Irish themes in ballad form. Yeats saw himself as one of them. Much is foretold in the title of the first book to contain Yeats's verse, *Poems and Ballads of Young Ireland* (1888). In 'To Ireland in the Coming Times' he had expounded an artistically unsuccessful marriage of folk superstition with symbolist spiritism. Laboriously he would make this union work; in 1892 he was not yet able poetically to hold together these disparate worlds of experience, although he had already long known that an essential unity linked them together.

III

Yeats began as a ballad writer by taking his subjects from local traditions. 'The Ballad of Father O'Hart' is typical of these early efforts. The subject is a former priest of Collooney, a village adjacent to Ballisodare, who inspired a legend of the birds. At his death,

> There was no human keening;
> The birds from Knocknarea
> And the world round Knocknashee
> Came keening in that day.
>
> The young birds and old birds
> Came flying, heavy and sad;
> Keening in from Tiraragh,
> Keening from Ballinafad . . .

The simplicity of these quatrains is borrowed not from the vigorous stanzas of folk poetry but from hundreds of earlier literary ballads. The young Yeats is daubing on the local color, the picturesque Irish place-names and dialectical terms requiring authorial gloss. The grammatical inversions and comment that intervene between the action and the reader guarantee that this is no folk ballad, nor is its rhythm that of a song. Nonetheless, this weak poem is valuable to an understanding of Yeats's balladry. The source of the legend, Yeats indicates, was *The History, Antiquities, and Present State of the Parishes of Ballysodare and Kilvarnet in the County of Sligo*, published in 1888 by Archdeacon Terence O'Rorke, then rector of Collooney where Father Hart had officiated in the mid-eighteenth century. O'Rorke's book is filled with legendary oddities and possible subjects; why did Yeats take only this tale from page 207 for the subject of his ballad? Perhaps because Father Hart had an intrinsic connection with Irish bardic poetry his tale had a special appeal for Yeats. O'Rorke a few pages earlier celebrates this priest as 'famous for hospitality':

> Carolan was often with the Harts, and showed his admiration of the bishop's general nature and many virtues by composing two songs in his honour . . . No doubt, Caro-

lan put forth all his powers while under the bishop's roof, as knowing well that in no other place could bard or musician encounter more exacting critics.

This Turlough O'Carolan had been celebrated over a century earlier in Goldsmith's twentieth essay, where he is compared to Pindar and called 'the last and greatest' of the Irish bards. One of his more boisterous ballads had been adapted into English by Jonathan Swift ('O'Rourke's noble fare will ne'er be forgot'). Another poem of Carolan's praised the O'Harts as belonging to Tara.

In these raw materials Yeats could not fail to notice several conceptions brought together which were important to him: the tradition, in a great house, of hospitality and patronage for successive generations of harpers and poets (Carolan's predecessor, Thomas O'Connellan, was also entertained by the Harts), including the Irish bard praised by the two great authors of the Eighteenth Century Ascendancy. And in one of Lady Wilde's collections of folklore which he reviewed in 1890, Yeats marked this passage:

> . . . the fairy music seems to be lost forever. In all the hills of Erin the most beautiful tunes were thus caught up by the people and the native musicians. Carolan, it is said, the celebrated bard, acquired all the magic melody of his notes by sleeping out on a fairy rath at night, when the fairy music came to him in dreams, and on awaking he played the airs from memory; but since his time the fairies seem to keep silence on the hills and no more exquisite airs have been added to the pathetic music of Ireland.[1]

---

[1] Lady Wilde, *Ancient Cures, Charms & Usages of Ireland* (London, 1890), pp. 102–3, transcribed from Yeats's marked copy by courtesy of Mrs. W. B. Yeats. The tradition of Carolan's supernatural inspiration is repeated by Yeats in his note to the first section of *Irish Folk and Fairy Tales* (New York, n.d., Modern Library), p. 3, and is attested in the definitive study, *Carolan*, by Donal O'Sullivan (London, 1958), II, 33.

Yeats himself, after seeing from his cousins' house in Ballisodare supernatural lights ascending Knocknarea, 'wandered about raths and fairy hills,' longing 'for some such end as True Thomas found. I did not believe with my intellect that you could be carried away body and soul, but I believed with my emotions and the belief of the country people made that easy.'[1] The theme of abduction by a fairy lover he had heard from many countrymen, including the old woman in Ballisodare whose Irish song became his ballad 'The Host of the Air.' The theme, as we shall see, becomes for Yeats a constant symbol. But to embody it in his poems he must first be struck, as Carolan had been, by the magical power of the Others. And he claimed to have heard their supernatural music. When twenty-eight years old he avowed it in a speech to a society of amateur scientists, the Naturalists' Field Club of Belfast. Their secretary dutifully records the young poet-folklorist as having said:

> When he was a child he was told that there was a submerged city at the bottom of Sligo Lake, and that from its tower came up sometimes at evening a far-off murmur of fairy bells. Once when eight years old he gazed upon that lake, and he imagined, so much did the story possess his mind, that he could hear the murmur of the bells creep up through its waters.[2]

This has the sound of the speech of that young 'Visionary,' Yeats's self-portrait in *The Celtic Twilight*, whose poems were 'all endeavours to capture some high, impalpable mood in a net of obscure images' as he wandered the hills to speak with peasants, whose humble talk was truer

[1] *Autobiography* (New York, 1944), pp. 46-7.
[2] Report of Yeats's speech on 'Irish Fairy Lore,' 20 November 1893. in *Proceedings* of the Belfast Naturalists' Field Club, Ser. II, Part I, vol. 4 (1893-94), 47-8. See W. G. Wood-Martin, *History of Sligo . . . 1688 to the Present* (Dublin, 1892), p. 392.

poetry than his own imaginings. As yet he knew his ballads had not touched the power he felt vibrant within their sources.

I V

In his ballads on Moll Magee, on the old foxhunter, and on Father Gilligan, Yeats drew on popular traditions and local-color novels for native subjects. These early ballads all suffer from the faults we have noticed in 'The Ballad of Father O'Hart.' In none did he use a refrain, which he later recognized as essential to the best ballad poetry. In a revealing letter to Katharine Tynan in 1888 he analyzed the direction of this early work:

> I have noticed some things about my poetry I did not know before. . . . It is almost all a flight into fairyland from the real world, and a summons to that flight. The Chorus to the 'Stolen Child' sums it up—that it is not the poetry of insight and knowledge, but of longing and complaint—the cry of the heart against necessity. I hope some day to alter that and write poetry of insight and knowledge.[1]

In time Yeats so fused together intellect and emotion that 'the cry of the heart against necessity' became a part of his 'poetry of insight and knowledge.' In the process he remade his style to accommodate a new interpretation of his traditional materials, and he applied that new style to his ballads.

It is curious that when Yeats began to write ballads he could not find in Irish folk tradition the best models of the verse form so favored by the Anglo-Irish poets of the nineteenth century. For Irish balladry in English is singularly

[1] *Letters of W. B. Yeats*, ed. Allen Wade (London, 1954), p. 63.

lacking in those spare, intense, dramatic ballad-poems that heroically embody man's tragic fate. That great tradition, about which Edwin and Willa Muir have written with such understanding and from which Robert Graves learned so much, had not come into being in Ireland. Instead, when after Cromwell's time English replaced Irish as the popular language, Gaelic songs were adapted into English and broadside ballads were created on new themes. Unlike the older Scots and English ballads of oral tradition, broadsides originated in the towns and circulated in print. Instead of the impersonality of the oral tradition, broadsides are sentimental or didactic in their plaints of the homesick emigrant, the repentant brigand, the rebellious patriot. Imitating the internal correspondence of Gaelic poetry with insistent interior rhyme,[1] these broadsides sacrifice conciseness for the rhymes' sake; rarely does their language rise above bathos or bombast, or their verse above doggerel. Such broadsides have no analogues with the Scots and English ballads, centuries old, in which Lady Isabel meets her daemon lover, princesses are enchanted into serpents of the sea, and Thomas the Rhymer is a captive of the Queen of Elphame.

This difficulty Yeats circumvented by making the rather unhistorical assumption that the Gaelic songs of the Irish folk poets—in which similar themes were treated—must have been like the best English ballads of the same period. Lending his help to Frank O'Connor's translations of some of these, he published them, along with broadside ballads and literary ballads by himself and his friends, in the Cuala Press *Broadside* series.

[1] *Broad-Sheet Ballads, Being a Collection of Irish Popular Songs*, with an introduction by Padraic Colum (Baltimore, 1914), p. x.

Yeats, as Richard Ellmann observes, turned to the ballad as did Wordsworth, Coleridge, and Scott—we might add Burns—partly to purify the diction of verse. Folk ballads were the natural place to seek that diction based on common speech and heightened by passion which Wordsworth had avowed to be the basis of his poems in *Lyrical Ballads.* 'It was a long time before I had made a language to my liking,' Yeats wrote in 1937—

> I began to make it when I discovered some twenty years ago that I must seek, not as Wordsworth thought, words in common use, but a powerful and passionate syntax, and a complete coincidence between period and stanza. Because I need a passionate syntax for passionate subject-matter I compel myself to accept those traditional metres that have developed with the language. . . . I must choose a traditional stanza, even what I alter must seem traditional.[1]

In his three books after *The Rose* (1893) Yeats seems to have given up ballad-writing, but in *Responsibilities* (1914) he returns to this traditional form. In the meantime he had written his heroic farce, *The Green Helmet* (1910), and chosen as the meter for this play the rhymed fourteen-ers characteristic of broadside balladry. This crudely forceful meter was admirably adapted to the boisterous energy of that play. Now, returning to the ballad as a lyrical form, he writes in 'Beggar to Beggar Cried' and 'Running to Paradise' with a toughness and a swiftness unanticipated in his earlier efforts. As the second title suggests these do indeed still treat his old theme of flight from necessity, but with a new strength and hardness that makes the attempt itself a part of his desired poetry of insight.

[1] *Essays and Introductions* (New York, 1961), pp. 523-4.

The new note is evident in 'Beggar to Beggar Cried':

'Time to put off the world and go somewhere
And find my health again in the sea air,'
Beggar to beggar cried, being frenzy-struck,
'And make my soul before my pate is bare.'

'And get a comfortable wife and house
To rid me of the devil in my shoes,'
Beggar to beggar cried, being frenzy-struck,
'And the worse devil that is between my thighs.'

Three notable innovations: the harsh sensuality; the harsh dissonances of 'house / shoes / thighs'; and the equally harsh refrain, deliberately off-key and displaced to the unexpected third line in the middle of the narrative. Such concentrated dissonance shows how functionally Yeats envisages his form, yet 'even what I alter must seem traditional.'

In this poem Yeats has uncovered the secret of the ballad. Hitherto, although he had written many lyrics with refrains, he had used refrains in hardly any of his ballads.[1] And until now the refrains of his verses had always been merely a reiteration, sometimes in a longer or shorter line than the stanza itself, of the prevailing mood. In 'The Madness of King Goll' the refrain offered after every twelve lines whispered, *'They will not hush, the leaves a-flutter round me, the beech leaves old,'* while the refrain to 'Red Hanrahan's Song About Ireland' invokes, in a line as mellifluous as the rest of the song, the name of 'Cathleen,

---

[1] In the only extended account of Yeats's technique in his ballad poems, Louis MacNeice discussed the use of refrains and remarked that the poet achieved 'some of the simplicity or directness or the swing of the primitive form but he does not pretend away (as the early Yeats tried to do) his own sophistication.' *The Poetry of Yeats* (London and New York, 1941), pp. 164–70.

the daughter of Houlihan.' But in the present ballad Yeats
has reversed our expectations by making the refrain line
discordant and unsingable. From this reversal comes a tonal
dialectic between refrain and stanza, between speech and
song, a contrast Yeats will develop further in later ballads.
This contrast opens the way to a deepening of texture, a
richness of meaning, a double movement embedded in
sound and rhythm as well as in image.

The argument of 'Beggar to Beggar Cried' projects the
beggar's thoughts of marriage and settling down to a re-
spectable life. His perplexity is suggested in the first two
lines of the ballad, in which thought of a pilgrimage of the
soul is immediately contradicted by the suggestion of a sea-
side holiday. Shall he make his soul? Shall he 'get a comfortable wife and house'?

> 'And there I'll grow respected at my ease,
> And hear amid the garden's nightly peace,'
> *Beggar to beggar cried, being frenzy-struck,*
> 'The wind-blown clamour of the barnacle-geese.'

The poem tries to objectify Yeats's own dilemma at a
time when he suspected 'an unmarried woman past her first
youth,' with whom he had had an anxious liaison, of trying
to ensnare him in marriage.[1] By envisaging himself as a
beggar he can take on the direct speech and natural syntax
of folk expression to universalize his feelings. The beggar-
man is one of Yeats's favorite devices, indeed becomes one
of his masks. Like the Shakespearean fool, the beggar is so
unfettered by the claims and bonds of the material world
that his simple or daft speech reveals ultimate truths and
spiritual mysteries. Here, 'being frenzy-struck,' the beggar
considers putting aside the wanderings of his soul for a

[1] Joseph Hone, *W. B. Yeats, 1865–1939* (New York, 1943), p. 321.

conventional marriage. But in the last line all the implications of 'respected at my ease' and 'the garden's nightly peace'—so inappropriate for a wandering beggarman—are suddenly reversed by the heavily accented 'wind-blown clamour of the barnacle-geese.' Reversed not only metrically but implicitly; the barnacle-goose is a bird well known in folklore, and there is a belief prevalent in the West of Ireland that it is hatched from barnacles and therefore is a fish. Its flesh is eaten on Fridays, hence a symbol of immortality.[1] But the significance is double. The flight of the geese is doubtless northward, toward the Back of the North Wind, the land of the dead, and their honking cry is associated with the widespread belief in the Wild Hunt, the fearful sound of unhallowed souls of the dead portending trouble and storm.

The companion ballad takes us also to the Otherworld, but this time the beggar is 'Running to Paradise':

> As I came over Windy Gap
> They threw a halfpenny into my cap,
> For I am running to Paradise;
> And all that I need do is to wish
> And somebody puts his hand in the dish
> To throw me a bit of salted fish:
> *And there the king is but as the beggar.*

'Perhaps his most consummate triumphs,' Edwin Muir wrote of this poem, 'are in his simple riddling songs, filled with the realistic yet credulous imagination of the peasantry. That is the kind of song the peasantry might make if they still made songs, with its shrewd evaluation of worldly good, and its belief in another world.'[2] Again the spokes-

---

[1] Maria Leach, ed., *Standard Dictionary of Folklore, Mythology, and Legend* (New York, 1949), I, 460; Charles Swainson, *The Folklore and Provincial Names of British Birds* (London, 1886), pp. 149-50.

[2] *The Estate of Poetry* (Cambridge, Mass., 1962), p. 58.

man is a beggar, partaking of fish. 'Windy Gap' is the spot at which the spirits of the dead would appear to a mortal, and summon or abduct him. Whether a gap in a wall or a pass between the mountains, this place of the wind is the 'Steep Gap of the Strangers' in Yeats's story 'Hanrahan's Vision,' and the motif is one he had himself collected from the peasant folk.[1] The wind contains the whirling dead, the trooping fairies, Herodias' daughters, a vivid image from folklore which Yeats could enrich with suggestions of dance pattern and gyre-like movement.

> The wind is old and still at play
> While I must hurry upon my way,
> For I am running to Paradise;
> Yet never have I lit on a friend
> To take my fancy like the wind
> That nobody can buy or bind:
> *And there the king is but as the beggar.*

Years later, in 'The Municipal Gallery Revisited,' Yeats would write of Synge, himself, and Lady Gregory,

> All that we did, all that we said or sang
> Must come from contact with the soil, from that
> Contact everything Antaeus-like grew strong.
> We three alone in modern times had brought
> Everything down to that sole test again,
> Dream of the noble and the beggar-man.

In Yeats's imagined heroic Ireland, noble and beggarman could put thought and art and act to 'that sole test' because culture was unified and all shared alike in its traditions. In 'Running to Paradise,' however, there is the sharp recognition that such a world is transcendent, to be found only in the perfection of death, when '*the king is but as the beg-*

---

[1] *Mythologies*, p. 248; 'The Broken Gates of Death,' *Fortnightly Review* (April 1898), p. 528; 'Irish Witch Doctors,' ibid. (Sept. 1900), p. 443.

gar.' In this lilting ballad, that is the one line that cannot be sung: reality breaking up the music of the dreaming heart.

V

In the great poems of his middle period Yeats spoke in the syntax and the stanzas of the noble rather than of the beggarman. In the 1930's, however, he returned to the passionate, plebeian, 'frenzy-struck' voice of the ballad tradition. His best ballads hitherto, as we have seen, were based upon supernatural themes; he had not found within himself the heroic or ribald sensibilities of the folk ballad singers who, like those in Ballisodare, celebrated war and 'porter-drinker's randy laughter' in their rhymes. As old age approached, however, Yeats's imagination reached fiercely toward these passions of youth which in his own youth he had so carefully evaded. And he reached also toward a directness of syntax which the ballad form provided. At the same time he so mastered the dynamics of that form, exploring further the possibilities of contapuntal movement between verse and refrain which he had discovered in *Responsibilities,* that his later ballad poems have an unexpected power, being both simple and dense, both direct and complex. They are the most accomplished literary ballads in our language.

At this time Yeats took over the editorship of a new series of *Broadsides* produced by the Cuala Press. As far back as 1914 his sister Elizabeth had published a monthly ballad sheet, printing ballads of murder and piracy, cowboy songs and sea shanties, as well as Irish come-all-ye's. These were illustrated by their brother Jack B. Yeats, who, Mrs. W. B. Yeats informs me, chose the texts. Now, after a long hiatus, the poet himself revived the Cuala ballad series with the encouragement of F. R. Higgins, an enthusiast of Irish balladry, and of Lady Dorothy Wellesley, equally a partisan of English ballads. This latter friend sent Yeats the *Oxford Book of English Ballads,* and in his correspondence with her he defined some interesting principles of verse composition based upon balladry. Meanwhile, he and Higgins projected a book of Irish ballads, including the music, for by now Yeats was insistent that ballads be sung. Indeed, he was deeply moved when, at a banquet of the newly formed Academy of Irish Letters, his ballad 'The Curse of Cromwell' *was* sung. It is touching that Yeats should confound this personal tribute from the Dublin literary community with the actual folk currency of a popular ballad. But he had followed his own precept which led him to feel that the folk spirit was in his ballads along with their folk form. For, as he wrote to Lady Dorothy on February 8, 1937,

> To perfect your style is to watch yourself to prevent any departure from the formula 'Music, the natural words in the natural order.' Through that formula we go back to the people. Music will keep out temporary ideas, for music is the nation's clothing of what is ancient and deathless.[1]

He is equally insistent in these letters on the requirement of an unvarying rhyme scheme and of a strong lilting rhythm. He exults that 'the folk lilt lost since the time of Burns has been discovered in our time,' and he advises that 'Regular rhyme is needed in this kind of work. The swing of the sentence makes the reader expect it . . . In narrative verse we want to concentrate the attention on the fact

[1] *Letters on Poetry from W.B. Yeats to Dorothy Wellesley* (London, 1964), p. 139.

or the story, not on the form. The form must be present as something we all accept,—"the fundamental sing-song." '[1] He was so possessed by the power of this strong natural rhythm that, in parsing the first line of *Paradise Lost*, he insisted that in its rhythm 'the folk song is still there, but a ghostly voice, an unvariable possibility, an unconscious norm.'[2]

Yeats had learned from the best ballad models to pare down the story so that there is only the core. It is now not the mere matter of folk ballads he borrows, it is their strongly accentual rhythm and muscular syntax, their association with song. From such ballads as 'Lord Randal,' 'Lady Isabel and the Elf Knight,' 'The Lyke-Wake Dirge,' —as from Shakespeare's ballad songs like 'Heigh, Ho, the Wind and the Rain'—Yeats had learned that the ballads derive intensity from internal oppositions. Between question and answer, between the tale and the refrain, between the nonchalant gaiety of the diction and the bare revelation of archetypal action in the unfolding of the story: the best ballads are built on structural principles akin, in miniscule, to those of a Shakespearean tragedy in which the clowns' underplot reinforces by contrast the fall of kings.

Compact with this realization of the ballad form is Yeats's clarification of the ballad singer as a *persona*. Now in the last decade of his life he brings into being as the singers of his poems, whether ballads or modeled on ballads, such characters as Crazy Jane, Tom the Lunatic, the Wild Old Wicked Man, and the old revolutionaries, serving-men, and lovers of *Last Poems*. These masks permit him the manipulation of emotion in dramatic speech, which the ballad-like form enhances with syntactical and rhythmic power.

[1] Ibid., pp. 37–8, 90.
[2] *Essays and Introductions*, p. 524.

Strictly speaking, in 'Words for Music Perhaps' there is not a single ballad, and only the first seven of the twenty-five poems are given to Crazy Jane. She opens up the subject of the succeeding words and their music with her passionate memories, her ghostly lover, her scorn of the bishop, her knowledge of a glimmering immortality. Though her songs are not really ballads, yet the flavor, the lilt, the concision of speech and the unequivocal facing of tragic emotion which are in the best of the ballads are put into her words. In these poems it is the character of Crazy Jane and the other speakers, rather than slavish fealty to a form, which makes inevitable an association with transcendent peasant poets and their ballad songs. Did Yeats imagine all this as coming from the mouths of the daft old woman he had known and of the satirical crone who wandered near Lady Gregory's estate in Gort? It seems not too fanciful to suppose that Yeats blended with these real, pathetic persons the legendary figure of the Shan Van Vocht, the old woman who represents the spirit of Ireland. He had summoned her before, in his most directly political play *Cathleen Ni Houlihan*, where the old woman calls the youth away on his wedding eve. There the choice was between fulfilled love or a heroic death: the two themes of balladry. What must have blended in Yeats's mind this traditional figure of the old woman with the visionary and satirical crones he had known was Frank O'Connor's reading aloud one night a translation of the fourteenth-century song fragment, 'Ich am of Irlant.' This becomes the basis of the refrain in 'Words for Music Perhaps, xx':

> 'I am of Ireland,
> And the Holy Land of Ireland,
> And time runs on,' cried she.
> 'Come out of charity,
> Come dance with me in Ireland.'

In this 'dance song,' as Yeats called it in a note to *The Winding Stair*, the meaning turns on the lines ' "And time runs on," cried she. / "Come out of charity . . ." ' where charity is used, of course, in its Biblical or Elizabethan sense of love. Although the narrative presents a woman dancing to a band before a tavern and inviting a man to come with her, what she cryptically promises is to take him to 'the Holy Land of Ireland' in their dance: a dance of transfiguration, of ecstasy. Therefore the Ireland of her song is the Land of the Blessed. And that is where the dance of love has taken Crazy Jane.

Her songs explore the nature of such love in a debate with the Bishop who expounds the soul but degrades the body. Jane, being crazy, cannot accept such abstract division. For her there is no satisfied love 'That cannot take the whole / Body and soul.' The Bishop preaches the love of God, yet

> A lonely ghost the ghost is
> That to God shall come

for Jane knows another love beyond this life; although 'love is but a skein unwound / Between the dark and dawn,' in that momentary ecstasy she knows transfiguration, her soul being bound 'ghost to ghost' with her dead lover Jack's. In 'Crazy Jane Grown Old Looks at the Dancers' she acknowledges the destructive power of love, its affinity with hate, yet that transcendent passion is all that she lived for or will die for.

This debate is carried on in stanzas of simultaneous simplicity and complexity. The simplicity is in the natural syntax, the complexity in its occasional interruption, as in the long suspension after the pronoun in the second line of 'Crazy Jane and the Bishop':

Bring me to the blasted oak
That I, midnight upon the stroke,
(*All find safety in the tomb.*)
May call down curses on his head
Because of my dear Jack that's dead.
Coxcomb was the least he said:
The solid man and the coxcomb.

Such an interruption of the natural order by a modifying
time-phrase seems to go against the rhythm of balladry; but
the second interrupting clause is a refrain, which ballad tradition allows to be inserted between the lines of the stanza.
Not until well on into the poem do we realize that the refrain has a meaning too, and sets up an inner debate between itself and the verse, between song and argument.
Meanwhile, so strong is the forward movement of Jane's
sentence that this double interruption is accommodated. It
is the direct active verbs, *bring me* and *call down curses*,
which move the sentence along. By the end of the stanza
we meet *The solid man and the coxcomb*, which rhymes
with and completes the refrain begun above. Now we look
for the recurrence of these two lines, and find them, as the
song goes on, shifting their references so that it is the
Bishop, not dead Jack, who will find safety in the tomb.
And Jack, whom the Bishop denounced as a coxcomb,
proves the solid man, for though dead he 'bids me to the
oak,' while the coxcomb is the Bishop, with his 'heron's
hunch' and 'a skin, God knows / wrinkled like the foot of
a goose.'

Whatever the suspensions or divagations of the argument, the refrains in Crazy Jane's songs bring the syntax
back straightway to direct simplicity:

And that is what Jane said.

'*That's certainly the case,*' said he.

> *All things remain in God.*

> *Love is like the lion's tooth.*

Even her nonsense is direct and musical:

> *Fol de rol, fol de rol*

—an irrational mockery of the argument in 'Crazy Jane Reproved.'

In *Last Poems* Yeats treats similar thematic material again in ballad and song. Immediately following the poem 'Sweet Dancer' ('Let her finish her dance'—she too is 'crazy') comes 'The Three Bushes,' which opens a seven-poem series. These poems combine an allegory of the soul's search for eternal love with ribaldry and wit. This time there is a tale rather than an argument, a tale the opening ballad tells and on which the succeeding songs make comment.

> Said lady once to lover,
> 'None can rely upon
> A love that lacks its proper food;
> And if your love were gone
> How could you sing those songs of love?
> I should be blamed, young man.
> > *O my dear, O my dear.*

She then, as his Muse, must offer him her love; but she loves her virginity as well and sends her chambermaid to his room by night. For she will offer him the love of her soul but will not soil her body. Her lover is deceived for a year, and on the anniversary of what he thinks her first visit he leaves the tavern for their tryst, with the crowd pleading for ' "A laughing, crying, sacred song, / A leching song," they said.' But he is thrown from his horse and dies,

and his lady dies for grief. The chambermaid however
'lived long,' and planted a rose on their adjacent graves. At
her death she makes full confession, and the priest

> . . . bade them take and bury her
> Beside her lady's man,
> And set a rose-tree on her grave,
> And now none living can,
> When they have plucked a rose there,
> Know where its roots began.

It will be seen that the lady's abstract philosophy prevails
only after death. In this life she was triply undone, first by
her own sensuous nature which knows, despite her strict
theology, that 'What hurts the soul / My soul adores, / No
better than a beast / Upon all fours.' The lover undoes her
divisive philosophy too, for he *is* deceived into mistaking a
chambermaid for his lady, and it is 'For the womb the seed
sighs,' not for the soul. And the chambermaid, with her
pun on spirit, has the last word—'His spirit . . . has fled
/ Blind as a worm.' Yet it is the priest, far wiser than the
Bishop who denounced Crazy Jane, who reunites what the
lady's conventional morality had sundered, and who plants
the rose of immortality to unify, as does the ballad, the
soul, the body, and the lover who was devoted to both.

The theme makes yet another ballad in 'The Wild Old
Wicked Man,' reminiscent of Blake. This is a 'sacred
song, / A leching song' in which the Wild Old Man is put
off by a holy virgin who has given 'all to an older man: /
That old man in the skies.' He admits,

> . . . a coarse old man am I,
> I choose the second-best,
> I forget it all awhile
> Upon a woman's breast.

Yeats could argue all sides of the philosophy of love in these ballads. In these, as in 'John Kinsella's Lament for Mary Moore' and 'A Drunken Man's Praise of Sobriety' he remakes the tradition of love balladry in the images suggested by his own transcendent philosophy as well as by sensuous delight. This kind of love poetry, as Miss Muriel Bradbrook has suggested, [1] is anticipated by the sophisticated ballad-like verses of such Renaissance poets as Raleigh and other courtly makers. Yeats alone in our time has successfully combined the traditional movement and refrain of balladry with a content at once philosophical and lubricious, a tone at once elegant and popular. But Yeats's love ballads differ from poetry of popular provenience in their intellectual dialectic. Both Crazy Jane and the Lady are philosophers as well as lovers. Folk balladry attends only to action and its consequences, not to its bases or justifications.

VI

The other major theme in popular balladry is likewise active and unreflective. Whether the subject be war or politics, such ballads combine heroism with patriotic feeling. Yeats's early poems on public controversies attack 'Those That Hated "The Playboy of the Western World" ' and the opponents of Hugh Lane's intended gift of paintings to Dublin; he could hardly have found balladry appropriate in contentions so limited to the aesthetic community. But after the Easter Rising it was indeed natural for him to use such a popular meter to invoke the 'Sixteen Dead Men'. Balladry was appropriate, not only to praise the new national heroes, but as a vehicle for apotheo-

---

[1] 'Yeats and Elizabethan Love Poetry,' *The Dublin Magazine* (Summer 1965), IV, ii, 40, 51–5.

sis. In this respect it was Yeats's lowly analogue to the Noh play, a literary form designed for the speaking of ghosts:

> 'O words are lightly spoken,'
> Said Pearse to Connally,
> 'Maybe a breath of politic words
> Has withered our Rose Tree;
> Or maybe but a wind that blows
> Across the bitter sea.'
>
> . . . .
>
> 'There's nothing but our own red blood
> Can make a right Rose Tree.'

Here, if anywhere, Yeats succeeds in merging the theosophic Rose of 'To Ireland in the Coming Times' with the matter of 'Davis, Mangan, Ferguson.' He did not write ballads of 1916 again until *Last Poems*, where the two on Roger Casement and the songs on Parnell and the O'Rahilly are strong and bitter, sharpened by retrospective indignation and by the celebration of that 'beautiful, lofty thing,' the reckless giving of a life. Moments before a British sniper cuts him down in an alley beside the Post Office, the O'Rahilly, chieftain of his clan, sings,

> 'Am I such a craven that
> I should not get the word
> But for what some travelling man
> Had heard I had not heard?'
> Then on Pearse and Connally
> He fixed a bitter look:
> 'Because I helped to wind the clock
> I come to hear it strike.'
> *How goes the weather?*

This ballad may well fix Yeats's surprised, if not bitter, look upon the conspirators who failed to tell him that the clock was about to strike. Perhaps they did not think to ask, as he asked of himself,

> Did that play of mine send out
> Certain men the English shot?

At any rate Yeats was visiting Rothenstein in England and did not 'get the word' until the Rising was over. It seems likely, in his ballad, that the inconsequent refrain is actually 'the word,' the conspirators' pass-word.

The Roger Casement ballads, struck off in the heat of indignation after reading a book attacking the Casement diaries as forgeries, would seem as near to poetry as political invective can come. Of the drinking-song 'Come Gather Round Me, Parnellites,' no such qualification need be made. Perhaps because the passions of the case were so old as to be already legendary, this ballad, celebrating Ireland's lost leader, is filled with poignance rather than hatred. For

> . . . stories that live longest
> Are sung above the glass,
> And Parnell loved his country,
> And Parnell loved his lass.

When Yeats set himself the task of writing ballads on events at hand the results were not likely to be first rate. Indeed, the marching songs he composed for General O'Duffy's Blue Shirts, and then, after his disillusionment with that demagogic leader, rewrote so they couldn't be marched to, are by all odds from the bottom of his drawer. The fanatical opinions of the old man in *On the Boiler* were not in themselves poetic emotions. His hatred of the present age, however, could be turned into magnificent poetry when the poet found means to control it. Such a means was the mask of a ballad character, projected backward in time so that the tone is one of visionary lamentation rather than vindictive rage. In 'The Curse of Cromwell' the speaker is an aged minstrel of centuries gone by, allied by birth to the lower orders, by talent a ballad singer, and by station in the service of the vanished aristocracy he celebrates and mourns. This remarkable poem has the vigorous movement of a broadside ballad, its meter strongly accentual in lines of great elasticity. Four heavy beats to the line is the normative rhythm:

> You ask what I have found, and far and wide I go:
> Nothing but Cromwell's house and Cromwell's murderous
> crew,
> The lovers and the dancers are beaten into the clay,
> And the tall men and the swordsmen and the horsemen,
> where are they?
> And there is an old beggar wandering in his pride—
> His fathers served their fathers before Christ was crucified.
> > *O what of that, O what of that,*
> > *What is there left to say?*

This stanza is clearly suggested by Frank O'Connor's version of 'Kilcash,' a seventeenth-century Irish lament for a great house torn down by Cromwell's invaders:

> > And the great earls where are they?
> > The earls, the lady, the people
> > Beaten into the clay.

Not only did Yeats publish 'Kilcash' in his Cuala *Broadsides* only three months before 'The Curse of Cromwell' (May and August, 1937), but O'Connor has said the translation 'was one of his favorite poems, and there is a good bit of his work in it.'[1] I think the Irish poem suggested not only the borrowed images but the character of the lament-

[1] O'Connor, *Kings, Lords, & Commons* (New York, 1959), p. 100.

ing gleeman, who, like Carolan, had been harper and poet to 'the tall men and the swordsmen and the horsemen.' Juxtaposed to our mean time when 'we and all the Muses are things of no account' and 'money's rant is on' is this bard's apocalyptic vision of the dead he still serves 'though all are underground':

> I came on a great house in the middle of the night,
> Its open lighted doorway and its windows all alight,
> And all my friends were there and made me welcome too;
> But I woke in an old ruin that the winds howled through;
> And when I pay attention I must out and walk
> Among the dogs and horses that understand my talk.
> > *O what of that, O what of that,*
> > *What is there left to say?*

The bitterness of the last line is compounded not only of the old poet's preference for his master's beasts to our 'money's rant,' but of our catching the echo of Gulliver in the stable after his return to England. Thus the ghost of Swift speaks through the ballad poet too.

This image of the great house all alight recurs often in Yeats's work. It is an image from folklore, his most powerful symbol of transfiguration. It appears here as an embodiment of historical truth, and in 'Crazy Jane on God' as a memory of personal ecstasy. The play *The King of the Great Clock Tower* concludes with a ballad of transfiguration—sung by the lover's severed head—that brings together two such images of spiritual reality. 'Castle Dargan's ruin all lit, / Lovely ladies dancing in it,' says the rambling, shambling travelling man, who is answered by his opposite, the crooked hawthorne tree, 'I have stood so long by a gap in the wall / Maybe I shall not die at all.' For there, as we know from the ballad of Windy Gap, are the souls among the Sidhe, who never die. Ruined wall and ruined castle are the domains of the living dead, whose spirits we shall join. By means of such images from folk belief, set forth in meter and form based on folk verse, Yeats made a part of his own myth the folklore he learned as the Matter of Ireland.

Throughout *Last Poems*, ballad meters and ballad refrains in stanzas not actually ballads dominate the texture of the verse. These conventions make possible the openness of diction, the intellectual muscularity, and the accessible passion that move in these poems with such seeming simplicity.

> 'The work is done,' grown old he thought,
> 'According to my boyish plan;
> Let the fools rage, I swerved in naught,
> Something to perfection brought';
> *But louder sang that ghost, 'What then?'*

As though to answer Plato's ghost, Yeats wrote, in a letter three weeks before his death,

> It seems to me that I have found what I wanted. When I try to put it all in a phrase I say, 'Man can embody truth but he cannot know it.' I must embody it in the completion of my life. The abstract is not life and everywhere draws out its contradictions. You can refute Hegel but not the Saint or the Song of Sixpence.[1]

His calendar of Saints includes the aged minstrel, the sacrificed revolutionaries, the transfigured lovers—his ballad singers and ballad characters, who cannot be refuted because their knowledge is a tradition as old as our culture, and their songs are in meters as old as our language.

[1] *Letters*, ed. Wade, p. 922.

:3:

THE TOWER AND THE BEGGARMAN

'Three types of men have made all beautiful things,' Yeats wrote in 'Poetry and Tradition':

> Aristocracies have made beautiful manners, because their place in the world puts them above the fear of life, and the countrymen have made beautiful stories and beliefs, because they have nothing to lose and so do not fear, and the artists have made all the rest, because Providence has filled them with recklessness. All these look backward to a long tradition, for, being without fear, they have held to whatever pleased them.

From this passage, as indeed from many of his poems, we can infer that Yeats would be the artist who in his work unites the long traditions of the nobleman's manners and the countryman's beliefs. No wonder he endows his ballad-singing beggars with the imaginations of Neo-Platonic philosophers, in rhythms so captivating that we forget to cavil at the implausibility of the combination. But, then, is the combination of high thoughts in a lowly head so implausible? 'Folk art is, indeed, the oldest of the aristocracies of thought,' Yeats had written at the end of *The Celtic Twilight*, '. . . and because it has gathered into itself the

simplest and most unforgettable thoughts of the generations, it is the soil where all great art is rooted. Wherever it
is spoken by the fireside, or sung by the roadside, or carved
upon the lintel, appreciation of the arts that a single mind
gives unity and design to, spreads quickly when its hour is
some.'

Sending beggars to a learned school is one way that a single mind can give design and unity to the heritage of its
culture. Another is to put into a noble mind the same
thought that the beggar thinks, and have that mind express
its thought in forms and meters as appropriate to its station
as are the ballads to its lowly counterpart's. The later work
of Yeats in fact does dramatize such a division into two
voices, each with its own traditional meters, forms, and
masks. As we have seen in the ballad poems, the syntax is
that of passionate speech counterpointed by refrains. Their
rhythms, as Thomas Parkinson has ably shown, bear out
Yeats's acceptance of the prosodic theories of Thomas Mac-
Donagh, who held that the scansion of Anglo-Irish verse
differs from that of English in distributing the accents
musically, as in singing, rather than metrically, as from a
norm of spoken verse. Therefore the line, not the foot, is
the metrical unit. In these poems most of the speakers and
singers are stylized characters: Crazy Jane, Tom the Lunatic, the rakehell warriors who chant the marching songs,
and the old Parnellites and revolutionaries who sing 'their
chosen man.' There are John Kinsella, mourning Mary
Moore; the half-sordid, half-mystical woman who sings 'I
am of Ireland'; and the lady, her lover, and her chambermaid.

To this list of lovers, warriors, and divine beggars in his
ballads we must compare the speakers and meters of another group of Yeats's poems. These are the long medi-

tative poems, aristocratic in tone and in character, which use his distinctive eight-line iambic stanzas, whether in *ottava rima* or in the alternating line-lengths of the stanza he used for 'In Memory of Major Robert Gregory.' These poems, include 'A Prayer for My Daughter,' the Byzantium poems, parts i and iv of 'Ancestral Houses,' the long first section of 'Nineteen Hundred and Nineteen,' 'Among School Children,' the two poems on Coole Park, 'The Gyres,' 'The Municipal Gallery Revisited,' 'The Statues,' 'Hound Voice,' and 'The Circus Animals' Desertion.' To these we may add the poems in *rime royale*—'Parnell's Funeral' and 'A Bronze Head.' These obviously are spoken, rather than sung, by, variously, an aristocrat or celebrant of aristocrats, or by an adept of 'mysterious wisdom won by toil.' The knowledge given in Byzantium does not differ in kind from that on Cro-Patrick, but the speaker who has endured this world and the voyage toward the holy city has won his wisdom by renunciation, discipline, and experience, while Tom the Lunatic has received his as a gift of God and accordingly sings it in a style whose seeming naturalness disguises all the labor that makes its syntax passionate and strong.

It is rarely that these two voices, these two *personae* and the traditions they represent, actually coalesce. In the long center section of Yeats's great poem 'The Tower' they do come together with a poignance and power unexampled even in Yeats's other major poems. 'The Tower' itself belongs to a series of poems Yeats wrote every few years or so throughout his career. It is one of his conscious attempts to summon up, combine, and unify the properties of his multivalent imagination. It takes its place—I think it a central place—in a series extending from 'The Song of the Happy Shepherd' through 'To Ireland in the Coming

Times' and 'The Grey Rock' to his last summations, 'The Circus Animals' Desertion' and 'Under Ben Bulben.' In 'The Tower' the first and last sections are philosophical discourse, the first posing the agonized question, what is the passionate and fantastical imagination to do now it is 'tied like a dog's tail' to that absurdity, a decrepit body. Shall he abjure the Muse and be content with argument and abstraction, choosing Plato and Plotinus for companions? In the third section he triumphs over this reasonable but despairing counsel, writing his will—like Blake and Keats *making* his soul, 'Compelling it to a study / In a learned school' until imagination itself can triumph over old age and death. But to do so he had first to 'pace upon the battlements' of his tower, and 'send imagination forth to summon 'Images and memories' from his youth. It is these, and these alone, which can bring him the consolation and the courage to face his mortal fate.

The versification of this central section of 'The Tower' uses that eight-line iambic stanza, with the line length varied from four to five stresses, which Yeats first borrowed from Cowley's 'Ode on the Death of Mr. William Harvey' for his own elegy on Robert Gregory—another poem, like this one, of retrospection and of consolation against death. This is indeed the voice of an aristocratic *persona;* in 'The Tower,' what is that voice invoking?

One stanza sets a vivid scene of dinner in a Great House beneath glistening sconces (a scene to which I shall return in a moment). But the greater part of this section is given to an elaboration, indeed a poetic resurrection, of two ballad-singing peasant poets, Raftery and Red Hanrahan. The one was an actual person, one of the last of the Gaelic folk poets, famous in the nineteenth century; the other was Yeats's invented character, based on an earlier folk poet, and the hero of a book of Yeats's stories published in 1897. By bringing these ballad characters at such length into 'The Tower' Yeats would fuse the tradition of peasantry with that of the aristocracy.

But before he summons up his ballad poets he tells an anecdote he has experienced only in a book, a tale so barbarous as to outrage many a reader's sense of justice and decorum:

> Beyond that ridge lived Mrs. French, and once
> When every silver candlestick or sconce
> Lit up the dark mahogany and the wine,
> A serving-man, that could divine
> That most respected lady's every wish,
> Ran and with the garden shears
> Clipped an insolent farmer's ears
> And brought them in a little covered dish.

Yeats seems to relish playing off the savagery of emotion and deed against the formal courtesies of the gleaming table. Why this barbarity, where we might have expected instead the 'traditional sanctity and loveliness' he celebrated in 'Coole Park and Ballylee'?

It is no doubt to emphasize the unity of culture of noble and peasant, as well as to make the most dramatic contrast possible to Plotinus and 'abstract things,' that Yeats prefaces the adventures of Raftery and Hanrahan with this violent stanza. The Tower itself, which he had made his 'symbol' in 'Blood and Moon,' represents in this poem both the seat of his own family (he had purchased Thoor Ballylee from Lady Gregory a few years before), and the 'bloody, arrogant power' of the nobility with whom he allies his imagination, his family, his future. He had peopled Thoor Ballylee imaginatively with the ghosts of Goldsmith, Swift, Berkeley, and Burke, his intellectual forebears in the

Ascendancy. Now he brings into 'The Tower' a tale that emphasizes the unity of culture, in days gone by, of the nobility and their companions, the serving classes. The key to the stanza is the phrase 'an insolent farmer'; when we consult Yeats's source we find the unfortunate man described as 'a sturdy *half-mounted* gentleman,' that is, a social upstart who had the temerity to put himself on an equal footing with Mr. French. The tale is told by French's grandson, the barrister and diarist Sir Jonah Barrington, who certainly had his tongue in cheek as he admits the 'feudal arrogance' of his forebears, Mrs. French's 'rather violent' disposition, and her husband's excessive pride. Railing against the upstart neighbor at dinner, Mrs. French expressed a wish which her butler, like King Henry's nobles in the matter of Thomas à Becket, took for a command. Barrington offers this bit of eighteenth-century feudalism as an instance of 'the extraordinary devotion of the lower to the higher orders of Ireland in former times.' [1] From Yeats's point of view (which I think the faintly ironic tone both here and later in the poem invites us to accept) this instance of a servant acting as the hands of his mistress, though unlovely, is yet a defense of the old order's 'traditional sanctity,' against the insolent self-made class that lacks all culture and therefore gives no assent to the soul-mysteries in which both traditional orders believe.

II

Now, from the *Anima Mundi*, Yeats summons the images of Raftery and Hanrahan to learn from them the wisdom by which alone he may deal heroically with time and age. Why should imagination bring *them* forth, thirty years

---

[1] *Personal Sketches of His Own Time*, 2d ed. (London, 1830), I, 45-6.

after he wrote the tale of Blind Raftery's love for Mary Hynes in *The Celtic Twilight* and the *Stories of Red Hanrahan*, rather that such other symbolic figures as Oisin or the Rose, or Michael Robartes, or from his plays Seanchan or Naoise, or the annunciations of the unicorn, the swan, the great beast? It is because the begging ballad poet out of the eighteenth century and the peasant poet and seer renowned in Yeats's youth most forcefully bring together folk art, countrymen's beliefs, and aristocracy of thought. In the name of love they cross 'the broken gates of death' among 'the windy desolate places.' Their songs and their adventures, retold in the reflective voice of the artist-aristocrat, exemplify both unity of spirit and unity of culture.

And so, directly after the servant's vengeance in devotion to Mrs. French, we meet 'A peasant girl commended by a song'—

> And certain men, being maddened by those rhymes,
> Or else by toasting her a score of times,
> Rose from the table and declared it right
> To test their fancy by their sight

a song so passionate that men rushed out—or was it because they had toasted her 'a score of times'?—to 'test their fancy by their sight.' But 'Music had driven their wits astray,' and mistaking moonlight 'For the prosaic light of day,' one of her admirers 'drowned in the great bog of Cloone.'

The song of course was Raftery's, who could curse a thornbush to barrenness and put a doom on any man. But it was his love songs that made him most famous, in which he embellished the praises of beauty with comparisons to Deirdre and Helen. Whether Anthony Raftery really was the great bard Lady Gregory claims, or, as Frank O'Connor maintains, his 'gentle maunderings . . . are as close as genuine poetry has ever approached to doggerel,' [1] Yeats was greatly taken with the *idea* of a folk poet who knew Homer and Virgil and the Irish epics and improvised songs and satirical ranns. In *The Celtic Twilight* Yeats had told his tale of Raftery and titled it with a line from the Renaissance lyric by Nashe, 'Dust hath closed Helen's eye.' The beautiful Mary Hynes is dead, and it is said that the faeries claimed her and took her away, for they are the ancient gods, and Raftery made verses in praise of her beauty. Retelling their story, Yeats says,

> These poor countrymen and countrywomen in their beliefs, and in their emotions, are many years nearer to that old Greek world, that set beauty beside the fountain of things, than are our men of learning. . . . These old men and women, when they tell of her, blame another and not her [they blame the Sidhe], and though they can be hard, they grow gentle as the old men of Troy grew gentle when Helen passed by on the walls.

With Mary Hynes as a Galway Helen of Troy, Raftery becomes the Homer of Ballylee. Assuredly Yeats found in this folk story a fable fashioned from the same emotions as his own doomed love for Maud Gonne, whose beauty he would like to think had the same supernatural source as his own gift of poetry. Yet the tale, pathetic and fantastic as it is, seems imperfectly articulated. Not yet, he wrote, were Mary Hynes and Raftery 'perfect symbols of the sorrow of beauty and the magnificence and penury of dreams.' They would become so only after he had transformed his style into a verse as sinewy and filled with gaiety as the

---

[1] *Kings, Lords & Commons* (New York, 1959), p. 132; Lady Gregory, *Poets and Dreamers* (London, 1902), pp. 1-46.

strophes he imagined Raftery to have sung in praise of a
beauty he could not have seen:

> Strange, but the man who made the song was blind;
> Yet, now I have considered it, I find
> That nothing strange; the tragedy began
> With Homer that was a blind man,
> And Helen has all living hearts betrayed.

Homeric similes to describe the emotions of Irish peasants may seem a fanciful literary embellishment. But Yeats
does not make such comparisons casually. The interchange-
ability of the Matter of Ireland with the Matter of Greece
is of great importance to his thought as well as to his
metaphors. In his study of Irish antiquities Yeats had come
repeatedly upon authoritative claims that the folk beliefs of
the Irish peasants resembled the religion of Greek antiquity, and that the culture of Bronze Age Ireland was almost identical with that of Homeric Greece. D'Arbois de
Joubainville compared Irish beliefs in transmigration with
the Pythagorean, and Alfred Nutt had claimed 'that Greek
and Irish alone have preserved the early stages of the happy
other world conception,' indeed that Ireland preserved
these beliefs 'with greater fulness and precision than the
Greeks.' [1] Standish O'Grady, 'his mind full of Homer, retold the story of Cuchulain that he might bring back an
heroic ideal,' and despite manifest flaws it was his work,
says Yeats, 'which founded modern Irish literature.' [2] The
identity between Celtic heathendom and ancient Greece
was of pivotal importance to Yeats, for this supposition
gave him warrant to imagine both the folk religion of Ire-

[1] Joubainville, *The Irish Mythological Cycle* (London, 1903), ch. XV.
(Yeats read the original French edition, Paris, 1884.) Nutt, *The Celtic
Doctrine of Rebirth*, quoted by Yeats in his review, 'Celtic Beliefs about
the Soul,' *Bookman* (Sept. 1898), XIV, 159.
[2] *Explorations* (London, 1962), p. 371.

land and the stories of the Celtic pantheon as central to the great tradition of European culture. This assumption re-deems the uses Yeats made of the Matter of Ireland from the parochialism inherent in the work of almost all the other writers who have used it.

In 'The Tower' Yeats celebrates this humble Irish Homer whose songs of love drove men to madness and to death, for he too would, like Raftery, mingle sun and moonlight in one inextricable, illusory light. 'For if I triumph I must make men mad.' The third episode, follow-ing these gestures of devotion to Mrs. French and to Mary Hynes, is still more intense, more mysterious, requiring even more than theirs that we be maddened by his rhymes.

III

And I myself created Hanrahan
And drove him drunk or sober through the dawn
From somewhere in the neighbouring cottages.
Caught by an old man's juggleries
He stumbled, tumbled, fumbled to and fro
And had but broken knees for hire
And horrible splendour of desire;
I thought it all out twenty years ago:

Good fellows shuffled cards in an old bawn;
And when that ancient ruffian's turn was on
He so bewitched the cards under his thumb
That all but the one card became
A pack of hounds and not a pack of cards,
And that he changed into a hare.
And followed up those baying creatures towards—
Hanrahan rose in Frenzy there

O towards I have forgotten what—enough!

Of course Yeats has not 'forgotten what.' He has given clues enough for the reader to remember—if that reader has prepared himself with certain of Yeats's earlier writings. I shall retrace Hanrahan's journey as he follows the pack of cards enchanted into hounds and hare, for his destination is of first importance to an understanding of one of Yeats's major themes. To retrace this journey we must follow Yeats as he himself discovers where it is that Hanrahan must go. We can begin, as with Raftery, in *The Celtic Twilight*, where so many of the *données* of Yeats's mature work appear in the earliest forms his imagination gave them.

He first published in the *Scots Observer* for 15 June 1889 the sketch in *The Celtic Twilight* called 'Kidnappers.' This sketch presents several accounts from country people of persons being kidnapped by the people of faery—the very theme of 'a flight into fairyland from the real world' in his poetry of 'longing and complaint' which, in his letter to Katharine Tynan a year earlier, he had hoped to replace with 'poetry of insight and knowledge.' Almost forty years later, in the stanzas just quoted from 'The Tower,' Yeats still dramatizes the pattern of action that once seemed an evasion of reality. Now it has become part of the poetry of knowledge and insight.

The story in 'Kidnappers' [1] is identical with that in his early ballad 'The Host of the Air,' except that the young man of the prose version has now become a poet, like Carolan or Raftery:

> He heard while he sang and dreamed
> A piper piping away,
> And never was piping so sad,
> And never was piping so gay . . .

[1] See *Mythologies*, pp. 73-4.

Despite the echoes of Blake, Yeats writes, 'I heard the story on which this ballad is founded from an old woman at Balesodare, Sligo. She repeated me a Gaelic poem on the subject, then translated it for me.' O'Driscoll, as the lover is named in the ballad, dreams that he sees his bride Bridget among young men and girls 'Who danced on a level place.' The dancers crowd around him and offer him wine and bread, but, as Yeats's note continues, 'Any one who tastes fairy food or drink is glamoured, and stolen by the fairies.' To prevent her lover from suffering her fate, Bridget draws him away 'To old men playing at cards / with a twinkling of ancient hands.' O'Driscoll, who 'thought not of evil chance,' joined their game—until one of the 'host of the air' bore Bridget away in his arms. Then,

> O'Driscoll scattered the cards
> And out of his dream awoke:
> Old men and young men and young girls
> Were gone like a drifting smoke.

This is the first appearance in Yeats's work of the uncanny card game in 'The Tower.' It seems a folktale version, scaled down to peasant life, of a dimly remembered mythic motif. It is the test or wager against the creatures of the Otherworld, such as the 'game' in *Sir Gawaine and the Green Knight*. What is suppressed in 'Kidnappers' and 'The Host of the Air' is the point of the game: the girl's return to life is what is at stake. By winning the card game against the men of the Sidhe, O'Driscoll could, like Orpheus, have brought his wife back from the dead. This image, not yet fully developed, comes into Yeats's folklore collecting again and again. Each time it recurs something is added to the synthesis that would eventually disclose its meaning. An excerpt from his projected book on the people of faery, published in 1899, contained this same motif:

An old woman from the borders of Sligo and Mayo says
that she remembers seeing, when she was a child, 'a wild
old man in flannel who came from Ennis.' He and the
men used to sit up late at night, playing cards in a big
barn. She was not allowed to go into the barn because
children kneel down and look up under the cards, and a
player has bad luck if anyone kneels when he is playing,
but her father often told her that when they had been
playing a long time 'the wild old man' would take up the
cards and move them about and a hare would leap out of
the cards, and then a hound would leap out after the hare
and chase it round and round the barn and away.[1]

The players' fear of a kneeling child of course marks this as
a devil's or a witches' game. A dozen years later Yeats re-
called that Glanville had quoted testimony of the witch
trial of Julian Cox in 1663: pursued by hounds, the hare
took to earth and turned into herself. 'Lady Gregory's
story of the witch who in semblance of a hare, leads the
hounds such a dance, is the best remembered of all witch
stories,' writes Yeats.[2] Robert Graves has a poem in *The
White Goddess* based on similar testimony from another
witch trial in 1662.[3]

A set of images is taking shape in Yeats's mind. We are
moving from the banalities of his early poems toward
something much more powerful. The fairy abduction as it
appears in 'The Stolen Child' and perhaps even in 'The
Hosting of the Sidhe' is probably the theme of Yeats's with

[1] 'Ireland Bewitched,' *Contemporary Review* (Sept. 1899), p. 390.
[2] 'Witches and Wizards in Irish Folklore,' Yeats's essay in Lady Gregory's *Visions and Beliefs* (New York and London, 1920), I, 248. The
motif is still in oral tradition in Ballisodare, where I heard it in August
1965.
[3] *The White Goddess*, 3d ed. (London, 1952), pp. 399–400. The poem,
'The Allansford Pursuit' is reprinted in Graves's *Collected Poems 1955*
(New York, 1955), pp. 244–5, but is omitted from his subsequent collections.

which the modern reader is least likely to have patience. Indeed, it seems to combine whimsy with *fin du siècle* escapism. Yet to achieve the poetry of insight and knowledge Yeats would not merely have to write poems on real people or on political subjects. Yeats conceived of the 'real world' as the instant's manifestation of a history as old as time, a history of the individual soul, of the perpetual symbolism of the *Anima Mundi* ever revealing itself through change. 'For things below are copies, the Great Smaragdine Tablet said,' he wrote in 'Supernatural Songs.' Of what things above is his early theme of flight to fairyland a copy then?

We must remind ourselves that in Irish folk tradition the fairy people have never been reduced to seedpod size, as Englishmen since Shakespeare's day conceive of them. In Ireland, as Yeats had explained in his article 'The Prisoners of the Gods,' quoted in the last chapter, the Sidhe are of a size like ourselves and are ever among us, at the crossroads or the marketplace, and their kingdom, from which they emerge to dance upon the raths, may be entered by descending into the raths. Some of these, such as Newgrange in County Meath or, in County Sligo, Carrowmore under Knocknarea or Magherahanrush above Lough Gill, were kingly burial mounds with still extant tunnels leading into their midst. This entry into the Otherworld of the dead is an analogue of Aeneas' descent into the netherworld by plucking the golden bough.

The Sidhe inhabit also the land of the blessed, an island which, Alfred Nutt wrote in a book Yeats reviewed with enthusiasm,

> may be reached by mortals specially summoned by denizens of the land; the summons comes from a damsel, whose approach is marked by magically sweet music, and who bears a magic apple-branch. . . . Its inhabitants are

free from death and decay, they enjoy in full measure a
simple round of sensuous delights.[1]

This summons is, of course, the opening episode in Yeats's
'Wanderings of Oisin.' The Happy Otherworld, as it appears in such romances as *Oisin in the Land of Youth, The
Voyage of Bran, The Conception of Mongan* and *The Adventures of Connla*, is, properly understood, not merely the
pagan indulgence in perpetual fulfillment that it seems.
Yeats had already collected much corroborative material
from folk informants when he reviewed Nutt's survey of
the Happy Otherworld and the Celtic doctrine of rebirth,
saying,

> He describes the Celtic and Greek doctrine of the rebirth
> of the soul, of its coming out of the happy other world of
> the dead, and living once more, and of its power to change
> its shape as it desires. By comparing the Greek cult of
> Dionysius and the Irish cult of the fairies, he concludes
> that its rebirth and its many changes are because 'the
> happy otherworld' is the country of the powers of life
> and increase. . . . He describes the old orgiac dances in
> which the worshippers of the powers of life and increase
> believed themselves to take the shapes of gods and divine
> beasts, and first, he thinks, imagined 'the happy other
> world' in which their momentary and artificial ecstasy
> was continual and natural ecstasy.

Had Nutt had access to fuller collections of Irish fairy
legends, Yeats writes, 'he would have had even more
copious evidence to prove the association of continual
change . . . with the inhabitants of the other world, with

[1] Nutt, 'The Happy Otherworld in the Mythico-Romantic Literature
of the Irish,' in *The Voyage of Bran*, translated by Kuno Meyer (London,
1895), I, 143.

the dead as well as with the fairies,' for 'all that is told of the fairies is told of the dead who are among them.' [1]

Thus understood, Yeats's theme of 'the flight into fairyland from the real world' can become summons not merely to a nebulous escape from necessity but to the repossession of original energy, the powers of life and increase grasped by a mortal at their supernatural source.

But in his ballad of the ghostly card game Yeats had not yet so fully understood the implications of his folk and legendary materials. The theme emerges with much greater clarity in Yeats's story 'Red Hanrahan.' In the first magazine publication of *Stories of Red Hanrahan* the hero was called O'Sullivan, for Yeats modeled his imaginary hedge-schoolmaster and poet on Owen Roe O'Sullivan (Roe means Red), a rather scapegrace itinerant Irish poet who lived from 1748 to 1784. 'Red Hanrahan,' Yeats wrote to a friend, 'is an imaginary name . . . there were many poets like him in the eighteenth century in Ireland. . . . I think the stories have the emotion of folklore.' [2] In the first of these tales Red Hanrahan comes to a house on Samhain Eve (All Souls' Night), summoned by a mysterious message from his sweetheart, and finds a group of men are playing cards. An old man is moving the cards about, muttering 'Spades and Diamonds, Courage and Power; Clubs and Hearts, Knowledge and Pleasure.' He entices Hanrahan into his card game, and after a time his hands and the cards have all but hypnotized the players. In a moment the cards are enchanted into a hare and hounds, and only Hanrahan has the courage to follow the hounds into the night. The

---

[1] 'Celtic Beliefs About the Soul,' *Bookman* (Sept. 1898), XIV, 159–60.
[2] Inscribed in John Quinn's copy of *Stories of Red Hanrahan*, dated June 1905; quoted in Allen Wade, *A Bibliography of the Writings of W. B. Yeats*, 2d ed. (London, 1958), p. 72.

cry of the hounds 'went up all of a sudden into the air . . . northward till he could hear nothing at all.'

It is clear that this pack of hounds, like the flight of barnacle-geese in 'Beggar to Beggar Cried,' represents the common folklore motif of the Wild Hunt. The association here of this flight of unshriven souls with the enchanted card game and the witch in the shape of the hare makes for Yeats a promising constellation of meanings. The yelping pack is known in Celtic tradition also as the Hounds of Annwn; for in the *Mabinogi* of Pwyll, Prince of Dyved, the Welsh king Pwyll goes out hunting with his own hounds but is overtaken by the pack of the king of Annwn, the Otherworld, with whom he must exchange places. A year later the kings of this world and the other can regain their right shapes after an exchange of blows. This tale was known to Yeats, who called the pack 'the Hounds of Annwoyn or of Hades' and thought them 'probably related to the hounds that Irish country people believe will awake and seize the souls of the dead if you lament them too loudly or too soon.' [1] Thus the hounds Hanrahan followed were at once the souls of the dead and the Hounds of Hades; further, Hanrahan, it is implied, would have to exchange shapes with a man of the Sidhe for a year in recapitulation of the fertility ritual which comprises the game in *The Mabinogion*. And indeed a year passes before he comes back to his own self and senses.

But we have yet to account for the hare which the hounds pursue. In Celtic Britain, as Caesar recounted in his *Gallic Wars* (V, xii), the hare was a sacred animal; consequently in Christian times it was associated with the exorcised paganism, witchcraft. In popular tradition and in

---

[1] Yeats's note to 'He mourns for the change. . . .' in *The Wind Among the Reeds*, repr. in *The Variorum Edition of the Poems of W. B. Yeats*, ed. Peter Allt and R. K. Alspach (New York, 1957), pp. 806-7.

theology alike, witchcraft has always been linked with fertility and sexual abandon,[1] a tradition Yeats follows in 'Nineteen Hundred and Nineteen' when he invokes 'love-lorn Lady Kyteler' (the only witch tried in Ireland) and her familiar. There he links the witch to 'Herodias' daughters' in 'the labyrinth of the wind,' an image combining the Sidhe with yet another form of the Wild Hunt.[2] In the story 'Red Hanrahan,' the hare is the shape into which the soul of the poet's sweetheart Mary Lavelle has been shifted, and she is being chased by the Hounds of Hades whom the hero Hanrahan pursues, so that he may—if his adventure fall out well—reclaim her spirit from the Happy Other-world.

In Yeats's tale the pack, rushing northward, disappears, and Hanrahan comes upon a doorway to another country where, 'although it was night-time outside, it was daylight he found within.' Now an old man (no doubt the same wizard who had dealt him the cards in which the queen became a hare) leads Hanrahan toward a great house all lit up, so we know a revelation is at hand. Within are a queen and four crones who hold a cauldron, a stone, a spear, and a sword. These objects the crones identify with the same virtues symbolized by the suites of the card deck. 'And every one after she had spoken, waited as if for Hanrahan to question her, but he said nothing at all.' They say, after his silence, 'He is afraid . . . Echtge, daughter of the Silver Hand, must stay in her sleep.' When Red Hanrahan awakes he knows not how he came to the hillside of Slieve Echtge. In his sleep a year has passed and Mary Lavelle has disappeared from the earth.

[1] I have discussed the folk, theological, and literary traditions of witchcraft in *Form and Fable in American Fiction* (New York, 1961), pp. 157–68.
[2] Q.v. in *Standard Dictionary of Folklore, Mythology and Legend*.

This much elaborated version of the enchanted card game brings into the pattern the Parsifal theme of the seeker's failure in the Grail Castle to ask a question of the ruler of the Otherworld, and thereby to relieve the loveless waste land in this world. Introducing the four Celtic symbols, Yeats is trying to unite elements from the legendary Matter of Ireland with their analogues in Romance literature and in folk tradition. The Cauldron which represents Pleasure in Echtge's castle is patently the Cauldron of Regeneration in the *Mabinogi* of Branwen, familiar to Yeats in Lady Guest's translation and cited in Rhys's *Celtic Heathendom*, one of the books over which Yeats and Maud Gonne pored together in their early studies of the Irish gods. The cauldron is the original in Irish legend of the Holy Grail,[1] while the Stone of Power is the Lía Fáil, 'one of the four precious things brought to Ireland by the Tuatha De Danaan,' or the Sidhe; Rhys connects it with the worship of the sun god.[2] The sword and spear, identified by Jesse Weston as sexual symbols in the Grail legend, appear with stone and cauldron as the sacred objects in an outline written by Yeats for the initiation ceremony into a mystical cult, probably the Celtic Order in which he and Maud Gonne collaborated.

'Red Hanrahan' is most probably, like the tale of Raftery and Mary Hynes, a fable of Yeats's unassuaged passion for Maud Gonne. In the apotheosis of this tale she becomes, in the Otherworld, Echtge, Daughter of the Silver Hand. A reader as conversant with Irish mythology as Maud Gonne would recognize Mary Lavelle's spiritual father as Nuada

[1] Roger S. Loomis, 'Irish Origin of the Grail Legend,' *Speculum* (1933), VIII, 415; Helaine Newstead, *Bran the Blessed in Arthurian Romance* (New York, 1939).

[2] John Rhys, *Lectures on the Origin and Growth of Religion as Illustrated by Celtic Heathendom* [1887], 2d ed. (London, 1892), pp. 206–7.

of the Silver Hand, the war god who conquered chaos and established the kingdom of the Sidhe,[1] a lineage which elaborates the claim in *The Celtic Twilight* that Mary Hynes's beauty was a gift of the Sidhe. But Red Hanrahan fails to redeem Mary Lavelle from the Happy Otherworld. In subsequent adventures he sees a vision of the Sidhe going into a white door on the side of the mountain (it was on Ben Bulben), and in that whirling mist he recognizes the lovers of olden time. In his dying hour he hears fairy music and knows 'that it was but the continual clashing of swords.'

The change in the description of that music which came to Carolan and to himself from fairy bells to the clashing of swords portends Yeats's progress from the poetry of escape to the poetry of insight. He is still under the pall of late Romanticism, 'half in love with easeful death,' and can but state the theme of conflict, not yet embody it as he would do in the Cuchulain plays, where the clash of swords pits mortal ambition against a fate beyond mortality's comprehension.

Yet of all Yeats's imagined characters it is Hanrahan whose experience seems most indispensable in 'The Tower' as a defense against old age. Yeats dismisses all the others he has summoned,

> . . . but leave Hanrahan,
> For I need all his mighty memories.

This 'Old lecher with a love on every wind,' who has 'Reckoned up every . . . unseeing plunge . . . Into the labyrinth of another's being,' can best answer what the poet called up all his ghostly troupe to learn:

> Does the imagination dwell the most
> Upon a woman won or a woman lost?

[1] Ibid., pp. 119 ff.

What can Red Hanrahan say to that? It is his creator who answers,

> If on the lost, admit you turned aside
> From a great labyrinth out of pride,
> Cowardice, some silly over-subtle thought
> Or anything called conscience once;
> And that if memory recur, the sun's
> Under eclipse and the day blotted out.

It is to himself that the poet is speaking, of course, since if Hanrahan turned aside he can yet 'reckon up,' with his transcendent knowledge, the experience that he missed. The image of the labyrinth here is one of Yeats's 'masterful images because complete,' suggesting as it does the love of Theseus and Ariadne, the woman's gift which would lead the hero unscathed from his peril, the passage of the lover through a mysterious tunnel, and his encounter with a beast that can be mastered only by not turning aside. But Yeats *qua* Hanrahan did turn aside from these, the possibilities of love in action, finding instead his 'mighty memories' of transfiguration. Yet he must admit,

> . . . that if memory recur, the sun's
> Under eclipse and the day blotted out.

We might have recourse to *A Vision* to see what this means. A full moon, eclipsing the sun, would be in Phase 15, Pure Subjectivity, when 'nothing is apparent but dreaming *Will* and the Image that it dreams.' This is the phase when

> contemplation and desire, united into one, inhabit a world where every beloved image has bodily form, and every bodily form is loved. This love knows nothing of desire, for desire implies effort, and though there is still separa-

tion from the loved object, love accepts the separation as necessary to its own existence.[1]

But we must recall that in this phase human life is not possible. In the terms proposed in section ii of 'The Tower' itself, the poet must suffer defeat 'if memory recur'; for had he not cried out, after Raftery's song had driven men into the bog of Cloone,

> O may the moon and sunlight seem
> One inextricable beam,
> For if I triumph I must make men mad.

IV

Yeats's heroes never triumph. Or if they do, their victories are Pyrrhic. In *The King's Threshold* Seanchan dies; in *Deirdre* Naoise is executed; in *A Full Moon in March* and *The King of the Great Clock Tower* the lover is beheaded; in *The Herne's Egg* Congal is turned into a donkey; and Cuchulain wins nothing but fame in the songs of harpers to come. Triumph in this world is incompatible with the condition of mortality. Only the soul can triumph, in transfiguration. And so in the final section of 'The Tower,' the artist, his imagination renewed and refreshed by the 'mighty memories' of the peasant poets in whom he had dramatized the transcendent passions of his youth, subsumes them all—blind beggar, peasant visionary, great house, noble hero—in his transfiguring cry:

> And I declare my faith:
> I mock Plotinus' thought
> And cry in Plato's teeth,
> Death and life were not

---

[1] *A Vision* (New York, 1956), pp. 135-6.

> Till man made up the whole
> Made lock, stock and barrel
> Out of his bitter soul . . .

And after the death of the body, even Paradise is a dream of the soul. Hanrahan's quest had led him through 'The Broken Gates of Death' to his dream of Paradise, and now that memory recurs the poet has 'prepared his peace' with all learned things, with

> Poet's imaginings
> And memories of love,
> Memories of the words of women,
> All those things whereof
> Man makes a superhuman
> Mirror-resembling dream.

In 'The Tower' Yeats successfully unites the high with the low Matter of Ireland. He combines the vigorous energy and common character of his ballad poets with the reflective voice of the spiritual philosopher. He holds together thematic materials drawn from peasant folklore, from the aristocratic medieval Romance literature of the Grail and *The Mabinogion* and, in the first and third section which enclose these amatory and spiritual adventures, philosophical speculation and 'learned Italian things.' Seldom in his verse is such an eclectic fusion unified with such dramatic authority or such sustained imaginative energy. His vision of transcendence is far more effective here than in the earlier writings to which 'The Tower' alludes because it is no longer pursued for its own sake but, in the present context, to offer the ageing man his only consolation against 'the wreck of body' and the 'slow decay of blood.'

Hanrahan's dream of Paradise had not the fulfillment of

the frenzy of Crazy Jane, whose mighty memories held no turning aside from the fullness of love in this life. But Yeats's unique authority, as Edwin Muir has said, is that 'He had mastered his art so completely that he could express all his moods with equal power.'[1] And Crazy Jane's randy transport led her, also, to a great house all alight. Translunar Paradise is our common dream, however we pass out of the light of common day to achieve it, whether in visionary trance, in sexual ecstasy, or in the death of the body. Hanrahan's adventures have their counterpart too in the epic action of Cuchulain. Unlike the peasant poet, however, that noble warrior did not turn aside from the labyrinth of love. Yet he too suffers defeat in this world, though he is transfigured in the next.

[1] *The Estate of Poetry* (New York, 1962), p. 56.

: 4 :

CUCHULAIN AND THE EPIC THEME

'What can I but enumerate old themes?' *

The most ambitious poem of Yeats's youth was an attempt
at epic, as though to answer his own call for an Irish literature based on epic and legend as well as balladry. But *The
Wanderings of Oisin* is more legendary than epical. In old
age Yeats rather wryly wrote that he had led his hero 'by
the nose' through 'allegorical dreams' of 'Vain gaiety, vain
battle, vain repose.' The tale is based on one of the countless stories of abduction to the Otherworld which Yeats
found in both his reading and his folktale collecting. Oisin
has been summoned by golden-haired Niamh, daughter of
the gods, to three enchanted islands, adventures which he
tells retrospectively to Saint Patrick on his return three
hundred years later. One source of monotony, however, is
the fact that the world from which Oisin was spirited away
in the poem is all but as nebulous as the islands to which he
traveled. The style of *The Wanderings* is ornate and pic-
torial, the rhythms langorous. The poem is much more suc-

---

* From 'The Circus Animals' Desertion.'

cessful as an extended narrative in the Pre-Raphaelite style than as an epic, despite Yeats's illusion that he was treating epic materials.

In a letter to Katharine Tynan, Yeats said that his first notion of a long poem was 'as a region into which one should wander from the cares of life. The characters were to be no more real than . . . shadows. . . . Their mission was to lessen the solitude without destroying its peace.' He was describing an earlier poem as 'a region,' to differentiate *Oisin* as rather 'an incident or series of incidents.'[1] But most readers of *Oisin* find the atmosphere stronger than the action. In fact, this is not an epic at all but a decorative evocation of a theme from that Ossianic literature which Irish scholars like Gerard Murphy classify as romance rather than epic. In his synoptic essay *Saga and Myth in Ancient Ireland*, Murphy sums up the qualities of that epic literature which flourished from the ninth through the twelfth centuries, earlier than the romantic tales of Finn and his son Oisin:

> Heroic literature is aristocratic in outlook. As virtues it praises loyalty, prowess, and fulfilment of one's word. . . . It idealises its heroes, yet remains fundamentally realistic: those heroes are made of flesh and blood; their success or failure depends more on character and action than on accident or magic, though fate and the gods may be regarded as inscrutable yet necessary factors in life.[2]

Literature from the epic tradition had an even greater appeal to Yeats than did the Fenian material. In such tales which he first read in the translations of Ferguson, O'Grady, P. W. Joyce, and other nineteenth-century scholars, and then in Lady Gregory's romantic retellings

[1] *Letters*, ed. Wade, p. 106 (13 January 1889).
[2] (Dublin, 1961), pp. 26-7.

—the Fenian stories in *Gods and Fighting Men,* the epic tales in *Cuchulain of Muirthemne*—Yeats found epitomes of the brave warrior, the seeker of vengeance, the plotter of discord, the seeker of wisdom. He found in this ancient literature, already patterned, the themes of the son struggling against the father, of man struggling against fate, of the coming of a new faith and the destruction of an ancient world. Further, this national literature of myth and epic action was the aristocratic analogue of folktales and supernatural beliefs. Its forms were aristocratic forms, the world in which its characters moved was one of noble manners and high courtesies in war and in love, and both realms of action were interfused by divine personages and magical powers.

It was all very well for the young poet to propose epic themes for Irish letters, but how, at the end of the nineteenth century, could such materials be treated? Ever since Wordsworth, epic, as it was understood from Homer through the eighteenth century, had been impossible because of the difficulty in imagining a hero whose actions would be equally significant to both a national and a personal history. A new conception of epic appeared in *The Prelude*—the man of sensibility replaced the man of action as the heroic figure, and the modern subject of the epic became the growth of a poet's mind. Whitman, also, managed an epic theme; he called it 'Song of Myself' and made the self a container of the entirety of American experience. Much though he admired these poets, Yeats could not have undertaken so radical a repudiation of all tradition as did Whitman. 'Whatever I alter must seem traditional.' Yeats had access to what Whitman and Wordsworth lacked, a tradition about a national hero, half mythological, in which he could still believe and assume belief by others—at least that 'suspension of disbelief' which, as Coleridge said, is the necessary illusion in the reality of poetry.

The five plays he wrote about this Homeric man, Cuchulain, differ widely in technique. Written and rewritten between 1904 and 1939, their dramatic forms reflect Yeats's changing attitudes toward the theater. One devolves from Jacobean stage drama, another from farce, and three from the Japanese Noh play; the first two were designed for a popular theater, the Noh plays for an elite audience of no more than a hundred. The Noh play proved exactly right for the extended lyric emotion in a formalized, hieratic setting which Yeats needed for his theme. As my present interest in these plays is conceptual rather than theatrical, I wish to examine their significant action in hopes of elucidating Yeats's treatment of an epic character.

The Cuchulain plays seem to me Yeats's most successful version of an epic theme—not the growth of a poet's mind but the tragedy of a heroic personality struggling against necessity. Yeats became an epic poet not by writing an epic poem but by imagining successfully an epic character. Alone among a dozen countrymen who wrote on Cuchulain, Yeats pursued the significance of character to its ultimate reward, an understanding of tragedy. Yet considering the five plays together, we find that, while the character and action from epic sources are interpreted freely in a mode of tragedy, the action is manipulated in a fashion more characteristic of traditional romance than of either tragic drama or epic poetry.

In the Cuchulain series the two heroic themes of love and of war are fused together in a knot of concentrated power. Yeats used the materials he found in Lady Gregory's books so freely as to baffle the efforts of Birjit Bjersby and others who have tried to trace the sources in his versions. A study of the revisions of his early poem 'Cuchulain's Fight with the Sea' (which must have seemed, in 1892, merely an Irish imitation of Arnold's impressive 'Sohrab and Rustum') with the versions of *On Baile's Strand* would show how skillfully Yeats remolded his materials to the needs of his synoptic theme. While the originals of these plays were heroic sagas of a medieval people, Yeats dramatized the plots so as to embody a spiritual content and a lyrical emotion characteristic of late Romanticism, rather than of the work of a heroic age. Yet in this a circle is fulfilled; for to spiritualize these stories, Yeats incorporated into them beliefs from Irish folklore, while the saga material itself contained the detritus of earlier myths expressing religious conceptions similar to those still extant in country superstitions.

This side of Yeats's Cuchulain epic appears in his treatment of the hero as lover, in which are developed convictions already embodied in *Stories of Red Hanrahan*. The other side of his epic, the warrior theme, as Yeats works it out in *On Baile's Strand*, becomes cunningly dependent upon Cuchulain's spiritual adventures as lover. And there are further syncretions in Yeats's handling of these themes. Cuchulain as warrior-hero must surrender his autonomy to a human king, but as spiritual hero Cuchulain acknowledges no human law and seeks identity with the divine forces beyond this life. It is the consequence of his spiritual quest which dooms him in his worldly prowess, as we shall see. And there Cuchulain is trapped not only by an oath he reluctantly has sworn, but also by his own mortality as a man: as a son and as a lover, as a father and as the subject of a king. This is the web of dark necessities which is thrown over Cuchulain's head. His vain and tragic struggle against this web leads to his near-death, and to the surrender of his

soul into the keeping of the malicious, fateful gods of the
Sidhe. There the sacrifice of a human love redeems him to
our life, but in the end all of his glories cannot save him
from a mean death. His heroism accomplishes nothing, and
exists only for its own sake, in images of fearlessness and
pride that haunt us from the stage.

II

In his *Collected Plays* Yeats arranged the five Cuchulain
episodes not in the order of their composition but in that of
the adventures of the hero. I shall follow his order in discussing them. These plays have been summarized to advantage by, among others, Peter Ure and Helen Vendler;
nonetheless, I propose to trace the hero's course once more,
in the hope that, by attending to certain patterns in the action and elucidating the significance of certain relationships
between the characters, we can more fully understand both
the significance of Cuchulain and the intensity by which
Yeats made the Matter of Ireland his own *materia poetica*.

Yeats makes no use of the saga material recounting
Cuchulain's birth and upbringing. When the hero first appears he is already a young man in *At the Hawk's Well*
(1917), a man, we are told by the musician's song which is
a prelude to this Noh play, 'climbing up to a place / The
salt sea wind has swept bare.' This image of a man seeking
an encounter in a high windy place is juxtaposed, in the
second verse of the song, to the image of a bent old man
with 'speckled shin,' whose mother, could she see him,
would think 'How little worth' were her hopes, her fears,
her birth-pangs. This song, then, invokes a brief, heroic life
as preferable to a long, prudent, submissive one. Each of
these options is soon personified in action.

The action in the play is very brief. There is a sacred well whose waters grant immortality to any man who drinks them. The well is guarded by a hawk woman, and for many years a fifty-year-old man has been waiting, without success, for the waters to appear. They rise, but when he is asleep, and fall leaving no drop behind. This timorous man of fifty is an emblem of the poet who, in *Responsibilities,* had begged pardon of 'old fathers, that for a barren passion's sake,' although he was nearly forty-nine, he had 'no child . . . nothing but a book.' The Old Man's barrenness and sterility are set off by the vigor of Cuchulain, who strides confidently onstage. The prudent Old Man warns him against Aoife, the Woman of the Sidhe who will 'allure or destroy.' Any man who has 'gazed in her unmoistened eyes' will be cursed:

> Never to win a woman's love and keep it;
> Or always to mix hatred in the love;
> Or it may be that she will kill your children . . .
> Or you will be so maddened that you kill them
> With your own hand.

The Guardian of the Well throws off her cloak, revealing her hawk-like body. 'Do what you will,' Cuchulain says, 'I shall not leave this place / Till I have grown immortal like yourself.' As the hawk woman begins her dance—it is an orgiac dance, at once inviting and menacing—the Old Man falls asleep, and Cuchulain '*drops his spear as if in a dream*' and follows the dancer offstage. She eludes him there, and the water rises and falls while he is gone, as the Old Man discovers on awaking. Cuchulain returns and the Old Man says, 'She has but led you from the fountain.' But the musicians are crying 'Aoife! Aoife!' to the striking of a gong, and the young man asks, 'Who are they that beat a sword

upon a shield?! . . . I will face them'—and seizing his
spear, he goes out *no longer as if in a dream,* calling, 'He
comes! Cuchulain, son of Sualtim, comes!' The Musicians'
coda is a song in which first an empty well, then a leafless
tree, praise a man who calls the milk cows home and sets
store on a hearth with children and dogs. But the refrains
ask

> Who but an idiot would praise
> Dry stones in a well?
>
> .　.　.　.　.　.　.
>
> Who but an idiot would praise
> A withered tree?

So their final stanzas repeat the burden of the Musicians'
opening song, that a brief heroic life is preferable to a timid
longevity.

In *At the Hawk's Well* the action is simple, the verse
spare and swift. Yet the play has proved a puzzle to its
readers, in part because the Noh form presents them with
an alien stage tradition, in part because the Cuchulain
legends in the *Táin Bó Cúailnge* seem as unfamiliar (despite the long bibliography of English translations from
Standish O'Grady on) as do the Japanese mystery plays.
Besides, even to persons who know the Irish legends Yeats's
play can seem confusing because of his free handling of tradition. There is disagreement about such elementary matters as what the well and the hawk represent, who are
Aoife and the Guardian of the Well, and whether Cuchulain is seeking heroism, or immortality, or love. One critic
has it that '*At the Hawk's Well* . . . is superficially the
representation of an Irish heroic myth and really the (uni-
versalized) statement of Yeats's own gathering despair.' [1]

---

[1] F. A. C. Wilson, *Yeats's Iconography* (London, 1960), p. 32.

First let it be said that the legendary sources—including Lady Gregory's adaptations in *Cuchulain of Muirthemne*, the most proximate source for Yeats—are themselves pretty confusing. For instance, in the Irish legends Cuchulain marries not only Emer but also Eithne (whom Yeats makes Cuchulain's mistress) and among women of the Sidhe he is married, at one place or another, to Uathach and Aoife, while yet another, Fand, steals him away to be her lover. But, as Rhys says, 'Much consistency is not to be looked for in these matters.' [1] What is to be sought is the manner in which Yeats imposed consistency upon the contradictions of his material. With Yeats's artistic needs in mind it is of no consequence that Aoife was in reality not the ruler to whom Cuchulain was apprenticed to learn the trade of war (as in *On Baile's Strand*) but the enemy of that queen.[2] Nor does it matter that Cuchulain was held captive under enchantment by Fand, the deserted wife of the sea-god Manannan, who came to him as a white bird. Mr. F. A. C. Wilson thinks this episode suggested the description in *At the Hawk's Well* of Cuchulain's trying to stone the hawk who attacked him as he climbed the mountain, and supposes that the Guardian's dance occurs 'when Fand possesses a human body to seduce Cuchulain from the Well.' [3] Yeats does introduce the figure of Fand in a later play, *The Only Jealousy of Emer;* in a few pages I shall discuss her significance there. Suffice it here to say that the point is strongly made by Yeats that Cuchulain acts in *At the Hawk's Well* by his own choice: he knowingly and voluntarily forsakes the rising of the water in order to seek a different kind of immortality by gazing on Aoife's 'unmoistened eye,' hazarding the curses which the Old Man

[1] *Celtic Heathendom*, 2d ed. (London, 1892), p. 466.
[2] See *Cuchulain of Muirthemne* (London, 1902), pp. 32-8.
[3] *Yeats's Iconography*, pp. 29-30, 34-5.

has foretold in order to become as immortal as herself. The well water offers not this immortality of the soul, but, as Mrs. Vendler suggests, merely the longevity of a Tithonus.[1] It is therefore apt that the Old Man, representing timidity and prudence, should seek no more than a physical immortality—and be cheated of it—while Cuchulain chooses to seek a more heroic sort of immortality. True, he is also cheated by the Sidhe. But the point of the relationship between Cuchulain and Fand is that it is involuntary on his part: she comes from the Otherworld to choose him. Cuchulain is whipped by Fand and her sister and for a year he lies as though dead, a condition relieved only by his taking Fand as his wife. He remains her captive until Emer reclaims him.[2] Yeats, as we shall see, unified his rather intransigent materials. Quite wide of the mark is Mr. Wilson's comment that the plays, 'planned independently, do not cohere in any essential respect, and Yeats's attempt to interrelate them is largely wasted ingenuity.'[3] Because these plays dramatize a consistent character, they do cohere, as a careful reading buttressed by some relevant supplementary information should demonstrate.

Lady Gregory had told in a bald, condensed way, of Cuchulain's combat against Aoife: apprenticed to the warrior queen Scathach, the hero defends her realm against Aoife, who begs for her life and, evidently as a condition of surrender, 'gave her love to Cuchulain.'[4] Yeats coalesced this account of a relationship, which he enriched to one of love and hate, with a separate legend of the guarded well. In Irish legend and folklore the well of immortality or wis-

[1] Helen Hennessey Vendler, *Yeats's Vision and the Later Plays* (Cambridge, Mass., 1963), p. 209.
[2] Rhys, *Celtic Heathendom*, pp. 458–64.
[3] *Yeats's Iconography*, p. 41.
[4] *Cuchulain of Muirthemne*, p. 38.

dom is one of the most common motifs,[1] and in his reading Yeats had come upon yet further variants of the widespread folktale of the loathly lady who guards a sacred well.[2] He made this loathly lady into a Hawk Woman, one of Aoife's troupe, whose hawk body, hidden until she removes her cloak for her orgiac dance, is an image of fierce nobility, as the bird's rapacity is a part of its grace.

To understand *At the Hawk's Well* we must decide who is this Guardian of the Well and what she represents. It is true, as Peter Ure says, that as she 'becomes possessed by the hawk, the terrible life of the deity slides through her veins.'[3] This Guardian, and Aoife—who was herself the hawk that attacked Cuchulain as he climbed her sacred mountain—are of that company of Yeats's divine birds and beasts—the heron, the swan, the unicorn, the 'great beast' of 'The Second Coming'—who violently bring supernatural energies into the human world. In the Cuchulain plays such creatures are of the Sidhe—to put it in terms of *A Vision*, they are from Phase 15, Pure Subjectivity. Thus Cuchulain, in pursuing the Guardian, in drawing his sword against Aoife and then, after mastering her, ravishing her, is reversing the theme of fairy abduction. He is trying to make his way, recklessly, by main force and sexual energy, into the life beyond our life of the Otherworld. The analogy is plain in Hanrahan's heedless pursuit of the hounds and hare to the Castle of Queen Echtge, where not only the action but the symbols are parallel: the Cauldron of the Head of Hades, which represented Pleasure in Queen Echtge's castle, is equated by Rhys with the Well of Wis-

[1] Most notably the Well of Connla, subject of a poem by AE; see Birjit Bjersby, *The Cuchulain Legend in the Works of W. B. Yeats* (Upsala, 1950), pp. 41-4. There were fifty-seven such wells in County Sligo (Wood-Martin, *History of Sligo . . . from 1688. .* , p. 355).

[2] Wilson, *op. cit.*, pp. 35-7, cites two examples.

[3] *Yeats the Playwright* (New York, 1963), p. 70.

dom in Irish legend.[1] But where the tone of Red Hanrahan's story was wonder, here the mood is that of mortal
danger and the need for superhuman courage. Only on his
deathbed did Hanrahan recognize that fairy music was the
clashing of swords, but Cuchulain's first adventure combines sword-play with sexual ecstasy.

Like the still older hero of the first recorded epic,
Gilgamesh, Cuchulain is himself the son of a god and a
mortal, and journeys to the other world seeking immortality he cannot be granted.

III

The Green Helmet (1910) is Act II of Yeats's Cuchulain
plays. Here we have another demonstration of the hero's
transcendent courage. Yeats based this play upon two Irish
legends. In Lady Gregory's version of Bricriu's Feast [2] he
found the boastings of Cuchulain and two rival Ulster warriors over which should be given the champion's portion,
and the corresponding contention between their wives.
This provides the outline for the farcical humor of *The
Green Helmet*, in which rhymed fourteen-syllable couplets
canter on to the end, encompassing a theme of terror as
much as of hilarity. For the dispute is to be settled by an
exchange of blows with the Red Man who has come out of
the sea to challenge the Champion of Ulster. He has left a
green helmet upon the shore, for that champion to wear.
The blows they are to exchange are beheadings. This tale,
from the Irish *Cennach in Rúanada*, is the earliest known
appearance of the beheading motif used three centuries
later in *Sir Gawaine and the Green Knight*. For the original

---

[1] *Celtic Heathendom*, p. 373.
[2] *Cuchulain of Muirthemne*, pp. 48–61.

giant Yeats substitutes a character he calls the Red Man, who is clearly based on one of the nine types of evil fairies Yeats had classified in his anthology *Irish Fairy Tales* (1892). This is the 'Far Darrig,' whose name in Irish means 'red man'; he is 'the practical joker of the other world' who 'presides over evil dreams.' [1] Cuchulain is the only champion who dares accept the Red Man's challenge, but instead of beheading the hero the supernatural challenger crowns him with the green helmet, saying,

> And I choose the laughing lip
> That shall not turn from laughing, whatever rise or fall;
> The heart that grows no bitterer; although betrayed by all;
> The hand that loves to scatter; the life like a gambler's throw;
> And these things I make prosper, till a day come that I know,
> When heart and mind shall darken that the weak may end the strong,
> And the long-remembering harpers have matter for their song.

The farce of *The Green Helmet* strikes a tone unique among Yeats's works, one which has seemed heavy-handed to most readers. The play is not taken very seriously. Yet its combination of *rodomontade* with the marvellous, of an earthy realism with an apprehension of supernatural terror, is both true to the spirit of the Irish epics and appropriate to the adventures of Yeats's hero. The virtues praised in the last speech are the aristocratic ones of reckless courage, love of life, generosity, and these are associated with a suggestion of the hero's role as guarantor of the fertility of the

---

[1] *Irish Fairy Tales* (New York, n.d. [First pub. 1888]), p. 227. Yeats's elaborate classification is adapted from those in T. Crofton Croker, *Fairy Traditions and Legends in the South of Ireland*, 3 vols. (London, 1825-28), and Thomas Keightly, *Fairy Mythology* (London, 1850), pp. 362-72.

land. In the first version of the play the champion's helmet was golden, but a green helmet better suggested the connection between the hero who would accept a challenge from the Otherworld and the continuing fruition of his country.

Cuchulain is often described as the son of Lugh, the sun god, and Rhys in his *Celtic Heathendom* interprets Cuchulain, according to the then-prevalent mythographic theory, as a solar myth. The Red Man coming out of the sea is patently an image of the rising of the sun, which Yeats allies with the figure of the sea god Manannan in order to make plausible the continuity of *The Green Helmet* with Cuchulain's fighting the waves in the next play, *On Baile's Strand*.

This play also takes place on the beach where the realms of sea, air, and land meet: the kingdoms of Manannan, the Sidhe, and King Conchubar. Here we have the working out of the conflict between power and knowledge, a theme explored as early as in the poems 'Fergus and the Druid' and 'Who Will Go with Fergus Now?' in which Fergus abjured his crown for a druid's bag of dreams and gained, in the latter poem, the knowledge that controls the four elements. The problem is much more complexly imagined now. Cuchulain is king of Muirthemne, himself in fealty to the High King of Uladh, Conchubar. Cuchulain is a warrior-hero, not a druid or a philosopher; his knowledge is but to be true to his own character, demonstrating in every breath and action the proud, careless virtues that Yeats so much admired. It is Cuchulain who now represents power, and Conchubar knowledge. But Conchubar is no druid either; he is but the High King, the executive ruler whose 'wisdom' is merely prudential, not divine. He represents the demands society makes upon the will of each of its members to conform to custom, law, order, so that the continuity of culture may be assured. Cuchulain, on the other hand, is, like Achilles, heroic because anarchic. His will is the free expression of a personality that submits freely to nothing, recognizes no limits upon its own expression or fulfillment. And Conchubar holds his throne only because Cuchulain's power has held off the enemies of his kingdom.

All this is made clear in the final version of the play (1906); little of it appears in Yeats's early poem or in the first printing of the play (*In the Seven Woods*, 1903). By degrees he enriched this background, barely suggested by the relationships between the characters in Lady Gregory's *Cuchulain*. Yeats has dealt freely with the original tale, inventing incidents and characters which make possible the thickening interplay of motive and theme.

When the play opens it is not the High King and rebellious warrior who hold the stage but a Fool and a Blind Man, wrangling about their dinner. *On Baile's Strand* is modeled on a Jacobean revenge tragedy in its structure and versification, and Yeats has adapted to his own needs the Shakespearean device of an underplot. Yeats's Fool is the lowly parallel and shadow-image of his reckless hero; the Blind Man, who, the Fool complains, is 'always thinking,' is the shadow-image of King Conchubar. They are also the chorus, filling in for the audience the necessary background and interpreting, after the denouement, what has happened offstage.

When the king and hero enter they are wrangling too. A strange warrior has landed from Aoife's country, under a *gesa* or bond not to reveal his name, and he has challenged the champion of the land. Conchubar, in this emergency, must rely on the unpredictable Cuchulain. The king would leave his children 'a strong and setted country' but his

champion frolicks and riots without regard to the needs of
the kingdom. Therefore, Conchubar bids Cuchulain take
an oath of obedience. The hero scornfully refuses to 'Give
up my will to yours; go where you please; / Come when
you call . . .' but the king is insistent. He says that
Cuchulain defies civil authority only because he has no
children to inherit his reputation or his realm. Conchubar's
own children are afraid of their wild protector and have
urged the king to put him under bonds. Conchubar says
that since Cuchulain despises the queens of the realm he
should have begotten children on 'Some daughter of the
air.' This touches a spring of memory in Cuchulain, and he
recalls that 'daughter of the air' he had fought, overpowered, and briefly loved while in Scotland where he
learned his warrior's trade.

> Ah! Conchubar, had you seen her
> With that high, laughing, turbulent head of hers
> Thrown backward, and the bowstring at her ear . . .
> Or when love ran through all the lineaments
> Of her wild body—although she had no child,
> None other had all beauty, queen or lover,
> Or was so fitted to give birth to kings.

Conchubar then reasonably replies that it is Aoife whom
Cuchulain is praising, the very one who now hates him and
plots the ruin of the kingdom that he serves. But Cuchulain
knows that Aoife's vengeance is not inconsistent with her
love, for the love that moves him is

> a kiss
> In the mid-battle, and a difficult truce
>
> .   .   .   .
>
> A brief forgiveness between opposites . . .

The king continues with regal patience to argue reason-
ableness and obedience to this unruly, anarchic, demonic
hero on whose strength the stability of his own realm depends. 'You are but half a king and I but half,' he says; 'I
need your might of hand and burning heart / And you my
wisdom.' Cuchulain, for all his primordial energy and instinctual independence, is not wise, at least not in the way
of Conchubar's prudence. For in the end he tires of argument and says 'I'll take what oath you will,'—the rash boon
by which heroism becomes ensnared in the net of tragic
necessity. The oath Conchubar gets him to swear is 'to be
obedient in all things / To Conchubar, and to uphold his
children.' The worldly-wise king replies, as, in a ritual of
intensification, they thrust their swords together over the
flame,

> We are one being, as these flames are one:
> I give my wisdom, and I take your strength.

At this point, if Conchubar's wisdom is truly wise, unity
of being has been achieved. With power and wisdom
welded by the one flame, the kingdom of Uladh is now im-
pregnable. But Conchubar's 'wisdom' proves to be not that
of Fergus, who 'rules the brazen cars . . . And the white
breast of the dim sea.' Conchubar's rule extends only over
Uladh, the everyday world of time-serving, where, as
Cuchulain had taunted him, he'd have no women near who
would not cringe to please him. Over the tumultuous world
of unruly energies in which Cuchulain revels at whatever
the cost, the world where love is 'a difficult truce' between
'hot-footed sun' and 'cold, sliding, slippery-footed moon,'
Conchubar does not rule, any more than he understands it.
No sooner has Cuchulain sworn his oath of allegiance
than the young stranger from Aoife's country appears,

challenging him to battle. From this point onward Yeats not only develops the ominous consequences of the foregoing action but provides, with great concision, a much fuller working-out of the Sohrab and Rustum theme than appears either in his Celtic sources or in Arnold's poem. Yeats's play reaches deeper and brings out more clearly the psychological roots of a similar tragic situation. Now Cuchulain is struck with admiration at the young stranger's noble bearing, his dignity under his *gesa* not to reveal his name, his heroic mien. This lad is no timorous administrative mind like Conchubar's sons; he is no cautious diplomatist nor subject of any civil code. The old hero, half-recognizing the lineaments of Aoife, salutes the young, his own kind, and offers a gift that Aoife would recognize as Cuchulain's own and so not accuse her young warrior of cowardice. The gift is a cloak. Cuchulain says,

> My father gave me this.
> He came to me to try me, rising up at dawn
> Out of the cold dark of the rich sea.
> He challenged me to battle, but before
> My sword had touched his sword, told me his name,
> Gave me this cloak, and vanished. It was woven
> By women of the Country-under-Wave
> Out of the fleeces of the sea . . .

> . . . .

> Boy,
> If I had fought my father, he'd have killed me,
> As certainly as if I had a son
> And fought with him, I should be deadly to him . . .

But no such show of forgiveness between enemies can be tolerated by Conchubar or by his other subservient kings.

They mutter that Cuchulain has been bewitched, till, in a rage, he seizes Conchubar and defies him. The other kings berate Cuchulain until in a daze he acknowledges that only witchcraft could have made him break his bond and lay hands upon his high king. Suddenly drawing his sword, he drives the young challenger out to the strand. All follow but the Blind Man and the Fool, the Fool reporting what he sees from the door, the Blind Man telling him what he should think of it. Then Cuchulain comes back, and throws himself on the other end of the bench from the Blind Man, who has already told the Fool that the youth was Aoife's son, for he, before he lost his sight, had visited Aoife's country.

The Blind Man is therefore probably the Old Man of *At the Hawk's Well*, who was already in Aoife's country. We may be tempted to think of him as a Tiresias who has lost the sight of one world for knowledge from another, but his blindness surely objectifies the impotence of the one who waited by a leafless tree and a dry well. The *peripatea* of this play has been rightly praised by Lennox Robinson and others as one of the great moments of the modern theatre. Cuchulain questions the Fool and the Blind Man about the father of the youth he has killed. The Blind Man insists that nobody knows, but the Fool reveals, 'He said a while ago that he heard Aoife boast that she'd never but the one lover, and he the only man that had overcome her in battle.'

> *Blind Man:* Somebody is trembling, Fool! The bench is shaking. Why are you trembling? . . . It was not I who told you, Cuchulain.
>
> *Fool:* It is Cuchulain who is trembling. It is Cuchulain who is shaking the bench.
>
> *Blind Man:* It is his own son he has slain.

Driven mad by this knowledge, Cuchulain first attacks the vacant throne of King Conchubar with his sword, then rushes down to the beach. The Fool looks through the door and tells the Blind Man what is happening.

> *Fool:* Ah! now he is running down to the sea, but he is holding up his sword as if he were going into a fight. (*Pause*) Well struck! Well struck! . . . . O! he is fighting the waves!
>
> *Blind Man:* He sees King Conchubar's crown on every one of them.

And then, while all the nobles are running down the strand and the Fool is transfixed watching Cuchulain slash and slash the surf till the waves roll over his body—then the Blind Man, thinking of dinner, says, 'There will be nobody in the houses. Come . . . We will put our hands into the ovens.'

This is Yeats's own modification of the heroic tale in which Cuchulain fought the waves while under a spell cast by Conchubar's druid to protect the king from his madness. Now the Blind Man, as Conchubar's double, even though he has been in Aoife's country cannot understand the desolate fury that has driven Cuchulain mad. He can think only of vengeance on the king. But Cuchulain is driven by a far deeper, more primordial impulse to avenge his own outrageous fortune. He must sacrifice himself to his own father who once before had spared him as he has not spared his son. Like him, his son was born from the union of a mortal with a god, and, being like him bound by a *gesa*, bore Cuchulain's own fate: a heroic soul in a mortal body, doomed to suffer, not to understand his suffering, and to die.

Yeats is using the convention of the oath to dramatize the individual's inescapable bondage to necessity. Although he nowhere uses the terminology of Freud we can readily see that what is being dramatized here is an Oedipal conflict between fathers and sons. (Yeats adapted the two Oedipus plays in versions for the modern stage.) Cuchulain has ravished and deserted Aoife, the mother, who is idealized as a creature of the Otherworld at the same time that she is made terrifying as a bird of prey. The youth has set out under bonds to avenge his mother's spoliation. And this too is but part of a recurring pattern, since Cuchulain himself has had an earlier combat against his own father. In a late play, *Purgatory*, this theme is re-enacted yet again, not by a hero but by a loutish beggar and his son, emphasizing the sordidness of the body before the splendor of an illuminated castle in which the soul of the mother relives her ecstasy and ruin.

The last of the curses foretold by the Old Man in *At the Hawk's Well* has come true. In the remaining Cuchulain plays the other penalties the gods exact of the mortal who would thrust himself into their immortality remain to be fulfilled.

I V

> Thy great leaves enfold . . . him
> Who met Fand walking among flaming dew
> By a grey shore where the wind never blew,
> And lost the world and Emer for a kiss . . .*

The fourth play in the series, *The Only Jealousy of Emer*, is perhaps the most obscure on a first reading or in performance. The analogues as well as the sources of its symbolism have been exhaustively reviewed by F. A. C. Wilson, whose researches present the play as a synoptic exposition of a Neo-Platonic philosophy in which Yeats's

* From 'The Secret Rose,' 1896.

'symbolism is Florentine as much as it is Gaelic.'[1] I prefer
to regard *The Only Jealousy* as a dramatic work whose
symbolism, affiliated though it is to Renaissance expositions
of a spiritual theory, grows organically out of the given interrelationships of the characters. And the significance of
these characters was already fully present in the Gaelic
sources—which to be sure Wilson has traced with perse-
verance. Indeed he shows us how skillfully and ruthlessly
Yeats condensed the duplications and triplications of character and incident in the original story of Fand's seduction
of Cuchulain. But rather than rehearse this complicated
myth let us see what action Yeats has contrived for his
hero, now vanquished beneath 'the bitter tide.'

In the play we find Cuchulain lying as though dead after
his fight against the waves. His wife Emer has summoned
his mistress Eithne Inguba in hopes that she can call
Cuchulain back to life. But his body is misshapen, and
Eithne is repelled by it. Alone again with Cuchulain's
body, Emer recognizes that there is a changeling in it, and
this changeling, called the Figure of Cuchulain, speaks to
her. He says he is the 'Maker of discord among gods and
men, / Called Bricriu of the Sidhe,' and he tells Emer,

> I do not ask
> Your life, or any valuable thing;
> You spoke but now of the mere chance that some day
> You'd be the apple of his eye again
> When old and ailing, but renounce that chance
> And he shall live again.

As early as 1902 Yeats had worked out the symbolic significance of this occult and mysterious action, finding in
Cuchulain's abduction by Fand a pattern which his later
readings in the Renaissance Neo-Platonists, in Swedenborg

[1] Wilson, *Yeats's Iconography*, p. 103.

and in the Noh plays of Japan would confirm as a universal attribute of his native mythology. In an article of that year titled 'Away'—by which is meant a trace-state or coma or a fainting fit—Yeats gives several instances from his folklore collecting of the Irish countrymen's belief that the afflicted person has been taken by the Sidhe. 'It was probably one who was himself "away" who explained, that somebody or something was put in your place, and this explanation was the only possible one to ancient peoples, who did not make our distinction between body and soul. . . . This substitution of the dead for the living is indeed a pagan mystery, and not more hard to understand that the substitution of the body and blood of Christ for the wafer and the wine in the mass.' Recovery is effected by propitiating the interloper. And this pattern Yeats finds also in the intricate story of Cuchulain's abduction by Fand. Indeed, there are other striking parallels in the Celtic myths which Yeats had already used elsewhere:

> Professor Rhys has interpreted both the stories of Cuchulain and the story of Pwyll and Arawn as solar myths, and one doubts not that the old priests and poets saw analogies in day and night, in summer and winter; or perhaps held that the passing away for a time of the brightness of day or of the abundance of summer, was one story with the passing of a man out of our world for a time. There have been myth-makers who put the mountains of the gods at the North Pole, and there are still visionaries who think that cold and barrenness with us are warmth and abundance in some inner world; while what the Arran people call 'the battle of the friends' believed to be fought between the friends and enemies of the living among the 'others' to decide whether a sick person is to live or die, and the battle believed to be fought by the 'others' at harvest time, to decide, as I think, whether the harvest is to stay among men, or wither from among men

and belong to 'the others' and the dead, show, I think, that the gain of one country is the other country's loss. The Norse legend of the false Odin that took the true Odin's place, when the summer sun became the winter sun, brings the story of a man who is 'away' and the story of the year perfectly together. It may be that the druids and poets meant more at the beginning than a love story, by such stories as that of Cuchulain and Fand, for in many ancient countries, as even among some African tribes to-day, a simulated and ceremonious death was the symbol, or the condition, of the soul's coming to the place of wisdom and of the spirits of wisdom; and, if this is true, it is right for such stories to remind us of day and night, winter and summer, that men may find in all nature the return and history of the soul's deliverance.[1]

These parallels in the Matter of Ireland were not forgotten by Yeats, for he used some of this same material fifteen years later in annotating Lady Gregory's *Visions and Beliefs*. Thus Yeats had in mind this conjunction of the Cuchulain-Fand episode with the patterns of fertility myths and 'the soul's coming to the place of wisdom' at the time when he returned to his Cuchulain series with *At the Hawk's Well*, of which *The Only Jealousy of Emer* is a thematic continuation. His Neo-Platonic researches had correlated the pattern he had long before uncovered in legend and in folklore with that doctrine of dynamic oppositions between the spirit world and the world of the living which Miss Raine has shown to be found also in Plato's *Laws* and to be the source of Blake's poem 'The Mental Traveller.'[2] In the 'harsh geometry' of *A Vision* this is the interaction represented by the interlocking gyres.

Although *A Vision* can be invoked as an interpretive aid,

[1] 'Away,' *Fortnightly Review* (April 1902), n.s. LXXI, 733–40.
[2] Kathleen Raine, 'Blake's Debt to Antiquity,' *Sewanee Review* (Summer 1963), 405–18.

in the play the doctrine is represented by the action that follows upon Bricriu's bargain with Emer. The doctrine itself is consistent with a religious belief in which the ecstatic suspension of consciousness, whether in dance or in sexual frenzy or in dream or in death, was thought to be an experience of the Otherworld. Yet in *The Only Jealousy* Yeats assigns the elucidation of this doctrine, learned from Alfred Nutt and Sir John Rhys, to Bricriu, the Maker of Discord. The state of being 'away' or in near-death summons up a world of hostile spiritual forces, inimical to all for which the mortal heart longs, and a race of gods hungry to devour our blessings. This is not the Happy Otherworld of the orgiac dance and of Queen Echtge's Castle but a nightmare Otherworld through which the soul must pass. For the ghost of the dead is unable to enter the Happy Otherworld until it has purged itself of all earthly memories.

Speaking as the Figure of Cuchulain, the evil Bricriu tortures poor Emer, who has already humbled her pride by inviting Cuchulain's mortal mistress to his side. Now Bricriu taunts her,

> You've watched his loves and you have not been jealous,
> Knowing that he would tire, but do those tire
> That love the Sidhe?

Bricriu 'touches' her eyes so that she may see the Ghost of Cuchulain, his spirit separated from his body, crouching beside the bed. But Bricriu withholds from Cuchulain's ghost the power to see Emer, and she must now watch unseen as the Maker of Discord summons a strange woman to his side, one who

> has hurried from the Country-under-Wave
> And dreamed herself into that shape that he
> May glitter in her basket . . .

Now Emer recognizes that this Woman of the Sidhe 'Has hid herself in this disguise and made / Herself into a lie.' Costumed, the stage directions tell us, to *'seem more an idol than a human being,'* she awakens Cuchulain's Ghost by her quickening dance. When they speak, the blank verse of the play is broken by their hypnotic rhymed couplets. Cuchulain's Ghost is not yet ready for the voyage the dead make to the country of the Sidhe, for he is yet weighed down by memories of Emer's love. As he is entranced by the Woman of the Sidhe, he is pulled also by other memories, away from this world:

> I know you now, for long ago
> I met you on a cloudy hill
> Beside old thorn-trees and a well.
> A woman danced and a hawk flew. . . .
> Half woman and half bird of prey. . . .

But, like Emer, we know that Cuchulain's Ghost is seeing a *false* vision of Aoife, a cruel illusion conjured by the malicious Bricriu. Now Bricriu is Yeats's own contrivance, an interpolation into the story given by Rhys, Lady Gregory, and other redactors. Yeats has introduced Bricriu (who figured as the cause of contention in the tale on which *The Green Helmet* was based) in what seems to me a brilliant adaptation of an episode from Spenser. For it was the evil magician Archimago whose substitution of the false Duessa for Fidessa led the Red Cross Knight astray in *The Faerie Queene*. Now the false Aoife tempts Cuchulain's Ghost, who cries again and again for Emer. Then, tempted at last beyond earthly memories, Cuchulain's Ghost rushes offstage to follow the Woman of the Sidhe, to kiss her and be forever in the land of forgetfulness. Bricriu turns on Emer—

> Fool, fool!
> I am Fand's enemy come to thwart her will,
> And you stand gaping there . . .

And now we know that the Woman of the Sidhe, who had appeared to Cuchulain's Ghost as Aoife, is in reality Fand. As is told in Lady Gregory's story of 'The Only Jealousy,' Fand is that deserted wife of the great sea-god Manannan who had taken Cuchulain for her lover but had had to relinquish him to Emer. Bricriu has brought her here not only to thwart her will but to thwart Emer's love—and to fulfill the curse brought on Cuchulain by his invasion, in *At the Hawk's Well*, of the land of immortality.

It is clear that Fand represents the role played in Irish fairy lore by the Leanhaun Sidhe, or fairy mistress, another of the malevolent types of supernatural creatures which Yeats classified in 1891. Of this creature he wrote, 'This spirit seeks the love of men. If they consent, they are her [slaves]. . . . Most of the Gaelic poets, down to quite recent times, have had a Leanhaun Shee, for she gives inspiration to her slaves and is indeed the Celtic Muse.' [1] Mr. Wilson, discussing Fand as a moon symbol, has pointed to William Larminie's neglected poem (from *Fand and Moytura*, 1892) as a probable source. This is most likely, as is Larminie's presentation of Fand as a Leanhaun Sidhe, a tradition which this earlier poet and folklorist would have known. [2]

Yeats's Cuchulain, then, has both Emer and Eithne Inguba in this world and two immortal lovers also, Aoife, his first love whom he chose, and Fand, his fairy mistress

[1] *Irish Fairy Tales*, p. 229.

[2] Wilson quotes excerpts from Larminie's 'Fand' in *Yeats's Iconography*, pp. 91–2. Yeats reviewed with great approval Larminie's beautifully translated *West Irish Folk-Tales and Romances* ('The Evangel of Folk-Lore,' *Bookman* [June 1894], VI, 86).

who chose him.[1] It is at this point, when Cuchulain's Ghost
is about to follow Fand to the Country-under-Wave, that
Bricriu exacts Emer's renunciation of all hope that Cuchulain will love her again. Now Eithne Inguba, his mortal
mistress, comes onstage again, calls him back to life, and
takes credit for his recovery. Cuchulain awakens and
speaks in his mortal person for the first time—

> Your arms, your arms! O Eithne Inguba,
> I have been in some strange place and am afraid.

Where *On Baile's Strand* had explored the hero's relations with worldly power, *The Only Jealousy of Emer*
complementarily explores his fate as lover, determined by
the powers of the Otherworld. Here Cuchulain is 'away,'
divided into an inert, misshapen body and a detached and
enchanted spirit. The life of our world is seen to be
doomed to suffering: Cuchulain will come back bearing
Bricriu's curse, unable to return the true love of Emer. We
see that Cuchulain's relations with women have been
schematized in this play so that Emer represents a true and
all-forgiving, all-sacrificing human devotion; Eithne
Inguba the pleasure of the body; and Aoife the unappeasa-
ble longing of the spirit. The Woman of the Sidhe, Fand,
represents the insatiable desire of the Otherworld for our
prowess, a sinister figure embodying Blake's apothegm that
'Eternity is in love with the productions of time.' For being
a creature of the full moon, the pure subjectivity possible
only at the extinction of human life, her desire for Cuchu-

---

[1] A further argument against identifying Fand with the hawk woman
of *At the Hawk's Well*, as Wilson does, is that Aoife, the hawk woman,
is a 'daughter of the air' who frequents the windy gap on the mountain,
where Cuchulain climbs to pursue her; but Fand, wife of the sea-god
(her name is etymologically derived from the word for *water*; Rhys, op.
cit., p. 463), claims him, both in the legend and in Yeats's play, when he
is fallen, having been beaten into insensibility.

lain cannot be fulfilled while he is in this life, any more than can his for Aoife, who is likewise of that transcendent phase. As always in Yeats, division undoes unity, and love so divided cannot be fulfilled. Cuchulain is defeated in love as in battle by the inscrutable fate imposed by the other world, which denies its perfection to our life.

The flight into fairyland of Yeats's early verse has now been comprehended as the obliteration of mortal energy. The life that Cuchulain lives is controlled and invaded by the spirits of the dead, claiming their portion in the unremitting equations of life and death, day and night, joy and woe, plenitude and desolation, which are ever being balanced between their world and ours. In such a world the heroism of the epic warrior and lover must be to hold fast to his soul's own behests, however impossible fate may make it for these to be fulfilled. For, as Yeats wrote of Cuchulain's adventures in his article 'Away,' '. . . in all these stories strength comes from among men, and wisdom from among gods who are but "shadows." '

V

What brought them there so far from their home,
Cuchulain that fought night long with the foam . . .
What but heroic wantonness? *

As Yeats lay dying in the Hôtel Idéal Séjour he worked upon his last heroic play, *The Death of Cuchulain*. Bending the legends to his own imaginative needs, he made the hero who, in *At the Hawk's Well* had chosen a brief glorious life rather than a timorous longevity, persist into old age, an undaunted and reckless warrior still. But now, after six

* From 'Alternative Song for The Severed Head' in *The King of the Great Clock Tower*.

mortal wounds, his time of death has come. This last play dramatizes his 'heroic wantonness,' his mean death, his transfiguration.

The starting-point for any discussion of this coda to the epic series might well be the letter which Yeats wrote in October 1938 to Ethel Mannin:

> Goethe said that the poet needs all philosophy but must keep it out of his work. I am writing a play on the death of Cuchulain, an episode or two from the old epic. My 'private philosophy' is there but there must be no sign of it; all must be like an old fairy tale. It guided me to certain conclusions but I do not write it.[1]

There has been ingenious commentary on this difficult play, notably by critics who insist upon explaining the 'private philosophy' which its author was at pains to conceal. My concern, however, is to follow out the ways in which 'all must be like an old fairy tale.' This comment of Yeats's reminds us of Coleridge, who told a woman who wanted a moral in 'The Rime of the Ancient Mariner' that the poem should show its moral no more than does a tale from *The Arabian Nights*. Yeats himself once called fairy tales 'stories [which] have no moral,' [2] and while I do not suggest that this play is based on the dreamlike illogic of the West of Ireland folktales that occasioned his remark—tales in which magic makes irrelevant the consequences of deeds —the point is that the meaning of his play must be inherent in, indeed inseparable from, the logic of its form.

Yet the structure of *The Death of Cuchulain* seems at first disarticulated and baffling; episode follows episode without connectives or, as in *On Baile's Strand*, exposition.

---

[1] *Letters*, pp. 917–18.
[2] In his review of William Larminie's *West Irish Folk-Tales and Romances*, *Bookman*, VI (1894), 86. A fairy tale in *The Celtic Twilight* is called 'Dreams That Have No Moral.'

After a prologue (which I shall discuss below) the play is divided into scenes in which Cuchulain confronts one character after another in turn: Eithne Inguba (from *The Only Jealousy of Emer*); Aoife (from *At the Hawk's Well*); and the Blind Man (from *On Baile's Strand*). This brings us to Cuchulain's death, but there are three further episodes or epilogues, as his obsequies are spoken by the Morrigu (a war-goddess newly introduced in this play), then danced by Emer, and finally sung by a harlot who closes the play with a lyric in the manner of the Japanese Noh form. In the first part of the play we are still in the world of the living, in the last in the spirit world; Aoife and the Morrigu appear in our world, Emer dances as though in theirs, dramatizing the interpenetration of the one realm with the other. The action of the first part again coalesces Cuchulain's roles as lover and as warrior. This fusion continues after his death, when his character is celebrated in both aspects.

Unlike the earlier Noh plays in the Cuchulain series, this last is not framed by songs which give lyrical expression to its themes. That is the function of the harlot's song at the end, but the prologue is instead a harangue against the audience, spoken by an irascible Old Man who much resembles the splenetic monologist of *On the Boiler*. Mrs. Vendler is put off by his 'contempt for the audience' and finds his demand that they 'know the old epics and Mr. Yeats's plays' a 'preposterous' requirement. But these are the only terms on which *The Death of Cuchulain* is comprehensible. To understand what's going to happen here one must at the least have in mind the four preceding plays; and of his Dublin audience Yeats was demanding no more than knowledge of a national mythology which he had dramatized and propagandized for fifty years. As T. R. Henn observes, 'All of that mythology that has survived its testing, that can still decorate or explain a poet's heroic mask, is there on the stage.[1]

Granting the preparation required for the play, its audience might still not find *The Death of Cuchulain* unified by the successful dramatic structure that Peter Ure discovers it to have.[2] The coherence of this play seems to me to be not so much dramatic as symbolic and poetic. As a piece of stagecraft *The Death of Cuchulain* would probably seem bizarre, but a coherence does reside in the conceptualization which brings the hero's relationships with his mortal and immortal lovers to their destined ends. The play's form is unique to its occasion. Let us see in what fashion the six episodes comprise a fit conclusion to Yeats's epic theme. We will find a rationale, too, for the ranting prose prologue of the Old Man, which is best considered in its relation to the final song.

1. *Cuchulain and Eithne Inguba.* Cuchulain's wife Emer has sent Eithne, his mistress, to warn him not to go into battle while facing insuperable odds. That is the message in the letter Eithne bears, but what she tells him is the opposite: to rush into battle against Queen Maeve. Cuchulain listens, then reads the letter. He accuses Eithne of trying to send him to his death because, being tired of him, she desires a younger man. Eithne protests that she has been bewitched, and indeed the evil-doer's shape appears before her: it is the Morrigu, the woman with the head of a crow. This goddess of war is in league with Cuchulain's enemy Maeve, plotting his destruction. But Cuchulain, unable to see the Morrigu, does not believe Eithne. Emer in *The Only Jealousy* and Eithne here are given the 'touch' or sec-

---

[1] Vendler, *Yeats's Vision and the Later Plays,* p. 238; Henn, *The Lonely Tower* (London, 1965), p. 294.
[2] *Yeats the Playwright* (New York, 1963), pp. 77, 82.

ond sight, but this gift of prescience is never granted to Cuchulain. It is part of his destiny not to be able to see behind the veil which hides the supernatural forces against which he, in his heroism, contends. Indeed, it is the essence of his heroic character to struggle against these forces which he cannot see and hence cannot comprehend. Consequently, he now misunderstands Eithne's intentions. Forgiving her of a treachery she has not committed, he is unmoved by her despair. He decides to do battle whatever the odds, and bids his servant, should he not return, bestow Eithne upon Conall 'because the women / Have called him a good lover.'

2. *Cuchulain and Aoife.* Eithne is led away, for Cuchulain, his time nearly come, has no more to do with mortal loves. Now the stage darkens to the sound of pipe and drums (always these instruments in Yeats's Noh plays denote supernatural influence), and when the light returns it is after the battle. Cuchulain staggers in, wounded. He recognizes Aoife, as she comes before him, now like the aged Maud Gonne 'erect' and 'white-haired.' Although faint from his six wounds, like the ancient chieftains in the poem 'The Black Tower' Cuchulain would die upright, and he asks Aoife to bind him to a stone pillar. He knows why she has come: 'You have a right to kill me,' to avenge his killing of their son. The scene between them is vibrant with remembered and rekindled passions as Cuchulain awaits the fatal blow from his murderous lover; for had not her love been a truce between battles?

But the curses foretold for the man who breached the immortality of the Sidhe in *At the Hawk's Well* did not include death at her hand. Accordingly, Aoife does not recognize that it is Cuchulain's slayer who comes; as he approaches she withdraws, saying 'I will keep out of his sight, for I have things / That I must ask questions on before I kill you.' And so she is cheated of her revenge. The one who comes, however, has no sight, for it is the Blind Man.

3. *Cuchulain and the Blind Man.* He is the same who told Cuchulain that it was his own son he had killed—Conchubar's double, and, as the Old Man in *At the Hawk's Well* who foretold the curses Cuchulain must endure, he had been in Aoife's country before he lost his sight. Now the Blind Man has been promised twelve pennies if he brings back Cuchulain's head in a bag. As he gropes his way toward the helpless hero, Cuchulain has a prevision that

> There floats out there
> The shape that I shall take when I am dead,
> My soul's first shape, a soft feathery shape,
> And is not that a strange shape for the soul
> Of a great fighting-man?

As the Blind Man feels his shoulder, then his neck—'Ah! Ah! Are you ready, Cuchulain?' The hero answers, 'I say it is about to sing.' The knife approaches, the curtain falls—but rises again to the sound of pipe and drum.

4. *The Morrigu.* We see a lone woman with a crow's head, holding a black parallelogram that represents Cuchulain's head. Behind her are six other parallelograms, the stylized heads of the warriors who gave him his wounds. 'The dead can hear me, and to the dead I speak'—she names each warrior slain, then concludes, 'I arranged the dance.' Placing the head of Cuchulain on the ground, she goes out.

5. *Emer.* The place of the Morrigu is taken by Emer, who begins a dance, first raging against the six heads, then dancing around her husband's 'as if in adoration or triumph.' About to prostrate herself before Cuchulain's head, she 'seems to hesitate between the head and what she hears. Then she stands motionless, and in the silence a few faint bird notes.'

The dance that the Morrigu arranged was, of course, not only Emer's stylized pantomime but the greater dance of which this is the imitation. A warrior hero must serve the Battle Goddess, and it is she who has decreed and arranged his death; for her power is greater than that of Aoife. Here Cuchulain's death is an ironic reversal of his death in combat as told in the original legend. Now, helplessly bound to a stone, he is cut down for a shillingsworth of pennies by the Blind Man. It is this seeming degradation of the hero which leads Mr. Ure to take the play as ironic and Mrs. Vendler to speak of its 'weariness and indifference.' But Emer dances 'as if in adoration or triumph,' and the tone of the final obsequy, the harlot's song, is one of exultation. We have the right to ask, however, what in this hero's equivocal death has prepared the way for exultation or triumph?

Perhaps in the closely woven net of interrelationships that bind together the characters in these five plays there is a connection between Cuchulain and his slayer by which we are to understand the meaning of his death. Otherwise, the mockery of his mean end so contradicts the transfiguration of his soul and of his survivors that the play would seem to end in confusion or despair. We have seen that this murderous Blind Man is the double or shadow-image of King Conchubar, who seemed, in *On Baile's Strand*, to exemplify Emerson's bitter apothegm that 'Society everywhere is in a conspiracy against the manhood of each of its members.' Little do Conchubar and his kind understand either the passionate independence of a soul like Cuchulain's or his spiritual loves and adversaries. Recalling the oath scene between Cuchulain and Conchubar, it is clear that the king is the hero's opposite, his mask. United by oath, ritual, and flame, the two comprised a unified character, each giving the other the qualities each alone lacked.

But we know that not even that fusion was proof against the fate that the Sidhe hold in store for the hero who has lusted after immortality. In the opening scene of *The Death of Cuchulain* he is as wanton and reckless as ever before.

His inglorious beheading by the Blind Man would seem, then, to symbolize his own fatal, mortal flaw. This is as clearly as Yeats can put onstage before us an action to signify that Cuchulain is slain by his inability to hold within his personality the qualities of submission to order which the Blind Man represents. This is by no means to exalt those qualities (as the presence of the king instead of his double in rags might have done); for these qualities are identical with the cowardly and contemptible prudence of the Old Man in *At the Hawk's Well*. But Yeats would acknowledge that such submission to order is a condition of physical survival, of the continuance of an individual as well as of a society.

Can it then be said, as Wilson proposes, that 'Cuchulain . . . conscious of the death-wish . . . goes out to meet his fate'? Surely he is passive before the oncoming knife; as for his going into battle though forewarned, when had he ever done otherwise? This is not to be 'conscious of the death-wish,' it is the 'wanton recklessness' that defines his courage. Yeats's point is not that Cuchulain now seeks death with a Romantic longing but that he has always defied it with heroic abandon. This is the quality that won the Red Man's praise, who tested the hero in *The Green Helmet*:

> The heart that grows no bitterer although betrayed by all;
> The hand that loves to scatter; the life like a gambler's throw . . .

If we see Cuchulain turning into a soul even before his throat is cut, it is not that he wishes for death but that he knows he is already dying.

If, as I have suggested, Cuchulain's heroism has dramatized his willed experience, despite his mortal dress, of the spirit's immortality in both love and battle, then Emer's dance of 'adoration or triumph' is a fitting accompaniment to his transfiguration. Cuchulain has outlived and transcended his mortality. Like the dead in the poem 'Cuchulain Comforted,' who 'changed their throats and had the throats of birds,' his soul takes on its first shape, whose song brings Emer's dance to its end. This moment of supernatural sensibility dissolves in blackout, and a different music breaks in upon the song of birds. It is the ballad music of a street singer in a present-day Irish fair.

6. *The Harlot*. In a daring reversal of the aristocratic tone of the entire Cuchulain series, Yeats gives its last words to a ragged minstrel: 'The harlot sang to the beggar-man,' this final ballad begins. In an earlier Noh play, *The King of the Great Clock Tower*, Yeats had used a ballad for the closing lyric; but sung there by two attendants of the king, the tone like the scene was hieratic still. Here it is the earthiness of both scene and singer which is important, for this brings us down dramatically from the remoteness in time and space of both the ancient world of heroic action and the Otherworld into which Cuchulain's soul has already entered. We are rudely thrust back into our own time, in which Cuchulain—as the Red Man foretold at the end of *The Green Helmet*—has provided 'the long-remembering harpers' with 'matter for their song.'

Although in a wholly different key, this ballad complements the Old Man's ranting prologue. The discontinuity between them, as well as the episodic structure of what in-

tervenes, gives *The Death of Cuchulain* its nonce form.
One might suggest that its episodic structure parallels in
miniature Shakespeare's analogous abandonment of a conventional fixed structure for the chronicle form in *Anthony and Cleopatra.* Had Yeats adhered to his fixed conventional structure, the Noh play, and introduced *The
Death of Cuchulain* with a supernatural song by dancers or
musicians (as in *At the Hawk's Well*) he would have seriously compromised the direction he meant his play to take.
For in it we move *from* the present world, in which the
Old Man rages against our own historical circumstances, to
the heroic world of Cuchulain, and thence toward the
achievement of spiritual perfection in the next world. It is
from that vantage point that the harlot sings to the beggar-
man, once more in our present time. She summons up those
images that, like others in 'Byzantium,' 'fresh images beget';
for the knowledge of heroism keeps alive the possibility of
heroic action. Although ours is not an heroic age, we being
doomed to live in what, in 'The Statues,' Yeats calls 'this
filthy modern tide,' individual men may yet participate in
redemptory heroism. Which men? The answer is the burden of the harlot's song:

> The harlot sang to the beggar-man,
> I meet them face to face,
> Conall, Cuchulain, Usna's boys,
> All that most ancient race . . .

Ghostly lovers, the ancient gods and fighting men. Meeting
their 'long pale faces,' hearing their horses, she realizes
'what centuries have passed' since they were alive, and she
recalls

> That there are still some living
> That do my limbs unclothe,

> But that the flesh my flesh has gripped
> I both adore and loathe.

Which is to say, her human lovers strip her down to sheer
spirit, but she cannot escape her loathing of the body as
well as her adoration of the spirit which the body clothes.
This was exactly the predicament of the Lady in 'The
Three Bushes,' the condition of loving and loathing which
Crazy Jane solved by her acceptance of the body as the en-
velope of the soul. The present harlot finds in her mortal
lovers the spiritual lineaments of the great immortals,
whom she knows and, in imagination, adores without loathing.

Her song is here interrupted by the supernatural music
of pipe and drum. To this she responds by asking, 'Are
those things that men adore and loathe / Their sole reality?'—a wholly rhetorical question, as is made plain by her
asking next,

> What stood in the Post Office
> With Pearse and Connolly?
>
> .   .   .   .
>
> Who thought Cuchulain till it seemed
> He stood where they had stood?

Padraic Pearse's invoking the spirit of Cuchulain as the
Dublin Post Office burned about him represents a reincarnation of the hero's spirit. Wilson is surely right in identifying 'the emotion of exultation' as 'our central response to
the play.' Some readers, however, have been misled by the
harlot's last stanza to think the play ends in disillusionment
and despair:

> No body like his body
> Has modern woman borne,

But an old man looking on life
Imagines it in scorn.

Does not the foregoing greatly qualify this spurning of a
base modernity? The 'old man' who scorns life is obviously
the splenetic spokesman of the prologue, who had promised
to teach the audience 'the music of the beggar-man,
Homer's music,' and had demanded a 'tragic dancer, upon
the same neck love and loathing, life and death.' But he
himself has only loathing of present life. Some critics have
taken his scorn in the ballad as warrant for relating the entire play to the place of the present age in Yeats's historical
system.[1] But is the old man or the harlot the spokesman of
Yeats's deepest thought? As he had said in the introduction
to his work, written only two years before his last play, 'I
can put my own thought, despair perhaps from the study
of present circumstance in the light of ancient philosophy,
into the mouth of . . . some imagined ballad singer of today, and the deeper my thought the more credible, the
more peasant-like, are ballad singer and rambling poet.'[2]
Yet the harlot's song is not of despair. For it is she who has
felt the resurrected spirits of 'All that ancient race' in the
flesh of her lovers, and she knows that Cuchulain has lived
again in the Post Office and 'Where men first shed their
blood.' It is she who follows her report of the old man's
imagined scorn for life with the last image in the Cuchulain
plays

A statue's there to mark the place,
By Oliver Sheppard done,

as though to balance against his bleak scorn the reality of a
work of art (the statue of Cuchulain in the Dublin Post

---

[1] F. A. C. Wilson, *Yeats and Tradition* (London, 1958), p. 190.
[2] *Essays and Introductions*, p. 516.

Office) in which heroic emotion does indeed live again in
our own age, as it does in these plays.

Although for Yeats ours is 'an age engendered in a ditch,'
in the Easter Rising, at least, the 'heroic wantonness' of
Cuchulain was in truth re-enacted. Indeed, Yeats seems
often to consider that the Rising itself was a drama, a work
of imagination:

> Come gather round me, players all:
> Come praise Nineteen-Sixteen,
> Those from the pit and gallery
> Or from the painted scene. . . .

At the moments of transfiguration, myth, history, and art
merge into one another 'as though god's death were but a
play.' Yeats's ballad heroes, whether sighted or blind, are
themselves poets as well as lovers, but in the Cuchulain
plays there are no such figures of the artist. Yet everywhere for Yeats the heroism of the lover, the warrior, the
visionary, and the artist are aspects of the same transfiguration. 'Like an old fairy tale,' *The Death of Cuchulain* is a
'tale that has no moral' save the participation of character,
artist, and audience in the re-creation of Cuchulain's heroic
virtues.

Yeats's use of the Cuchulain material seems to me an
exemplary modern instance of the poetic employment of
myth. The poet who concentrates upon archetypal materials runs the risk of being overpowered by the conventional
gestures they perpetuate. But Yeats kept Cuchulain alive
and his cast of characters consistent in a series of works remarkable for their flexibility of form and of treatment. He
relied only upon the outlines of character, holding to the
permanent values in the given relationships while he simplified in the interest of intensity. He freely invented incident,
dramatic form, and style to explore to the fullest the conse-

quences of his characters' dispositions, psychological conflicts, and spiritual struggles.

Yet Cuchulain remains an individual hero. His significance as a national figure is almost entirely putative. In his
plays Yeats placed the emphasis steadily upon Cuchulain's
struggle to free his soul from his fated mortality, not on his
worldly role. War is a vocabulary for inner conflict, not an
instrument of temporal power. The hero's courage is the
guarantee of his own spiritual worth, not that of a kingdom
or a country.

Perhaps more successfully than any other modern poet,
Yeats has used the metaphors and conventions of the
Heroic Age in the presentation of Romantic values. From
the first his view of his materials was consistent with such a
conclusion. For in his introduction to Lady Gregory's
Cuchulain of Muirthemne he had compared to the moral
reality of the medieval Church the 'aesthetic reality' created
by the Irish storytellers, who have left us 'a company of
heroes.' The defect of their work, Yeats writes, was their
failure to give their themes 'perfect dramatic logic or . . .
perfectly ordered words.' These qualities of aesthetic com-
pletion are what Yeats provides in his Cuchulain plays.

Two: ROBERT GRAVES

: 5 :

THE UNQUIET GRAVES

There's a spring drizzle in the air. Around the subway kiosk a twitter of vagrant sparrows suggests the migratory madrigals of greener April afternoons. Two raincoated figures loom toward each other in the mist; under their breaths, both are singing. One pauses at the caesura of his tune and hears the other, still unaware of his presence:

> The wind doth blow today, my love,
>   And a few small drops of rain;
> I never had but one true love—

In a surge of fellow-feeling the listener completes the verse —of the very song he had himself been singing:

> And in greenwood he was lain.

First Singer: 'In cold grave she was lain.' Who's that?
Second Singer: A blind crowder with no rougher voice than rude style.
First: Oh, I'm afraid we've been reading the same book. I always hope to find a real informant from oral tradition in the city, but they all turn out like you. Did you like *The Ballad Book?*

Second: A fine collection. You're making one of your own?

First: Trying to. Most of what I've got I've taken down from my classes. I teach a course in the ballad.

Second: Well, I'll believe in the oral tradition these days, professor, when one of your students turns in a garble of a ballad by me.

First: You're a poet? I'm glad to find we read the same books. It's not surprising I'm *au courant* the latest work in my own field, but why would a poet today bother with a form so traditional and unambiguous?

Poet: If I can answer for my betters, Yeats wanted to re-store the emotion of heroism to lyric verse, and found it in the ballad. He hoped his own poems would be sung by country folk who didn't know his name.

Prof.: Laudable humility. But not all ballads are on heroic themes. There's none in 'The Unquiet Grave' we were singing.

Poet: No. That's perhaps why the unquiet Graves has a different theory from Yeats's. He believes—

Prof.: By the way, are you sure about that last line? I'm certain the text reads, 'In cold grave *she* was lain,' not 'he.' And it's 'cold grave,' not 'greenwood.'

Poet: *The* text? Now, you know a ballad-proper hasn't any fixed text!

Prof.: I was singing the text as it appears in *The Ballad Book.*

Poet: I was singing the one in the ballad book I read.[1] You know, Graves used to believe that the group-mind composed the old ballads, and that was why the text can't be fixed. Not a single poet, but, he maintained, 'a group-

---

[1] *The English and Scottish Ballads*, ed. with an introduction by Robert Graves (New York, 1957).

mind which is more than the sum of the individual minds that compose it, more than the convictions of the strongest or most active clique.' And as for his new ballad book, he nowhere confesses it's a revision of the one he brought out thirty years ago.[1] Perhaps because his new ballad theory contradicts his old one.

Prof.: Graves? Are you speaking of a person?

Poet: Robert Graves. Graves the poet.

Prof.: I don't place him.

Poet: . . . Graves the mythographer, Graves the translator. Graves the critic, Graves the novelist—

Prof.: Oh, *Graves.* The *I, Claudius* man. But he can't possibly have written *The Ballad Book.* It was edited by MacEdward Leach.[2]

Poet: And how would I be likely to have come across his name?

Prof.: You'd certainly know it if you'd ever applied to him for membership in the American Folklore Society. Or if you'd used his edition of *Amis and Amiloun* or *Paris and Vienne,* or his *Methods of Editing Medieval Texts.*

Poet: Well, I'll bet his editing of medieval ballads has more than one quibble with Graves's.

Prof.: No doubt. One right off is that group-mind business. That's old hat, you know. Here's what he says about authorship: The ballad 'originated pretty much like any other form of art, by creation of individuals.' In folk cultures, he says, 'Generations of singers slowly, subtly absorb' the ballads. 'A process of communal re-creation sets in . . . change may bring power or buffoonery and degeneration.' Professor Leach would say that Graves, like

---

[1] *The English Ballad,* ed. with an introduction by Robert Graves (London, 1927).

[2] *The Ballad Book,* ed. MacEdward Leach (New York, 1955).

Grimm and Gummere and the other communalists, was 'studying the ballads in terms of a romantic philosophy, instead of studying them realistically in the field.'

Poet: Graves doesn't believe in the group mind any more. But before publishing *The English Ballad* in 1927 he'd been reading Rivers's *Instinct and Unconscious* and MacDougall's *Group Mind.* As a matter of fact, though, Graves *had* studied ballads realistically in the field, and his fieldwork convinced him that the group-mind theory was true.

Prof.: Really? Leach is a dean among American ballad collectors, and his experience points just the other way. Where did Graves collect?

Poet: In the army. He served in the First World War with the Royal Welch Fusiliers, and he wrote that 'A remarkable revival of the ballad-proper in modern times, not a literary or sentimental revival, took place in the trenches. . . .' For a time, when men of all ranks endured terrible hardships and dangers and the usual discipline wore off, there were 'remarkable instances of communal action.' At this stage the new ballads appeared, 'composed nobody remembers by whom. . . . Most of these were subversive of military discipline.' It's strange, though; a few weeks later normal discipline was restored, and the ballad revival was over.

Prof.: No doubt some one or two gifted soldiers made up the ditties. But that's not a proper revival. The ballad must persist through time in oral tradition to be admitted to the canon.

Poet: That depends on the caliber of the canon. Graves's war ballads may not be 'Chevy Chase,' but they're not bad. 'Chevy Chase,' by the way, was one of the first two real poems Graves ever read; the other was 'Sir Andrew Barton.' When balladry gets into a man's blood young, it's likely to stick.

Prof.: And you say Graves writes his own ballads too?

Poet: Used to. Another curious thing—he brought out his new ballad book just a couple of years after stripping most of his own ballads from his *Collected Poems*. I guess the ballad Muse won't be so easily exorcised. You know, Graves is about the only poet left who can remember from his own childhood the scenes you find in ballads. Of course Yeats had an uncle with a castle, a deer park, and swans. But Graves's Bavarian grandfather had *two* castles—a ninth-century, ghost-haunted armorial museum, and a hunting lodge of Renaissance kings with a banquet hall 'as big as a cathedral.' Ballad-writing poets any younger and less highly connected will have to get their ballad atmosphere only from ballads. That may be why the literary ballad is petering out. There won't be much of that subtle re-creation Professor Leach writes about from the television troubadours and hootenanny enthusiasts who sing the ballads nowadays. Any subtle re-creation will have to come from the poets. And, as I was saying, even among poets younger than Graves or Yeats the old folk ballads seem to speak from beyond unquiet graves. Auden's ballads are closer to popular broadsides than to the hieratic master-pieces of old oral tradition.

Prof.: I wonder if your poets' ballads wouldn't be better if they had a more realistic idea of what ballad tradition really is than their casual notions about heroic lyricism and the group mind.

Poet: What they're interested in is finding in balladry something viable for themselves. A poet has to rifle the past to cobble together his own tradition these days. And I can appreciate what Graves found in the ballads. Although he's thrown out the group-mind theory, it served him pretty well for a time in meeting a harsh creative problem.

Prof.: How's that? I should think a poet of all people would see the fallacy of attributing artistic creation to a group rather than to individuals.

Poet: Well, maybe he felt more painfully than others the isolating individualism of creative power. Perhaps he wanted to escape from his isolation, yet not deny the creativeness for which it is the price. In the war, Graves found a closer cameraderie in the Regiment, facing death, than he had ever known at Charterhouse School where makers of verses were derided. And he found that his fellow soldiers were capable of being ballad poets, like himself. That must have proved steadying through the rough years after the front. He's ever since been digging furiously into myths, folklore, oaths, nursery rhymes—all the proofs the popular mind has ever given that it can share the artist's shaping power.

And the group-mind ballad theory helped Graves formulate an important principle in his own writing. The devil knows he wouldn't wear Yeats's or Pound's or Eliot's hats —it's his crowning privilege to knock them off—but in his own quirky way Graves was reacting against the excessive intrusion of personality into the art of the generation Pound satirized in *Hugh Selwyn Mauberley*. The ballad has to be impersonal because it reflects the mind of a whole culture, and its view of life—stark, tragic, passionate—is greater than any comment an individual can make upon it.

Prof.: That's true. That's why none of the literary imitators has ever written a ballad you'd mistake for a folk poem. I'll venture that's as true of Graves himself as it is of William Morris.

Poet: I suppose that's why he cut the ballads from his

Collected Poems. In the '20's he was searching for traditions that corresponded to certain tensions of his own—and
to their resolutions. You have to take into account his sense
of relation to England. Having a motherland isn't as simple
as one might think. Graves, like Britain herself, is of mixed
blood and felt the tug of conflicting cultures. Half-Irish,
half-German, he was reared and schooled in England, yet,
he says, it was in Wales—a country to which he had no ties
of blood—that he 'found a personal peace.' Well, in British balladry Graves found a literary tradition uniting the
qualities of spirit he felt in himself and in his country.
Here's what he wrote in 1927:

> As warlike peoples [the British] all have the element of
> fire in their race. . . . In the English ballad . . . all
> these strains are in fusion. It is by this blending of humours
> that English poetry, ballad, lyric, and all, has won its great
> renown, for where the air and fire of the Gael, the sea
> and fire of the Norse, the earth and fire of the Saxons, can
> be reconciled in amity with other lesser contributions,
> that fifth essence or quintessence of poetry appears,
> which is variously known as the spirit of wonder, as
> genius, as divine inspiration.

Prof.: That's a happy thought, expressed with elevation.
But you say his mind has since changed about ballad tradition. Has Graves done more thorough scholarship in the
interim?

Poet: A prodigious amount. By the time Graves antholo-
gized ballads again he had traced the main problem to its
ultimate source.

Prof.: Earlier than 'Judas' in the thirteenth century? Did
he find an actual ballad in Latin, as Gerould supposes?

Poet: He found the ultimate source—not of the ballads;
he leaves that golden fleece for you—the ultimate source of

that fifth quintessence of poetry, genius, or divine inspiration.

Prof.: Indeed, there's news of the Phoenix. Where did Graves look for that?

Poet: He consulted the Nine Muses on Helicon, and as he approached them reverently, his heart filled with awe and adoration, all pride of intellect fell from his forehead. His reward was to behold a miracle enacted.

Prof.: Really!

Poet: Yes, the Nine Muses in their frantic dance merged in their frenzy into Three, and these, the phantoms propagated by intemperate rituals, disclosed their essence to be but One.

Prof.: Did they! And which one was she?

Poet: Haven't her green fingers stroked your pale temples, haven't her lissome arms held your mortal throat in passionate dalliance? Surely you've seen her approaching—

> Her skirt is o the grass-green silk,
> Her mantle o the velvet fine. . . .

Surely you've cried out,

> All hail, thou mighty Queen of heaven,
> For thy peer on earth I never did see.

Prof.: The Queen of Elphame may have led Thomas Rhymer astray, but she hardly holds me in thrall. And anyway, what has she to do with the Muses?

Poet: Oh, she's just a late, Scottish reincarnation of the same divine essence which the late Greeks twice tripled in their museology. The original of both the Muses and the elf queen was of course Demeter.

Prof.: Come, now, this is too much for credulity.

Poet: Not at all. She had a different name in every tribe

and valley of the earth, but whether Freya or Caridwen or the Queen of Elfland, her green garb and ecstasy of fruition are the same. It's always been worth your life to fall in love with her. Now you surely know that the old nature religion survived in England until the iron-heeled Puritans stamped out the Maydance, the Beltane Fires, the New Year's Wren Hunts, the Midsummer Eve festivals?

Prof.: I'd want to check my sources first. I believe E. K. Chambers says. . . .

Poet: Well, I'll tell you that the nature cult lingered for a thousand years after Christianity became the State Religion, and the fertility cultists *were* the elves and fairies of medieval folklore. That elfin queen who seduced mere Thomas Rhymer and raised him to the holy dignity of True Thomas was their high priestess, and his adventure in the ballad was a ritual of initiation. Now, since Graves was seeking the divine source of poetic inspiration, don't be surprised that he followed the ballads to the goddess who inspired them.

Prof.: It's certainly an intriguing argument. I suspect it has just enough plausibility to traduce my brightest students.

Poet: You might refer them to the twenty-fourth chapter of *The White Goddess*. In his new *English and Scottish Ballads*, Graves simply documents the argument of *The White Goddess* with a body of literature in English. Perhaps he resented the suspicion of having manipulated to his own purposes in *The White Goddess* texts nobody but he could understand—the gnostic riddles in Middle High Welsh from *The Mabinogion.* Here in the ballad book he deals with familiar materials from the public domain of English tradition.

Prof.: That reminds me, I'd still like to check the text

you were singing of 'The Unquiet Grave.' May I see the book?

Poet: Here you are—page 47.

Prof.: What! Look at this! The lover is usually a man, but no matter—it's this last stanza—a real discovery!—

> But plait a wand of bonny birk,
>   And lay it on my breast;
> Then get you hame, my May Margrét,
>   And wish my soul good rest.

A new text!—not in Leach, not in Sharp, not in Child! I'll have to check the English County collections, but I don't recall any stanza like this. Let's see what Graves says about it. Here: 'The birch laid on the corpse's breast would grant the ghost admission to the pagan Paradise, the grave being in the greenwood and not in a consecrated cemetery.' That certainly supports the interesting theory you've expounded, but Graves fails to say where he collected the text. Tell me, is this ballad in his earlier anthology?

Poet: Let's see. . . . Yes. Here's 'The Unquiet Grave.'

Prof.: Indeed . . . but look—it's the conventional text, without any wand of birk. This stanza, and three others in the new edition, aren't there. Does your Mr. Graves confess to having collected any ballads in civilian life? Has he actually found either a folk informant or a reliable printed text for his unique 'Unquiet Grave'?

Poet: Graves doesn't say whether he collected ballads after the war.

Prof.: What he has done to this one is as interesting as any metamorphosis in Ovid. Isn't it odd that the additions here are exactly what make the text support his own peculiar theory? Tell me, by what right does Graves revise texts? A ballad editor has to play fair with his readers: does he sing the song as it was sung to him, or does he muddle with his own hand the tradition he professes to record?

Poet: Well, now, he just does what Scott and Burns and Percy did before him. He makes a composite version of the best features from several original texts. And he says, too, that 'where all versions are obviously defective at some point or other . . . I have restored the missing lines in the spirit of the original,' as in 'The Death of Robin Hood,' where the manuscript lacks several pages.

Prof.: And no doubt in 'The Unquiet Grave,' where the ballad is defective only in failing to support his theory?

Poet: I can't speak to that. But I do know that Graves is one of the most gifted text-restorers now going. He has restored the incantations of Taliesin, the Greek myths, Tom o' Bedlam's Song, and the Nazarene Gospel. For each of these, Graves's restoration gives us the original, incorrupt form of the work. In the light of such a distinguished restorative career I think he should get the benefit of the doubt on a mere ballad.

Prof.: Quite a career. Do you know where he takes his warrant to 'restore' such a gamut of works from so many literatures?

Poet: From the divine inspiration of the poetic imagination. Surely you'll agree that however great a man's knowledge, without intuition he can't transform it into wisdom. And I imagine Graves was much encouraged in restoration by the success of a technique he worked out with Laura Riding at about the time of his first ballad book. He took the 1609 printing of Shakespeare's 129th sonnet and compared it to the alterations and restorations of Shakespearean scholarship. The conclusions were obvious: first, that Shakespeare was a better poet than were all his scholiasts combined, and second, that it takes a poet to read a poem.

His explicative-intuitive method brought Graves marvellous results. In *A Survey of Modernist Poetry* he was even able to write the nonexistent Georgian poem about a sunset that E. E. Cummings had defiantly refused to write, Cummings having written instead another poem that readily revealed its secrets to Graves's analysis.

Prof.: That achievement surely writes a new page in literary criticism.

Poet: Perhaps, but it's an old page in scholarship. Have *you* ever actually *heard* a native speaker of Indo-European? Or recorded from oral recital the Ur-form of 'Cinderella'?

Prof.: The cases aren't comparable. Linguistics is a science, folklore is a science. This doesn't justify rewriting 'The Unquiet Grave.'

Poet: I'm not as sure as you that Graves rewrote it, for he could have proved his case as easily with extant texts of dozens of ballads. Take the whole Robin Hood cycle. Or 'Robin and Gandelyn.' What do you make of that one?

Prof.: I make of it what all reputable scholars from Child to Leach have made of it. It has nothing to do with Robin Hood. There may be some borrowing from 'The Tale of Gamelyn,' although, as Leach says, even this is dubious.

Poet: I don't imagine you have any idea of what the refrain means—'Robin lieth in greenwood bounden'?

Prof.: Ritson took the second word to be part of Robin's name, since there is a place-name in Flamborough called 'Robin Lyth's hole,' a cave popularly supposed to have been the hideaway of a pirate so named. The pirate may have been confused with Robin Hood the robber, just as this ballad of a fight between archers has been confused with Robin Hood on that account. But these are mere conjectures. I suppose your Mr. Graves has the final answer to these problems which a century of scholarship has not un-riddled?

Poet: Yes, if you accept it. The 'real subject' of this ballad 'is the New Year's hunting of the wren in vengeance of the robin murdered at midsummer. The chorus shows that Robin is the spirit of leafy Spring whom Wrennock, the spirit of leafless Winter, has bound with a spell. . . . Gandelyn, the bold spirit of the New Year, releases the enchanted spirit of his father Robin by killing the wren.'

Prof.: Neither you nor Graves has disappointed me. But I'm still curious, if Robin is the Spirit of leafy Springtime, if the Queen of Elphame is the Nine Muses *qua* Demeter, if 'The Unquiet Grave' is a pagan paradise, then how do we interpret the hundred-and-fifty-odd ballads that have nothing to do with such arcana? Look, Leach reckons that 'Fully half of the ballads . . . concern themselves with human relations. . . . They read like the front page of a tabloid newspaper.' But Graves doesn't have to answer such an embarrassing question; he simply omits these inconvenient ballads from his slim book.

Poet: Why shouldn't he? He says, in *The White Goddess,* that 'Originally, the poet was the leader of a totem-society of religious dancers. . . . The word "ballad" has the same origin: it is a dance poem, from the Latin *ballare,* to dance. All the totem-societies in ancient Europe were under the dominion of the Great Goddess, the Lady of the Wild Things; dances were seasonal and fitted into an annual pattern from which gradually emerges the single grand theme of poetry: the life, death and resurrection of the Spirit of the Year, the Goddess's son and lover.' That defines the true poem and the true ballad; why print the others?

Prof.: Since Graves has been so ingenious as to present

his fantasy in the guise of historical scholarship, I must in all conscience tell you that he won't make the curriculum in *my* university. The absurdities you've entertained me with are an insidious assault upon the objectivity of scholarship. From the Nine Muses to the Spirit of Leafy Springtime the whole thing is a palpable tissue of misinterpretation of the facts. Indeed, it seems a willful misinterpretation, in view of his suppression of evidence and manipulation of texts.

Poet: I guess you don't see that Graves assumes the discourse of rational inquiry merely to render sacred mysteries intelligible to minds that can comprehend only the intelligible. How else can he speak to such souls of mysteries but in terms of their explanations? If the mysteries remain mysterious to them, why, that's the just revenge of the Goddess for their prying. In former times, she turned them into stags. If Graves's rational assault upon her secrets leaves them unconvinced that the secrets exist, then there's his triumph.

Prof.: His triumph! Where?

Poet: In the proof that although reason may affirm what the imagination has created or perceived, rational discourse doesn't have the power to prove the imagination's sanctity.

Prof.: That's a devilish way to prove a case!

Poet: Oh, it's the Devil's way.

> Nice contradiction between fact and fact
> Will make the whole read human and exact.

Graves calls that 'The Devil's Advice to Story-Tellers.'

Prof.: Well, I feel vindicated in my conviction that Graves and his book can't legitimately serve my enterprise.

Poet: Oh, I hardly thought they would, although for mine I wouldn't miss Leach's *Ballad Book* for anything. I'm not surprised that you find Graves antipathetic to your transcendental devotions.

Prof.: And to which devotions do you refer?

Poet: One never can—as I've been saying—explain the meaning of devotions. I will, however, try to define yours, and his, and mine:

> You are absolutely for the relative.
> He is resolutely for the absolute.
>
> Your world conforms to what the mind expects;
> His world soul's singleness of kind reflects.
>
> His thoughts are feelings and his feelings forms,
> Perception's root bears fruit into his arms.
>
> Your thoughts assay the ore of truth in fact
> And leave fools gold in the earth that they reject.
>
> I am relatively for the absolute.
> My mind sees many while my soul seeks one.
>
> From contraries my soul and mind squeeze truth.
> Perception slowly feeds on contradiction.
>
> To be a fabler in an age of fact
> Demands a stubborn stomach. Wry intellect
>
> And soul's intransigent passion may yet compose
> The resolute poem that threatens all our prose.

Prof.: Charming, charming. The scansion's a bit irregular, but for an impromptu piece it's delightful. How did you bring it off so quickly?

Poet: I sought a certain grove within the wildness of my mind, and, eyes tight closed, I reached a sacred place close by the Queen of Elphame's thigh. What I drew forth was metaphor.

Prof.: I see. Well, don't let me keep you any longer from your chosen work. And, before the Library closes, I must return to mine. As for the ballads, take the advice of an old enthusiast. Don't fall into any more unquiet graves before you check your sources.

Poet: I'll remember that. Adieu.

> Before I check my sources
> I first must seek them out—
> By the mind's prismatic light
> That breaks the primal white
> To spectral shades which cast
> Its primacy in doubt;
> My sources I must seek
> By that other single beam,
> My intuition's blaze:
> Wherever that light plays
> All things become, or seem,
> Relations of one theme
> In metaphor or praise.
> These lights that doubly fall
> Dazzling point my courses:
> Where both beams cross, my soul
> Exults to find my sources.

:6:

SIGNIFICANT WOUNDS

In a slightly sententious preface to one of his thirty-six books of verse, Robert Graves writes,

> A volume of collected poems should form a sequence of the intenser moments of the poet's spiritual autobiography, moments for which prose is insufficient: as in the ancient Welsh and Irish prose tales the lyric is reserved for the emotional crises.[1]

Here is a poet who has never subscribed to T. S. Eliot's encyclicals about the need for poetry to express the extinction of personality. Indeed, the personality expressed in Graves's poems is one that takes a wry zest in the knowledge of its own peculiar individuality. In a poem ostensibly about a butterfly who 'Will never master the art of flying straight,' he praises the creature that has the knowledge, not of flight, but 'of how not to fly.' The diction in the poem is precise, yet the effect of its precision is to leave us, like the poet, giving thanks for the 'flying-crooked gift' of lurching 'by guess' as well as by 'God and hope and hopelessness.' This backlash of gratefulness upon unaptitude is typical of Graves, as is a more frequent paradox, the back-

[1] *Poems and Satires 1951* (London, 1951), p. viii.

lash of terror upon ecstasy. But as one reads Graves with greater familiarity both paradoxes are resolved into still a third, one's recognition that his 'flying-crooked' *is* his gift, that his terror is intrinsic to his joy. And his beloved

> is wild and innocent, pledged to love
> Through all disaster . . .

> Here is her portrait, gazing sidelong at me,
> The hair in disarray, the young eyes pleading:
> 'And you, love? As unlike other men
> As I those other women?'

He is unlike them, and his poems are unlike other men's. Once, he wrote,

> The lost, the freakish, the unspelt
> Drew me: for simple sights I had no eye.
> And did I swear allegiance then
> To wildness, not (as I thought) to truth—

But in latter days he has learned 'There is one story and one story only / That will prove worth your telling.' This story is the theme of his stupefying and exhilarating book *The White Goddess*, which ransacks the mythology of the ancient world and the literature and scholarship of the modern to refashion its hidden yet absolute truth:

The theme, briefly, is the antique story, which falls into thirteen chapters and an epilogue, of the birth, life, death and resurrection of the God of the Waxing Year; the central chapters concern the God's losing battle with the God of the Waning Year for the love of the capricious and all-powerful Threefold Goddess, their mother, bride and layer-out. The poet identifies himself with the God of the Waxing Year and his Muse with the Goddess; the rival is his blood-brother, his other self, his weird. All true

poetry . . . celebrates some incident or scene in this very
ancient story, and the three main characters are so much
a part of our racial inheritance that they not only assert
themselves in poetry but recur on occasions of emotional
stress in the form of dreams, paranoiac visions and de-
lusions.[1]

Let us defer an examination of the argument in detail,
and instead seek out some obvious implications from this
brief summary. Graves finds the meaning of life in a
monomyth, the contemporary recurreces of an eternal
pattern of conflict. Yet this monomythic net swings wide,
containing, in the conflicts already described, the struggles
between increase and diminution, life and death, and the
seasons, as well as the contention between the sexes, and the
division of the self into the lover and the rival, his 'blood-
brother' and 'weird.' Further, these characters and the action of this theme are graven upon our souls from birth, in
the manner that Jung ascribes to inherent archetypes. Conditions of emotional stress, dream, paranoia, and delusion
offer the materials of true poetry, if not the finality of
poetic statement. Graves found his own poetic materials in
such emotional stresses long before he recognized their uni-
versality in myths. Or did he find in myths a way to
universalize his own 'paranoiac visions'? As the loquacious
narrator of his poem, 'Welsh Incident' says, 'I was coming
to that.' But first we can notice that Graves, following
Freud's *Totem and Taboo* and Otto Rank's *Myth of the
Birth of the Hero*, considers dreams the individual's access
to myths, and he considers myths the dreams of the race.

Graves maintains that his discovery of this theme made
obsolete and superfluous many of the poems he wrote be-

[1] *The White Goddess*, 3d ed. (London, 1952), p. 24. The first edition,
since 'amended and enlarged,' appeared in 1948.

fore *The White Goddess*. He feels, and many of his critics agree, that until then his work was unfocussed, disunified, and he has accordingly excised most of this early work from successive volumes of collected poems. The early work he retains, however, is among his very best, and, as I hope to show, not only compels admiration for its own excellences but forms an intrinsic part of his achievement. Graves's poems accorded with his 'grammar of poetic myth' even before he spelled its laws, and the myth is but another set of metaphors for solving contradictions he has always been rent by.

II

Since Graves directs us to his own 'spiritual autobiography' in his poems, we may approach the poet and his chosen theme by seeking evidence of his divided self. Despite the particularity with which the passage from *The White Goddess* describes this division, Graves does not, as Yeats did, elaborate his opposites in charts and tables. Yet the opposed *personae* of his poems and prose are self-revealing. 'In Broken Images' reveals them:

> He continues quick and dull in his clear images;
> I continue slow and sharp in my broken images.
>
> He in a new confusion of his understanding;
> I in a new understanding of my confusion.

From childhood Graves has been aware of his dual nature. In his autobiography he traces the conflict between the complementary strains of his inheritance. His mother's father's people were von Rankes, 'not anciently noble. Leopold von Ranke, the first modern historian, my great-uncle, introduced the von. I owe something to him. He wrote, to the scandal of his contemporaries: "I am a historian before I am a Christian; my object is simply to find out how the things actually occurred." ' His grand-nephew's like compulsion would equally have scandalized Leopold's contemporaries. To his grandmother Graves attributes his 'gentler characteristics,' which abounded in his 'gemütlich' mother. 'Our busy and absent-minded father would never worry about us children' (there were ten children, five by the father's previous marriage). But 'our mother did worry.' She looms over the Graves brood, 'noble and patient,' protective, Germanic.

Father was Albert Percival Graves, 'a very busy man, an inspector of schools for the Southwark district in London . . . He occasionally played games with us, but for the most part, when not busy with educational work, was writing poems, or being president of literary or temperance societies.' Robert Graves takes a rather ironical tone about his father's literary activities, which in fact were far more extensive than a reader of *Good-Bye to All That* would suppose. A. P. Graves was a minor figure in the Irish literary renaissance that Yeats, AE, and Douglas Hyde had led. Dr. Hyde in fact wrote an appreciative forward to one of A. P. Graves's books of translations from early Irish poetry. All told, the elder Graves published forty-three books—translations from Welsh as well as Irish verse, his own facile poems on traditional Irish themes, anthologies of Irish fairy tales and Irish poetry, four plays, and sixteen volumes of songs. Of all this Robert Graves comments, 'That my father is a poet has, at least, saved me from any false reverence for poets. I am even delighted when I meet people who know of him and not of me. I sing some of his songs while washing up after meals, or shelling peas.' No doubt Albert Percival Graves will in the end, as his son predicted, be chiefly remembered for writing the one popular song, 'Father O'Flynn.' His prolix career, however, made certain courses of action probable for Robert Graves, and certain others impossible. The literary tendency, though in part from the historian von Ranke, comes more strongly from father Graves and from various antecedent Graveses, minor poets of the eighteenth and early nineteenth centuries. As the poetry-writing son of a poetry-writing father who was besides a professional Man of Irish Letters—even were Robert Graves interested in Ireland, how could he have written a line about Diarmuid and Grainne or Cuchulain?

By leaving Dublin for London and Harlech, his father 'broke the geographical connection with Ireland, for which I cannot be too grateful to him.' Young Graves grew up in a home library of Celtic scholarship, which he would one day put to his own uses. But the Celtic land he made his own would not be Ireland. Wales became the adoptive home of the poet who found in *The Mabinogion* the threads through the labyrinth of myths that led him at last to the White Goddess. In a poem (since dropped from his *Collected Poems*) he once acknowledged his ambiguous patrimony. Graves's father, in an anthology, *The Book of Irish Poetry*, had translated twenty-two triads from the Gaelic, but not this one:

> Poetry is, I said, my father's trade,
> Familiar since my childhood; I have tried
> Always to annul the curse of that grim triad
>
> Which holds it death to mock and leave a poet
> In mockery, death likewise to love a poet,
> But death above all deaths to live a poet.[1]

[1] 'The Poetic State,' from *Poems (1914–1926)* (London, 1926), p. 171.

As for the rest of his inheritance, 'The Graves's have good minds for such purposes as examinations, writing graceful Latin verse, filling in forms, and solving puzzles. There is a coldness in the Graves's which is anti-sentimental to the point of insolence, a necessary check to the goodness of heart from which my mother's family suffers.' [1] The qualities of all the antecedent Graveses live again, in varying degrees, in Robert. He claims there is a turbulence in his blood between the Graves intellectuality, coldness, and orderliness, and the von Ranke goodness of heart. Pulled in both directions at once, he is both quick and dull, slow and sharp, an intuitive rationalist distrusting reason, yet using it to justify the hegemony of the imagination.

III

Three kinds of experience appear to have been so formative of Robert Graves's attitude toward life that all else which has happened to him seems but an elaboration of patterns already established. These are his early family relationships, his life at Charterhouse School, and his service in the trenches as a captain in the Royal Welch Fusiliers.

Charterhouse School was a closed society, a highly organized tribal system of exclusions and humiliations in which the bullying of the topdogs was only the obverse of the toadying of the underdogs. The masters were remote from the boys and had little knowledge of the emotional lives and problems of their charges. As a late-comer to the school, as a boy who wrote poetry, and as one who was not only Irish but had a German middle-name, young Robert

[1] All the foregoing and following biographical information is quoted or paraphrased from Robert Graves, *Good-Bye to All That*, rev. 2nd ed. (New York, 1957).

von Ranke Graves found himself very much the butt of jibes and the persecutions which the system seemed designed to encourage. 'The school consisted of about six hundred boys, whose chief interests were games and romantic friendships. Everyone despised school-work.' Charterhouse was strong on cricket; Graves finally made an impression on his schoolmates, he says, by knocking five of them out in a boxing competition. For all this hostility, 'There is a lot of love in boxing—the dual play, the reciprocity, the pain not felt as pain,' he writes, with a curious conception of love later to be elaborated. There was at Charterhouse (as at any public school) both 'amorousness (. . . a sentimental falling in love with younger boys) and eroticism, or adolescent lust,' for Charterhouse boys had no contacts with girls. Already young Graves thought of women as mysteriously different, his feelings an admixture of fascination and fear. For a romantic adolescent boy in such circumstances there was little alternative but to fall in love with another youth. Graves is quite frank in *Good-Bye to All That* about his schoolboy affair with 'Dick,' a younger boy. This was but a phase he passed through, painfully. Years later, in an Army hospital,

> I fell in love with Marjorie, a probationer nurse, though I did not tell her so at the time. My heart had remained whole, if numbed, since Dick's disappearance from it, yet I felt difficulty in adjusting myself to the experience of woman love.

Nonetheless, on brief acquaintance during one of his sick leaves from the front, Graves married Nancy Nicholson, a sister of Ben Nicholson the painter. She was an iconoclast like himself, a feminist who changed from her wedding gown into 'her land-girl's costume of breeches and smock' in the midst of her wedding reception.

It was by chance that Graves, as he finished Charter-house, enlisted as an officer in a nearby regiment. The Royal Welch Fusiliers was an ancient regiment of the line with standards and traditions, with honors long since won and examples from the past that weighed upon the present and the future. The young man who at school had been 'a potato out of a different sack from the rest' found this or-ganization quite to his liking. He entered into the clannish martial spirit of the regiment and has never relinquished the sense of specialness, of earned privilege, of having won his right under fire to be a captain in an outfit of such manly and historic virtue. Even in a sportive ballad about a tavern sign, 'The General Elliott,' he enumerates the battle honors of his own regiment.[1]

Graves's autobiography, written in his thirty-third year, is, in addition to a key source-book on the poet's early life and character, one of the great descriptions of war in the twentieth century. *Good-Bye to All That* has much in common with *The Red Badge of Courage* and with *A Farewell to Arms* in its concentration upon the effect of mechanized modern warfare on an individual sensibility. It is a record of the stratagems and charms, the psychological quirks and aggressive self-defenses by which an individual grimly hangs on to his identity while the world goes syste-matically mad around him. Some recent histories of the tac-tics of trench warfare in World War I have suggested that there was no intelligent strategy used by either side in that monstrous war of attrition. Both general staffs, in their rear-zone château or castle headquarters, concocted offensives

[1] And says so in *On English Poetry* (London, 1921), p. 60.

against solidly built-up machine-gun emplacements, launched, as like as not, in hub-deep mud, sacrificing half a million lives at a time in colossally stupid frontal assaults.[1] Graves's book is a record of survival through horror. One-third of the men and half of the officers of his brigade were killed in one engagement.

The prose, however, is circumstantial, accurate, terse:

> We waited on the fire-step from four to nine o'clock, with fixed bayonets, for the order to go over. My mind was a blank, except for the recurrence of 'S'nice smince spie, s'nice smince spie . . . I don't like ham, lamb, or jam, and I don't like roly-poly. . . .' The men laughed at my singing. The acting C.S.M. said: 'It's murder, Sir.' 'Of course, it's murder, you bloody fool,' I agreed. 'And there's nothing else for it, is there?' It was still raining. 'But when I sees a s'nice smince spie, I asks for a helping twice. . . .'

Not long afterward an eight-inch shell burst a few paces behind him.

> One piece of shell went through my left thigh, high up, near the groin; I must have been at the full stretch of my stride to escape emasculation. The wound over the eye was made by a little chip of marble, possibly from one of the Bazentin cemetery headstones. . . . This, and a finger wound which split the bone, probably came from another shell bursting in front of me. But a piece of shell had also gone in two inches below the point of my right shoulder blade and came out through my chest two inches above the right nipple.

Near-emasculation, near-blindness, near-stigmata, near-death. On his twenty-first birthday Captain Graves's obitu-

[1] E.g., see Graves's review of *In Flanders Field* by Leonard Woolf, a book attacking Field Marshal Haig, in *Food for Centaurs* (Garden City, 1960), pp. 326–30.

ary appeared in the London *Times*, his mother having received a letter of condolence from his C.O. But Graves lay
sorely wounded in a field hospital, and was soon evacuated
to the rear by train and thence by ship to England.

After recovery and subsequent service in the trenches
Graves was returned once again to England, this time for
treatment of what used to be called 'shell-shock.' Fortunately, at Craigloch, the Royal Army Medical Corps hospital, he came under the care of Dr. W. H. R. Rivers, a Cambridge psychologist and ethnologist who also treated
Graves's friends the poets Siegfried Sassoon and Wilfred
Owen. Rivers was a pioneering therapist of war neuroses.
While accepting Freud's view that a patient's dream-life or
traumatic hallucinations were keys to his psychological
condition, Rivers differed from Freud in rejecting the sex
drive as the principal controlling factor in man's make-up.[1]
As a psychologist who had studied primitive cultures as
well as the personality structure of modern man, who specialized in the diagnosis of war hysteria, and who was besides particularly interested in the problems of poetic com-
munication, Rivers did far more for Graves than cure his
neuroses. In Rivers's scientific attempt to understand the
self divided between the instinctual and the conscious life,
Graves found an intellectual framework that he used for
his own aesthetic for the next decade.

In 1925 Graves published a critique of the writing of
poems, *Poetic Unreason*, in which he wrote, 'It was personal friendship for Dr. Rivers, admiration for his book, *Instinct and the Unconscious*, and the encouragement he
gave me in my writing of *On English Poetry* [a similar
study (1921)], that has made this book take the shape and

[1] Rivers's views are fully stated in his *Instinct and the Unconscious*
(Cambridge, 1920; 2d ed., 1922).

title it has taken.' Graves adds in *Poetic Unreason* that 'The late Dr. W. H. R. Rivers, in his *Conflict and Dream* (published posthumously), supports the main contentions of this book in the following paragraphs,' which are here transcribed since Rivers provided Graves with an *apologia pro poetica sua:*

> While many may be ready to acknowledge the similarity of dream and myth the proposition that the mechanism of the production of poetry is closely similar to that of the dream will awaken more opposition. There is little doubt, however, that this similarity exists. It is possible to take the images of the manifest content of a poem and discover more or less exactly how each has been suggested by the experience new or old of the poet. It is also possible at any rate in many cases to show how these images are symbolic expressions of some conflict which is raging in the mind of the poet and that the real underlying meaning or latent content of the poem is very different from that which the outward imagery would suggest. Moreover it is possible to show the occurrence of a process of condensation by means of which many different experiences are expressed by means of a simple image.
> . . . The poem may come in a state closely resembling a dissociation from the experience of ordinary life.
>   . . . Just as I believe that a really satisfactory analysis of a dream is only possible to the dreamer himself or to one who knows the conflicts and experiences of the dreamer in a most unusual way, so I believe that only when poets and other artists have set to work to analyse the products of their artistry can we expect to understand the real mechanism of artistic production.
>   In this comparison of the poem with the dream, one fact must be emphasised. The poem as we read it is very rarely the immediate product of the poetic activity, but has been the subject of a lengthy process of a critical

kind, comparable with that which Freud called the secondary elaboration of the dream. It is only through the study of the immediate unelaborated product of the poet's mind that we can expect to understand the part of the process of artistic production which is comparable with the formation of the dream.[1]

From this passage by Rivers, Graves derived, or drew support for, several convictions.

First, the poem, like the dream, is a symbolic presentation and resolution of individual emotional conflicts. Graves holds this conception still, although he has modified an accompanying theorem he held in the 1920's, that the chief value of poetry is therapeutic.

Rivers's second point of use to Graves is that there is the *materia poetica* ('the unelaborated product of the poet's mind') which is subjected to 'a lengthy process of a critical kind, comparable with . . . the secondary elaboration of the dream.' Hence the completed poem requires the collaboration of both the intuitive and the critical faculties of the mind, the von Ranke and the Graves in him joined together.

From Rivers's statement that 'the real underlying meaning or latent content of the poem' is in fact quite different from that suggested by its outward imagery, Graves takes warrant for a reading of the poetry of others that can only be called idiosyncratic. And finally, the assertion—understandable indeed from a psychoanalyst—that only the poet himself can reveal 'the real mechanism of artistic production' leads Graves to deduce universal principles of poetry from the analysis of his own practice.

In such books as *On English Poetry* and *Poetic Unrea-*

[1] *Conflict and Dream* (New York and London, 1923), pp. 148–9, quoted by Graves in *Poetic Unreason* (London, 1925), pp. 99–100.

son, as well as *The White Goddess,* and in his lectures at Cambridge (*The Crowning Privilege,* 1955) and the *Oxford Addresses on Poetry* (1962), Graves offers his own philosophy of composition. The vocabulary changes over the years from psychological to mythographic, the frame of reference expands from Herbert, Burns, Francis Thompson, and Shakespeare to an acerb survey of the history of English poetry at Cambridge. Yet the quality and often the objects of his enthusiasm of detestation remain constant through forty years. The avowed purpose of each of these forays into criticism is the reassertion of principles that Graves would make universal for the writing and enjoyment of poems. He is indeed similar to Poe in drawing universal laws of poetics from his personal experience, a process that relegates to the limbo of nonpoetry any species of writing of which the theorist finds himself incapable. Like Poe, Graves maintains that there is no such thing as a true long poem, and that all poetry should, as we have seen, be dedicated to a single theme. Although he has made only passing allusion to Poe, he would doubtless accept Poe's theme—that 'Beauty is the sole legitimate province of the poem'—as true but fragmentary, a concentration upon the Muse in only one of her aspects. Graves would certainly discredit the strain of Platonizing that conditions Poe's conception of beauty. Yet Graves's often repeated remarks on the necessity of rhythm as a hypnotizing medium resemble Poe's, as they do Yeats's in 'The Symbolism of Poetry.' Without pushing too far the similarities between them, it may be observed that Graves resembles Poe further in his addiction to 'ratiocinative' puzzles—such as his historical reconstructions of texts, legends, and mysteries—and in his critical assertion that poetry must be assessed by poetic standards alone.

Some of these views are, it is true, the stock in trade of the symbolist movement. Surprisingly, Graves came to these literary convictions not by way of the French symbolists—he has a streak of Gallophobia, perhaps the result of his wartime impressions of the French; nor by way of the proximate English poets—he makes no use of Blake, took special pains to exorcise his early Pre-Raphaelite inclinations, and spurned the example of Yeats. Graves found the symbolist position perhaps nascent in the literary climate during the Georgian period, but it was made most readily available to him in the theories of his psychoanalyst.

I V

Graves's early verses show the influence of many models: the nonsense rhymes of Edward Lear appear in his earliest poems, published in his father's autobiography,[1] as well as in the zany logic of his later satires and grotesques; the lyrical sweetness and facility of Ralph Hodgson, the fantasy of de la Mare, and the simple structures and stock symbols of old ballads and nursery rhymes are also evident. These enthusiasms were appropriate to a young Georgian poet whose first book, *Over the Brazier*, was published in 1916 by Harold Munro.

Graves has confessed to a still more important influence:

Skelton has had a stronger influence on my work than any other poet alive or dead: particularly I have admired in him his mixture of scholarship and extravaganza, his honest outspokenness and unconventionality in life and writings, his humour, his poetic craftsmanship, and, in spite of appearances, his deep religious sense. . . . Time and time again . . . I have caught myself playing at being

[1] Albert Percival Graves, *To Return to All That* (Dublin and London, 1930), pp. 320-21. The title is a riposte to his son's *Good-Bye to All That*.

> Skelton, in literary affections, in choice of metre and hand-
> ling of words particularly: always admitting my hero's
> faults (by twentieth-century standards, that is) of long-
> windedness, over-exuberance, crabbedness and occasional
> formlessness; his vindictive attitude towards [his rivals],
> his childish conceit . . . and other by no means admirable
> examples of poetic conduct. I certainly quite often iden-
> tify myself with him.[1]

This confession is half-jocular, yet true; for everything,
except the final fault, which Graves says of Skelton is in
good measure true of himself. In some poems in *Fairies and
Fusiliers* (1917), Graves imitated the Skeltonic line, with
its stumbling rhymes and metrical freedom. William Nelson
in his study of this neglected Tudor poet observes that the
Skeltonic 'constituted a deliberate refusal to obey the rules
he had learned in school . . . The style he invented had
the liberty of prose and the sharpness of poetry,' and 'It
gave him room for the flow of his imagination and the tor-
rent of his anger. . . . It gave him liberty to speak.' [2] For
Graves these qualities, both personal and poetic, were extremely attractive. To resurrect Skelton in 1917, when criticism as yet had done little to mitigate Pope's scornful jape
that 'Beastly Skelton heads of houses quote,' took a bit of
nerve. Already Graves was determinedly going his own
way, against the grain of the literary establishment and
equally against the counter-establishment of the avant-
garde. To put his discovery of Skelton into perspective we
must recall that the literary ancestor of the hour was John
Donne. Professor Grierson's edition had appeared only in
1912 with an immediate effect upon young poets as different from one another as Rupert Brooke, Isaac Rosenberg,

---

[1] *Poetic Unreason*, pp. 240-41.
[2] *John Skelton, Laureate* (New York, 1939), p. 101.

and T. S. Eliot. Donne had an effect on Graves too—the tortuous quality of intellectualized passion, the boldness of his wit, struck a response in the young poet already torn between his Romantic and his Classical selves. But Graves would not accept everyone else's metaphysical ancestor as his own. He practically invented Skelton to be his own peculiar forebear and familiar.

It was a lucky discovery, for it helped Graves to jack himself out of the slough of too easy sentiment, too facile rhyming, which his early won mastery of late Victorian poetic convention had made a temptation. Skelton gave him an example of a bold metrical irregularity, a heavily accentual line taking its movement from common speech. His influence helped Graves to develop a craggy individualistic personal meter. Many of his best poems could not have been written without the aid of Skelton's ghost. Yet even Skelton's admirers—and I am one—may have been surprised when, forty-five years after the poems in *Fairies and Fusiliers*, Graves praised Skelton in his *Oxford Addresses* as a Muse poet:

> Muse poetry is composed at the back of the mind: an unaccountable product of a trance in which the emotions of love, fear, anger, or grief, are profoundly engaged, though at the same time powerfully disciplined; in which intuitive thought reigns supralogically, and personal rhythm subdues metre to its purposes.

In the next lecture in 1961 Graves defined the Anti-Poet, Skelton's opposite. He avoids taverns, is girlishly shy, has a facility for versification, but writes on themes suggested by his patrons. He divorces poetry from common sense, uses poetic license and grammatical inversions, never lampoons those in power, and maintains style to be more important than subject. Where Skelton joked in church about his illegitimate children, the Apollonian Anti-Poet is incapable of loving any woman, much less of adoring the Muse with whose powers a particular woman might attract him. Indeed, he may be a pederast. In time of war he does not bear arms.

The Anti-Poet of course is Graves's anti-self, the reverse image in the mirror that he would exorcise. In his Oxford lecture he told us that this specter goes by the name of Virgil.

Such dichotomies cleave all of Graves's poetry and theories. In *Poetic Unreason* he proposed to

> show Poetry as a record of the conflicts between various pairs of Jekyll and Hyde, or as a record of the solution of these conflicts. In the period of conflict, poetry may be either a partisan statement in the emotional or in the intellectual mode of thought of one side of the conflict; or else a double statement of both sides of the conflict, one side appearing in the manifest statement, that is, in the intellectual mode, the other in the latent content, that is, in the emotional mode, with neither side intelligible to the other. In the period of solution there will be no discrepancy between latent content and manifest statement.

Graves further characterizes his doppelgängers:

> The terms Jekyll and Hyde . . . are rather more than synonyms for 'deliberate' and 'unwitting' because Jekyll is always used in the restricted sense of action in conformity with the dominant social code of the community, while Hyde is the outlaw. When Jekyll appears, Hyde is the 'unwitting,' but it must not be forgotten that Jekyll is the 'unwitting' when Hyde appears.[1]

The terms as well as the logic of this argument derive from Rivers, who proposed 'unwitting' as descriptive of

[1] *Poetic Unreason*, pp. 52-3.

what Freud calls the unconscious.[1] In Graves's later work we see the doubling and redoubling of these antagonistic selves, striving to be reconciled. His Muse hands him a double-bladed axe: he writes only 'poems for poets and satires for wits'[2]—the poetry of Unreason, the wit the work of Reason. The conflict between Romanticism and Classicism is unassuaged in Graves; yet, he wrote in 1925, 'The interaction of the two bodies of literature has been so fruitful that pure Classicism and pure Romanticism are nowadays far to seek in English poetry.'[3]

Much later, when he found the reinterpretation of myths essential to validate his theories, Graves again showed both sides of his nature: the irrational (Romantic) in requiring myth, and the rational (Classicist) in requiring its validation. As readers of *The Greek Myths* are aware, his retellings combine a Dionysian compulsion to belief with an Apollonian clarity of presentation. Yet again in the *Oxford Addresses* he proposed the achieving of paradisal visions by use of a hallucinogenic mushroom to produce 'a controlled schizophrenia.' Graves would split the self by narcosis—yet never forgets the need for 'control.' While he would make 'intuitive thought reign supreme,' it must nonetheless be 'profoundly disciplined.' His poetic theories attempt to show us how the interaction of these dichotomous states comprises both the origin and the function of poetry. His poems demonstrate their interaction.

V

The divided selves of Robert Graves early found their homes in different countries. The rationalist recognized his in a mild and quiet valley, where nothing alters 'the set

[1] *Instinct and the Unconscious*, p. 16.
[2] 'Foreword' to *Poems 1938–1945* (London, 1946).
[3] *Poetic Unreason*, p. 139.

shape of things.' This place is called 'An English Wood.'
Here the dread creatures—harpies, rocs, gryphons—which
haunt the imaginative man are quite unknown. Here 'No
bardic tongues unfold / Satires or charms,' and 'Small path-
ways idly tend / Toward no fearful end.' A bland little
spot, recalling D. H. Lawrence's descriptions of Crève-
coeur's farm, of Ben Franklin's neat little moral garden,
fencing off the wilderness and the terrors of the soul.
Graves's other self inhabits the opposite landscape from
'An English Wood,' places where 'Mermaid, Dragon,
Fiend' abound and difficult paths are followed compulsively
toward fearful ends. His *paysage moralisé* appears as
'Rocky Acres':

> This is a wild land, country of my choice,
> With harsh craggy mountains, moor ample and bare.
> Seldom in these acres is heard any voice
> But voice of cold water that runs here and there
> Through rocks and lank heather growing without care.
> No mice in the heath run, no song-birds fly
> For fear of the buzzard that floats in the sky.
>
> He soars and he hovers, rocking on his wings,
> He scans his wide parish with a sharp eye,
> He catches the trembling of small hidden things,
> He tears them in pieces, dropping them from the sky;
> Tenderness and pity the heart will deny,
> Where life is but nourished by water and rock—
> A hardy adventure, full of fear and shock.

These acres are surely the 'desolate, rocky hill-country'
where Robert and his sisters used to wander in their teens.
'Above Harlech I found a personal peace independent of
history or geography. The first poem I wrote as myself
concerned those hills. (The first poem I wrote as a Graves

was a neat translation of one of Catullus's satires.)' [1] But I doubt that 'Rocky Acres' was this poem, for it first appeared in *Country Sentiment,* his fifth book, in 1920. By then he had been through the war, had endured and outlasted unmitigated disasters and useless battles which could not be won. 'Is this joy? to be doubtless alive again, / And the others dead?' he asked in 'The Survivor.' It was Wales he went to when sent home on sick leave, and it was then he found his 'personal peace' among its rocky acres. That 'peace independent of history or geography' is a paradigm of the state of being for which Graves in his poems is continually searching. As is true in 'Rocky Acres,' that peace, when found, offers a landscape more of menace than of comfort:

> Time has never journeyed to this lost land,
> Crakeberry and heather bloom out of date,
> The rocks jut, the streams flow singing on either hand,
> Careless if the season be early or late,
> The skies wander overhead, now blue, now slate;
> Winter would be known by his cutting snow
> If June did not borrow his armour also.
>
> Yet this is my country, beloved by me best,
> The first land that rose from Chaos and the Flood,
> Nursing no valleys for comfort and rest,
> Trampled by no shod hooves, bought with no blood.
> Sempiternal country whose barrows have stood
> Stronghold for demigods when on earth they go,
> Terror for fat burghers on far plains below.

Here is a primordial landscape outside of time where the seasons turn anarch against the calendar. We exchange the poised, calm elementals of England for the fearsome buzzard who 'scans his wide parish.' In this land of no valleys

---

[1] *Good-Bye to All That,* pp. 32, 34.

one feels newly delivered 'from Chaos and the Flood,' beside the ruined temples to the earliest forces that knew
man's frightened gratitude and worship. 'The country of
my choice' is of course a psychological landscape. This is
the country of man's mind, of forces whose atavistic power
Graves cannot and would not control with consciousness.
Here, 'bardic tongues unfold / Satires or charms,' the only
verses Graves admits as poems. But why charms? Because
charms are magical incantations arraigning the power of
the spirit to obey the importunate will of the poet. In *On
English Poetry* Graves had argued for the magical authority of poetry. This is the burden of his poem 'The
Bards.'

The scene in this poem suggests the court of an early
medieval Welsh king, where the bards entertaining at dinner are pelted with bones by the 'drunken diners': pelted
for stumbling in their song, stumbling for fear of 'an unknown grief'—and the rest of Graves's poem is an invocation of that grief which 'like a churl / Goes commonplace
in cowskins.' This churl, 'by a gross enchantment,' razes
the palace, where twelve kings play at chess, and leads
away their beautiful daughters.

Any reader familiar with medieval romance literature
will recognize the traditional properties on which Graves
draws, true though it is that he has put these familiar
materials together in a new way and for a new purpose.
This churl with his 'unpilled holly-club' is surely of the
same breed as the Ugly Herdsman in such well-known romances as *Aucassin and Nicolette* or, to approach the
rocky acres, Chrétien's *Yvain*, where, near Arthur's court
at Carduel in Wales, Sir Calogrenant met such a shepherd
guarding a sacred spring. Graves has disclosed his source as
an old Irish legend which probably lies at the root of this

tradition, 'The Pursuit of the Gilla Dacker,' a farcical yarn of an ugly giant of the Fomor who carries away sixteen Fenian warriors on his magical, hideous horse.[1] Graves takes from this tale merely the key motif of the invasion of a royal castle by an ugly giant; his churl 'by a gross enchantment' destroys the palace and kidnaps the beautiful queens. The luxuriousness of the palace, J. M. Cohen has suggested, may be a deprecatory allusion to Yeats's Byzantine artificialities;[2] I think it far more probable, however, that Graves has in mind the lapidary splendors described in a Welsh romance of the early thirteenth century, 'The Dream of Rhonabwy,' which he knew from Lady Charlotte Guest's translation of *The Mabinogion*. In this romance Rhonabwy comes to a mean and filthy cottage where an old crone grudgingly lets his party sleep on flea-covered skins on a floor of cow urine and dung; once asleep, he dreams of a game of chess between Arthur and King Owein, played while Owein's ravens fight dire battles against Arthur's men. The action is subordinate to the enameled beauty of the court and costumes; regal splendor and disdain are in contrast to both the slaughter of battle and the meanness of the real world from which Rhonabwy's dream is a magical escape.

Graves analogously creates a reduplicated escape from the conditions of life through incantation. First he evokes the banquet scene, brutal and primitive in the diners' hurling bones at the failure of the bards' spell. This first spell has been broken by a stronger one, that of 'unknown grief,'

---

[1] Graves mentioned the Gilla Dacker as his source to Douglas Day, but Day has misled his readers by calling the story 'a terrifying Irish myth' and suggesting it as the source, not of the churl, but of the game of chess (*Swifter than Reason*, Chapel Hill, N.C., 1963, p. 143n.). Graves probably found the tale in *Old Celtic Romances* by P. W. Joyce, 2d ed. (London, 1894), pp. 223–73. This was its first rendition into English.

[2] Cohen, *Robert Graves* (New York, 1960), p. 62.

which both overmasters the 'running verse' of the bards
and supplants, for us, the drunken rage of the diners. But
this churl intensifies the rage of the drunkards. Being pelted
by bones had made the bards stumble in their song, but the
blows of the churl magically transform the faltering song
into an unanticipated legend of disaster, as he leads the
queenly beauties off 'to stir his black pots and to bed on
straw.' We are made to take literally this churl, who was
introduced only in a metaphorical comparison—he is not
even a character, but merely what the 'unknown grief' is
compared to. Wholly a figment, a specter, he arrogates in
the poem the psychic energy that compels our belief; from
unreality the poet creates a reality.

This is the reality of imagination, linked, here and in
such other poems as 'Outlaws' and 'Rocky Acres,' with the
primordial figures and features of prehistory. Thus far—
through the 1920's—Graves had not attempted to synthe-
size or systematize his fearful fascination with a reality
'independent of geography or history.' No need to wonder
at this time at his emphasis upon an imaginary reality or his
suspicion of the world of appearances. For some years after
the war Graves was in a state of serious traumatic disorientation:

> Shells used to come bursting on my bed at midnight,
> even though Nancy shared it with me; strangers in day-
> time would assume the faces of friends who had been
> killed. When strong enough to climb the hill behind Har-
> lech and revisit my favourite country . . . I would find
> myself working out tactical problems . . . where to place
> a Lewis gun if I were trying to rush Dolwreiddiog
> Farm. . . .

One surcease from such exigencies was to retreat into the
assurance of childhood. In the books of these years—*Fairies
and Fusiliers* (1917) and *Country Sentiment* (1920)—

Graves wrote charming and seemingly carefree nursery rhymes and ballads, some of them for and about his own children. But even childlike ballads had a way of being haunted.

To a man who could not bear to use a telephone or ride on trains, whose daylit life was peopled by the reappearing dead, it was not possible to look directly at life, or to find reality other than in the confusion of his own dreams. The title poem of his 1921 volume is 'The Pier-Glass,' a mirror in which a murderess, haunted by her guilt and trapped by her past, vainly looks for a freedom it cannot give:

> Ah, mirror, for Christ's love
> Give me one token that there still abides
> Remote—beyond this island mystery,
> So be it only this side Hope, somewhere,
> In streams, on sun-warm mountain pasturage—
> True life, natural breath; not this phantasma.

In time Graves rejected the child's-eye view of reality, re-pressing most of his poems of escape to the nursery from the successive volumes of collected poems. By 1929 he could, both as a recuperated veteran and as a parent, write a 'Warning to Children,'—and in a dreamlike iteration and reiteration he admonishes them to beware of unwrapping the appearances of things, for appearance encloses appear-ance in boxes within boxes. If this is reality, the truth re-vealed by the poem is in its pattern of compulsive repeti-tion. This is one of Graves's most convincing poems about dream-states, in which the rhythms of feeling well up from the unconscious. 'Warning to Children' might be taken as a statement, or a demonstration, of the futility of conscious-ness and reason to discern the shapes of reality. He wrote it to repeat and display the confusion of his understanding, and so to understand his confusion.

In 'Alice' (1926), another mirror poem, Graves finds a symbolic *persona* (like that of 'The Pier Glass,' feminine), whom he can make a mediator between the 'unwitting' and the 'deliberate' in life. Alice, 'that prime heroine of our nation,' can represent the English mind's fascination with mind. But as a child she is exempt from the bland rationalism of older dwellers in an English wood. Courageously she follows her 'speculative bent' into the topsy-turvy world beyond the Looking Glass, where, playing the game with 'simple faith in simple stratagem,' she wins her crown.

> But her greater feat
> Was rounding these adventures off complete:
> Accepting them, when safe returned again,
> As queer but true—not only in the main
> True, but as true as anything you'd swear to,
> The usual three dimensions you are heir to.

Alice could understand that neither did Looking Glass logic affect

> the clean
> Dull round of mid-Victorian routine,
> Nor did Victoria's golden rule extend
> Beyond the glass: it came to the dead end
> Where empty hearses turn about: thereafter
> Begins that lubberland of dreams and laughter . . .

Whereas the lady gazing in the pier-glass was trapped by her own reflection, Alice is able not only to live among the creatures of Unreason but to keep her conscious and unconscious knowledge sorted out:

> Though a secure and easy reference
> Between Red Queen and Kitten could be found—
> She made no false assumption on that ground

(A trap in which the scientist would fall)
That queens and kittens are identical.

Alice's resolution is complete; but most of Graves's poems in the mid-1920's do not manage such a mediation between Hyde and Jekyll. For instance, 'In Procession' begins as an attempt to celebrate 'that lubberland of dreams and laughter' he would mention in 'Alice.'

Often, half-way to sleep
Not yet sunken deep—
The sudden moment on me comes

—a procession of 'coloured pomps,' 'Carnival wagons' from which he harangues a crowd 'in strange tongues' while 'the sun leaps in the sky.' When he awakens, however, he longs for the courage 'To renew my speech' and summon back the marvels of legend and imagination from 'the land where none grows old . . .'

But cowardly I tell,
Rather, of the Town of Hell—
A huddle of dirty woes
And houses in fading rows
Straggled through space:
Hell has no market place,
Nor place where four roads meet,
Nor principal street . . .
Neither ends nor begins,
Rambling, limitless, hated well
This Town of Hell
Where between sleep and sleep I dwell. [1]

[1] This poem seems based on Coleridge's 'The Pains of Sleep.' In the original version the present text is preceded and followed by lines in which Graves thinks of himself as in the procession of the early Romantic poets. (*On English Poetry*, pp. 137-42, reprinted in *Poems (1914-1926)*, pp. 102-7.)

Graves cannot escape into a 'lake isle' of imagery, for he knows it to be a dream. Yet it is clear that the distortion of reality into 'This Town of Hell' is also a dream-illusion. At this time, for Graves, reality is as illusory as is the hope of escaping from it. In such poems as 'The Witches' Cauldron,' 'Welsh Incident,' 'The Castle,' he recognizes entrapment without hope of release. Self-knowledge may be rendered humorously, as when the Welsh storyteller embellishes his tale of mythological creatures coming in from the sea, leaving out all the details that his interlocutor (obviously an English rationalist) wants to know. There may be the rage and aggression of the misdirected traveler moving through the mountain mist in ever-widening circles, coming always to the one sign, 'The Witches' Cauldron / One mile.' And in 'The Castle,' 'by definition / There's no way out, no way out——.' All machinery of escape is futile, even

> Cheating checkmate by painting the king's robe
> So that he slides like a queen

for imagined sexual reversal is ominous, and, as we know from 'The Bards,' the chess game can be blasted by disaster—

> Or to cry, 'Nightmare, nightmare!'
> Like a corpse in the cholera-pit
> Under a load of corpses . . .

In this recrudescence of the war-born fear of death, Alice's logic—playing the game by the rules of the game—can be of no avail. There is no recourse in this castle but 'To die and wake up sweating by moonlight / In the same courtyard, sleepless as before.'

Here, and in such poems as 'Down,' the form of the feeling is that of rebirth—into the same death. It is this pattern of action which produces the haunting effect of these poems upon the reader. <u>Incantatory and repetitive rhythms heighten the normative iambic meter and phrasal line.</u> The imagery, as in 'The Castle,' is chiefly visual, rendered with staccato emphasis and great clarity of definition: 'Walls, mounds, enclosing corrugations / Of darkness, moonlight on dry grass . . .' These descriptive notations set the scene; the main work of the poem is borne by the hallucinatory images of balked escape, the wild stratagems (painting the king's robes, escape by rope ladders or rockets) all coming to naught. Fear is the essence of the poem, defined by the inability of either speaker or reader really to abandon hope of escape. Therefore, despite the knowledge given at the start that 'by definition / There's no way out, no way out—' to have the poem end 'With apparitions chained two and two, / And go frantic with fear . . . In the same courtyard,' comes as an unexpected shock. The inevitability of movement toward nonmovement has the logic of hallucination or dream, the understanding of a reality revealed by the unconscious mind.

In a chapter of *On English Poetry* called 'The Pattern Underneath,' Graves discusses this movement in which the reversal of implication discloses the meaning. It is a movement characteristic of his poems:

> The power of surprise which marks all true poetry seems to result from a foreknowledge of certain unwitting processes of the reader's mind, for which the poet more or less deliberately provides. . . . The poet may be compared with a father piecing together a picture-block puzzle for his children. He surprises them at last by turning over the completed picture, and showing them that by the act of assembling the scattered parts of 'Red Riding Hood with the Basket of Food' he has all the while

been building up unnoticed underneath another scene of
the tragedy—'The Wolf eating the Grandmother.'[1]

To this passage he adds that 'The underlying associations
of each word in a poem form close combinations of emotion unexpressed by the bare verbal pattern.' In addition,
then, to the thematic movement which contains the sur-
prise played by the unwitting upon the conscious mind,
there is the further concentration of meanings inhering in
the associations of words. This property of language
(which Ernst Cassirer and Susanne Langer have linked to
the liberating powers of myth) is, for Graves, an aspect of
associative thinking. It comprises one of the most important
of the illogical elements which he values in poetry. 'The
creative side of poetry,' he wrote almost forty years later,
'consists in treating words as if they were living things—in
coupling them and making them breed new life.'[2]

VI

Before the convergence, in *The White Goddess*, of these
and other latent conceptions, Graves had already partially
articulated the organizing structure of his thought. Thus
far his work was more unified than has generally been supposed, and his view of life had constancy if not coherence.
At this time—until about his thirty-third year and the clari-
fications that followed his writing an autobiography and
moving from England—he conceived of poetry as therapeutic magic, creating from the unconscious a reality that
reason could not discover. The external world is unreal; in
it, appearance and conventional society are Dr. Hydes. But
they are really Jekylls in disguise, and only the unwitting

---

[1] *On English Poetry*, pp. 24–5.
[2] *Food for Centaurs* (New York, 1960), p. 360.

can discern this truth. By turning topsy-turvy the pleasant picture-puzzle that reason puts together as its image of the world, the unwitting reveals the latent meaning hidden in the picture: Wolf Eating Grandmother.

The unwitting meaning of life, which appear latently in the symbols of poems that derive from the unconscious mind, are contained and revealed in the language and the structure of the poem. Graves believes that the vocabulary of poetry should be drawn from the 'ordinary spoken language of the day'; [1] each word should be used with full awareness of its implications and meanings; and, by juxtaposition of language, the copulative power of words can breed new 'life'—which is to say, can create a new realization of reality.

Obviously, diction and form—what Graves's friend John Crowe Ransom would call texture and structure—must complement one another. In Graves's work we find an inherent conservatism of both diction and structure as compared with the contemporaneous experiments of Pound, Cummings, Marianne Moore, and Eliot. The means by which he divines the truth of Unreason do not—as in the case of Pound, whose work Graves has always detested—abandon such appurtenances of logic as normal syntax or causal relationships.

Although Graves's practices, like his theories, seem often conformable with symbolist assumptions, he has never knowingly been influenced by the French tradition which Eliot, Pound, Stevens, and Williams brought into the mainstream of poetic modernism. It is principally the symbolist renunciation of syntax which Graves renounces. He has no interest in verbal copulars without connectives, in the

---

[1] *On English Poetry*, p. 42; Graves is assenting to the view of Lascelles Abercrombie in *Poetry and Contemporary Speech*.

disjecta membra of the imagination undisciplined by the inherent order of language. One might compare with Graves's poem 'In Procession,' in which the images are those that occur to him as he falls asleep, a poem by Pierre Reverdy presenting an analogous condition (though to a different end).[1] Reverdy's 'Et Maintenant' is, like Graves's poem, three pages long, but it is unpunctuated and contains not one completed sentence. This is to his purpose, of course, for a completed sentence expresses a beginning, a middle, and an end, and contains a subject, an action, and often an object. The trance-like dissociated state his poem evokes is not so much illogical as pre-logical. But when Graves brings up from his unwitting mind the material of the unconscious, this material is always subjected to that 'secondary elaboration' described by Rivers, and the illogical element is revealed rather in the elaborated pattern than by an unelaborated lack of pattern. Graves combines a reverence for the truth of unreason with a reverence for the logic of language. The former must reveal itself to him, the latter he knows he must never relinquish. This is the last bastion to which intellect can cling, and it is from this assumption that the poet as rationalist can join the poet as

[1] Here is a translation of the opening lines of 'Et Maintenant,' from *Main d'Oeuvre* (Paris, 1948), p. 531:

> Tonight no spring
> No fruit under the leaves
> The storm abates too late
> Love can't be heard   reason can't
> The heart's scattered pieces in the alleys
> All that the morning gilds again
> After savage and tormented night
> Like the wind that bleats and blows
> And laughs
> Yesterday's wind swollen on the air
> Toward noon
> Bubbles of imprisoned air
> Ruined songs . . .

daemon in their common attack across the treacherous terrain of the seeming world. For the poet of unreason is also the traditionalist Captain and the classical scholar who abides no willful inaccuracy in translation. He is in fact the Dr. Syntax who so roundly thwacks the knuckles of schoolboy Pound.[1] These dual sides of Graves's nature of course operate simultaneously. Dr. Syntax is forever taking hold of the incantations of the Medicine Man.

In his own poetic rhythms, too, we see the interation of reason and unreason. Graves has been dogmatic in his insistence on the need for a formal rhythm in poetry. At first he explained this by the hypnotic quality of rhythm, needed to put the reader's logical mind into a trance-state and impose upon him the compelling magic of the poet–witch doctor. Later he acknowledged the need to individuate meter (the traditional element) by a personal rhythm. He has always found rhythm to be accentual, in the nature of the English language, and has rejected alike such deviations as Marianne Moore's syllabic line and the complete abandonment of meter by the vers librists. Graves does use a phrasal rather than a metronomic rhythm in such poems as 'To Walk on Hills' and 'To Bring the Dead to Life,' but his most characteristic line is strongly accentual, often incorporating a variable number of unaccented syllables, sometimes rhyming accented syllables with unaccented. Thus in 'Rocky Acres,'

This is a wild land, country of my choice,

an anapest is followed by a spondee, then after the caesura an anapest is followed by an iamb. J. M. Cohen has suggested the influence of Skeltonic meter in this highly indi-

[1] *The Crowning Privilege* (Harmondsworth, 1959), pp. 242-4.

vidual personal rhythm. There is probably also a touch of Hopkins in the rhythm of this poem, particularly in the description of the buzzard's flight.

A poem that brings together in a single net these concerns of Graves, articulated in one of his most profound and fully realized forms, is 'The Cool Web.' This appeared on the final page of *Poems* (*1914–1926*) and, with some minor revisions, has remained in Graves's successive books of *Collected Poems*.[1] In 'The Cool Web,' the innocent child-protagonists of 'Alice,' 'Warning to Children,' and the early ballads are now menaced by the scent of roses, the 'black wastes of evening sky,' and the 'tall soldiers drumming by'—that is to say, they are endangered by the indifference of nature, the fury of the elements, and the terror of war. The children in this poem have only speech to protect themselves: 'We spell away the soldiers and the fright.' As though we were fish, we are safeguarded by 'a cool web of language' that 'winds us in.' In this poem, as Martin Seymour-Smith has observed, Graves conceives of language as itself the network of relationships that holds culture together. 'In that sense it is the sea, what we swim in, where we move and live and have our being.'[2] The consolation Graves offers us, however, is minimal, for we must 'retreat from too much joy' as well as from 'too much fear,' and in the end we shall 'grow sea-green' and 'coldly die.' We perish into 'brininess and volubility.' The alternative, however, is to throw off 'language and its watery clasp.' Without the power of incantation to protect us from the 'wide glare' of inchoate experience, we would 'go mad no doubt and die that way.'

[1] Graves's revisions are a marvel of craftsmanship, almost always improving the text; his 'secondary elaboration' need not come in the same trance-state as the *materia poetica*.

[2] Seymour-Smith, *Robert Graves* (London, 1956), p. 24.

There are, then, two conceptions of experience in this poem. Life without articulation is terrifying to the impotent observers, helpless as children. Given the power of language, however, the child-protagonists are caught in the protective web of incantation and immersed in the cool sea. It is not maintained that the reality of the cruelly indifferent rose, the menacing sky, and the tall soldiers is in the least altered by the cool web of language. The children have the power only to 'chill the angry day' and spell away their fright. The ultimate manifestation of language's incantatory power to keep brutal reality in check appears in this poem to be the identification of the cold sea—colder than the merely cool web—with death.

> We grow sea-green at last and coldly die
> In brininess and volubility.

This is the final triumph of language over the heat of the war-torn waste land. Until it comes, Graves offers a stoicism abjuring the extremes of fright and ecstasy alike. In mid-career he summed it up in another poem, 'Midway':

> Between insufferable monstrosities
> And exiguities insufferable,
> Midway is man's station.

Such a poet is in worse state than the authors of 'Dejection' or 'Ode to Melancholy,' who at least could be passionate in their despairs. Graves's position had become so narrowed by the numbness of his feelings that the sources of poetry were in danger of being blocked. His life as well as his art was at a turning-point. 'Midway' was written in 1929, the year in which he also wrote *Good-Bye to All That*. As its title implies, this autobiography is a farewell to the world whose values had been blasted by senseless wars and could not be reassembled in the haunted souls of the survivors. The book completed, Graves left England for Majorca where, except for intervals during the Spanish Civil War and the Second World War, he has made his home ever since. The world he rejected was modern life, industrial society, English rationalism, contemporary political activity, bureaucratic materialism, hidebound academia —in short, everything in the twentieth century which threatened his own poetic vision.

This withdrawal, or retreat, or victorious re-establishment of himself on a then remote island, corresponded with a personal crisis about which Graves has little to say in his autobiography. His marriage to Nancy Nicholson, whose opinions seemed so like his own, proved in a few years to have been a mistake. In an epilogue to the first edition of *Good-Bye to All That*, dedicated to Laura Riding (and since dropped from later editions), Graves wrote,

> For could the story of your coming be told . . . ? How she and I happening by seeming accident upon your teasing *Quids*, were drawn to write to you, who were in America, asking you to come to us. How, though you knew no more of us than we of you . . . you forthwith came. And how there was thereupon a unity to which you and I pledged our faith and she her pleasure. How we went together to the land where the dead parade the streets and there met with demons and returned with the demons still treading behind. And how they drove us up and down the land.

Like Graves himself, Laura Riding had been given up for dead (after a spinal injury), but had survived. Her poems have a terse, gnomic intellectuality in a style determinedly flat, from which all Romantic abandon has been excised. Like Graves, she has a sensibility in which passion is haunted by fear, and every Romantic feeling straightened by a puritanical restraint. She went off to Majorca with Graves, whose marriage was soon terminated, and Laura Riding was for the next ten years Graves's companion, collaborator, instructress, and indeed his Muse. Together they wrote several polemical books of criticism—*A Survey of Modernist Poetry* (1927), *A Pamphlet Against Anthologies* (1928)—and published through the Seizin Press annual miscellanies of criticism and verse as well as limited editions of their own writings. Under Laura Riding's influence Graves redefined the theoretical bases of his poetry, but not until after their separation in 1939 could he consider his new position objectively and conceive of it as a contemporary example of an eternal, archetypal pattern. Since that pattern, as we know, identifies the Muse with the beloved, and the beloved appears in her threefold role as mother, bride, and layer-out, it may be that not until the breaking-off of their actual relationship, in which the poet would find his identity changed from God of the Waxing to God of the Waning Year and his beloved's changed, by her rejection of him, from lover to the goddess exacting vengeance, could Graves recognize that he had been re-living this myth, the 'one story and one story only.'

: 7 :

'UNDER THE SCEPTRE OF GUESS WHOM?'

Discussing the poetic situation in 1926, Edwin Muir used the work of Robert Graves, Edith Sitwell, and T. S. Eliot to define the sensibility of the times. From our point of view four decades later, Muir's remarks seem particularly relevant to Graves:

> The poet is not concerned because ideals do not corre-spond to realities (a great source of pessimistic poetry); he is hardly concerned with ideals at all. His bewilder-ment springs from something far more complex: the feeling that reality itself has broken down, that even the simple emotions, the instinctive reactions, are disorientated and lead us astray. This bewilderment has not the abso-luteness of pessimism, but it is nevertheless more com-pletely without consolations. . . . The suffering which is reflected in his poetry is . . . the suffering of uncer-tainty, which, unlike all other kinds of suffering, has no power to distil its own alleviation. . . . Everything is conditional, everything is potential. . . . His temptation in this quandary is to accept [a number of] possible worlds provisionally, and build fanciful hypotheses round them.[1]

No poet in our time save Yeats has built a hypothesis as

---

[1] *Transition* (London and New York, 1926), pp. 188-9.

'fanciful' as Graves's. His theory of the White Goddess has been explained by Randall Jarrell as 'an ordinary wish-fantasy reinforced with extraordinary erudition—a kind of family romance projected upon the universe.' Jarrell finds this theory 'fantastic' and 'astonishing,' yet 'logical and predictable.' Citing some of the autobiographical material I have summarized from *Good-Bye to All That*, Jarrell presents Graves as a case study wholly explicable by Freudian analysis. Further, he writes, 'Anyone familiar with what Jung has written about the *persona* and *anima*, and what happens when a man projects this *anima* upon the world and identifies himself with it, will more than once give a laugh of astonished recognition as he goes through "The White Goddess." '[1] Although Graves has vehemently denied that his 'grammar of poetic myth' is thus analogous to a psychiatric case study,[2] Jarrell's point is incontestable. But it does not sufficiently explain *The White Goddess*. In this chapter I shall try to show not only how this theory is the projection of one individual's condition upon the universe, but why his need for belief took this form; how this myth is conceived as an aesthetic, a basis for poetry, and what uses this theory has been put to in his poems by the poet who conceived it. Further, I hope to show that his theory, however idiosyncratic he has been in marshalling evidence to support it, has an authority of its own: it is indeed a modern reconstruction of the most ancient dispositions of human feeling, and thus defines an extreme of Romantic primitivism in the sensibility of modern literature—a manifesto made necessary as a response to conditions widely felt in our time.

[1] 'Graves and the White Goddess—Part II,' *Yale Review*, XLV (Spring 1956), 467–78. Part I is a lively discussion of Graves's poems.
[2] *Five Pens in Hand* (New York, 1958), pp. 67–71.

For while *The White Goddess* is a work whose patterns bring those of Jung and Freud to mind, it is at the same time also an aesthetic statement of first seriousness, and a declaration of belief. Like the best of Graves's poems, it is a part of his spiritual autobiography. What is so terrifying about those poems written before *The White Goddess* which record the breaking-down of reality that Muir defines is the absence of anything outside the self by which the significance of the self's adventures may be measured. As in 'Rocky Acres,' life is 'A hardy adventure, full of fear and shook.' Like Eliot's poems of the same period ('The Waste Land' and 'The Hollow Men'), Graves's show the confusion and vacuity of a world from which God has been removed. In Graves's world God does not exist because He is impossible, otherwise the world would not be as it is described in these poems.

J. M. Cohen in a usually perceptive little book on Graves misses this point when he writes that 'Religious tension has never played any part in Graves's poetry or thought.[1] What *is* 'Rocky Acres' but the evocation of a world in which, instead of a God who from Heaven watches every sparrow's fall, there is a naturalistic demon, the buzzard who 'scans his wide parish with a sharp eye': the terrible domain of tooth and claw? Another representation of the world left by the war is in the poem 'The Cuirassiers of the Frontier.' Its imagery is taken from Roman history, a subject Graves studied as background for his historical novels. The parallel between the decline of the Roman Empire and that of contemporary Britain is clear. Captain Graves would not be likely to hold that by the third or fourth century the center of authority in the Empire was in the sybaritic metropolis, among 'pederastic senators,' 'cutthroat factions,' or 'The eunuchs of her draped saloons.'

[1] *Robert Graves* (New York, 1960), pp. 22-3, 40.

He knows where to look for the solid virtues that still uphold this sick civilization, on the frontier in the plain camp
of old soldiers not taken in by new religious fads. To them,
'In Peter's Church there is no faith nor truth,' and all the
God they serve is a pennant 'puffed by the wind.'

> We, not the City, are the Empire's soul:
> A rotten tree lives only in its rind.

But even the code of the regiment proves an insufficient
faith by which to live after demobilization. In a facetious
hymn-meter Graves sings a grotesque song of nihilism,
'Song: Lift-Boy' (1930). Old Eagle, a wild-eyed evangelist,
boards the elevator and preaches Damnation: 'So I cut the
cords of the lift and down we went.'

   In a world without a God or the hope of salvation there
is no comfort to be found in nature either. For nature cannot be numinous. 'All it has of mind /Is wind, / Retching
among the empty spaces, / Ruffling . . . the sheep's
fleeces. / Whose pleasures are excreting, poking, / Havock-
ing and sucking.' Nothing is other than itself, and what
pleasures are possible to us are in the recognition of the
uniqueness of each created object in its silliness and absurdity. Looking at the physicality of the natural world unre-
lieved by the possibility of numinous meaning, how can
one help being disgusted? Like the sheep, man too has a
body that havocs in such country pleasures as this poem describes. Nonetheless, in these oafish, silly, melancholy, idiot
pleasures lurk the possibilities of ecstasy, for ecstasy can
come to us from nowhere else.

   Just as one numerous group of Graves's poems expresses
the dichotomies of reason and the unconscious, another explores the contrarieties of body and spirit.[1] I do not say

---

[1] G. S. Fraser had accurately traced the tension between body and mind
in Graves even before *The White Goddess* appeared, in the essay he
reprints in *Vision and Rhetoric* (London, 1959).

soul, for there's little in Graves's work about souls. He has no theosophic doctrines of transubstantiation, no assuaging of death with consolatory dogmas about the transmigration or even the survival of the soul, except as haunting ghosts. But spirit, as it is used here, represents our capacity in this life to possess a self-transcending and ecstatic experience. It would seem that until Graves understood his own contrarieties it was extremely difficult for him to experience self-transcendence because it had no meaning in a world where reality had broken down and there was no power worthy of worship. Fear of death and fear of unreality compelled terror, but nothing regenerative evoked awe. Yet from the beginning there had been 'Lost Love' and 'Love in Barrenness.' This latter poem, contemporary with 'The Cool Web,' recreates the landscape of 'Rocky Acres,' so unlikely for romance, as nonetheless the very spot

> Where slow cloud-shadow strayed across
> A pasture of thin heath and moss.
>
> The North Wind rose: I saw him press
> With lusty force against your dress,
> Moulding your body's inward grace
> And streaming off from your set face;
> So now no longer flesh and blood
> But poised in marble flight you stood.
> O wingless Victory, loved of men,
> Who could withstand your beauty then?

In this singularly joyless love poem the beloved appears at first as a woman in a dress, but by the end she has become a marble icon of 'wingless Victory.' The movement from flesh to stone resembles that in Poe's 'To Helen.' If we wonder over whom she has been victorious, the last line gives us already a suppliant lover. If there is any comfort for the spirit in that barren land, 'the country of my choice,' it will be in the transformation of human love into the worship of an ancient goddess who rewards her idolator with the indifference of marble. This poem was written in 1923, two decades before its assumptions made themselves fully apparent to the poet or his readers. By the time that occurred he was able to explore other vicissitudes of love, not only this one.

This movement from sensation toward transfixed frigidity is typical of Graves's early poems. In one entitled 'Pure Death' (1925) it is managed with unexampled strength and delicacy in a single extended conceit, a metaphysical play on a conception in the manner of Donne. Graves goes far beyond the mere pun on dying, for in 'Pure Death' he explores the psychology of lovers so abandoned to their passion that they have given each other everything but their 'ungivable pride,' the last impediment to selflessness. What happens, then, when passion so overmasters egoism that even this is given, each to each?

> . . . each with shaking hands unlocks
> The sinister, long, brass-bound coffin-box,
> Unwraps pure death, with such bewilderment
> As greeted our love's first accomplishment.

Paradox makes its claims upon pure passion, as in 'Pure Death' the final gift is but reiteration of love's first. The double exactitude of the last word 'accomplishment' bespeaks the mastery of language's cool web that characterizes Graves's poetry at its most intense.

In 'Pure Death' the feeling moves in two directions at once, toward a hoped-for, desperately sought fulfillment, and at the same time toward a feared yet endurable ecstasy of terror, the frozen passion of death. Not until much later does Graves arrive at poetic statement of ecstasy uncomplicated by the shaking terror of self-sacrifice. A similar double movement will be found in Graves's eventual myth; now, in the 1920's, he makes it the source of tension in his poems.

One poem that succeeds in celebrating Graves's sense of doomed ecstasy is called 'Sick Love.' Although in it every promise of joy is immediately blighted, 'Sick Love' does promise something better than negation. Its four stanzas present, in turn, a persuasion to enjoy, a warning of the impossibility of happiness, a persuasion nonetheless, and a conclusion that offers what meager consolation may be wrested from the foregoing argument between joy and fear. The beloved is urged to 'be fed with apples while you may,' to take warmth from the sun and go 'A smiling innocent on the heavenly causeway.' But such delight is threatened by 'horror' of 'the cry / That soars in outer blackness,' the inarticulate horror of 'paranoiac fury.' The imagery in the poem fuses together personal, mythical, and cosmic dimensions in man's and woman's foredoomed attempt to experience a love that is not sick. To be fed with apples is both to partake of the fatal fruit and to arrive at Avalon, the apple-island paradise of Celtic heathendom. What can the fury of 'the dumb blind beast' be but man's rage against his body with its twitching, oafish nerves and sheepcote lusts? But, as he says in another poem, 'midway is man's station,' between the 'heavenly causeway' of the sun and this howling inchoate horror; so 'lift your head, / Exquisite in the pulse of tainted blood, / That shivering glory not to be despised.' The glory is shivering both from the spasm of love, 'a shining space,' and from the cosmic cold in which we are enveloped. 'Between dark and dark' we may find a momentary glory, though not the peace of death. The relationship between the conceptions held together in the poem makes implicit the suggestion that death would bring peace, that the 'grave's narrowness' is like the bed's narrowness.

Graves can take lust itself as his subject and treat it with ironic levity and wit. In poems like 'Down, Wanton, Down' and 'Ogres and Pygmies' he writes with an overt salacity that has seldom been seen in English verse since the Earl of Rochester, although Graves's attitude toward lust is anything but libertine. His witty poems are satires against that part of himself which quakes haunted by the nightmare, as in 'Succubus.' Here such a she-monster as Breughel would paint in Hell embraces him, 'Gulping away your soul,' making him father 'brats . . . of her own race,' 'Yet is the fancy grosser than your lusts were gross?' Indeed, the ecstasy of love seems haunted always, if not by lust then by terror. In 'Parent to Children' the poet must ask pardon for having passed on 'the pulse of tainted blood,' for 'In fear begotten, I begot in fear.' He does not imagine procreation without fear, only escape from fear without procreation.

And yet it is in sexual love that Graves in the end discovered the source of all that is numinous in human life. The structure of ideas and historico-religious conceptions in *The White Goddess* is, of course, a structure also of feelings; and it is so contrived as to make ample room for both terror and ecstasy, because it promises that each comes inextricable from the other. Man's station is no longer midway, avoiding the extremities of passion and punishment. If ecstasy is doomed, that doom comes with a 'shivering glory not to be despised.' Terror and shock are man's portion, but so, now, is adoration.

I I

In a speech given at the YMHA Poetry Center in New York in 1958 and published in his book *Five Pens in Hand*, Graves has said that the clarification of his theme came to him, imposed itself upon him, during the writing of his novel, *Hercules, My Shipmate*, in 1944. This book, like most of Graves's fiction, started out as a reconstruction of an intriguing problem in history: what actually were the adventures of Jason and the Argonauts? In the midst of writing it, Graves felt another compulsion welling up within him, and he wrote furiously for three weeks, producing the first version of *The White Goddess*. Without in the least discrediting the author's own account of his work, it seems evident that what happened in 1944 was not so much a sudden discovery of something unanticipated as the clarification and restatement of tensions that had already been embodied, if not with full self-consciousness, in his poetry. The *annus mirabilis* in Graves's career seems to me to have been somewhere around 1929–30, with *Good-Bye to All That*, divorce, and departure from England with Laura Riding. It is as much in the poems I have discussed from this period and in some fugitive prose works of these years, as in the autobiography, that the unification of his sundered meanings can be seen.

In 'A Journal of Curiosities' (1929) he had opened up the theme of God as having originally been Motherhood, in the days when 'sex was a delightful experience,' as among the animals. 'As mother of sets of twins I was held in particular reverence,' writes God in this jocular divine autobiography. 'As Great Mother I was not a mere shame-wizard dispensing ju-ju or tabu; I was the Name Giver.

thereby ruling.' Further attempts at clarification appeared in the 'Alpha and Omega of the Autobiography of Baal,' a mock-anthropological report by the Male Godhead of his own progressive deterioration and his foreknowledge of his supercession. 'Do you remember my fable of the mistletoe, the disregarded tree not bound by my oath, that slew me once as the god Balder? That fable epitomises all my anxieties.' [1]

Beneath the facetious surface in these writings, Graves is trying to fill the religious void he inhabits; his thought is turning toward matriarchy, cultural primitivism, and myth. A far more powerful writing of this time is his story, 'The Shout,' in which his latent myth, humorously skirted in 'Baal' and 'A Journal of Curiosities,' is still in the background, a prime mover of the action. But this myth was not yet recognized by Graves for what it is, and consequently the story is haunted by the ineluctable necessity of an uninterpreted dream. In a note to the first printing Graves says that 'This story occurred to me one day while I was walking in the desert near Heliopolis in Egypt and . . . stopped to pick up a few misshapen pebbles; what virtue was in them I do not know, but I somehow had the story from them, and three years later found it coming true to me . . . with a most important character added, and with the macabre strangeness illuminated.' [2]

In 'The Shout' a visitor to a mental hospital arrives during a cricket match and is introduced by a psychiatrist to the score-keeper who tells the ensuing story. This inmate holds the delusion that he is a murderer whose soul has been split into pieces. He tells of a married couple who have each had the same dream—of a stranger walking on

[1] *But It Still Goes On* (London and Toronto, 1930), pp. 164–6, 204.
[2] *But It Still Goes On*, p. 79.

sandhills with a black kerchief and a shoebuckle in his pocket. The husband, Richard, goes out on the links for a walk—and meets this very man. The buckle he carries is the one missing from Rachel's shoe. The stranger (whose name is Charles Crossley) tells Richard that he has the ability to kill others with his shout. 'It is a shout of pure evil . . . pure terror.' Yet Richard invites him home for dinner, and Rachel soon enough falls in love with this forceful, fearful stranger and spurns her sensitive, ineffectual husband. Charles in fact exercises buckle magic over Rachel. Richard, skeptical of the shout, dares Charles to display its power, but as they walk out on the sandhills among the cromlechs Richard is afraid and stops his ears with wax. Charles's face becomes horribly contorted as he prepares to shout . . . Richard turns away, and falls in a dead faint. When he comes to he is clutching a stone. He has sudden knowledge of the craft of shoemaking, but on his letting go of the stone, the knowledge leaves him. He later discovers that the souls of all the villagers are residing in the stones on this wild place—he had been handling the soul of his cobbler. In despair at losing his wife to Charles, he decides to wreak revenge by breaking Charles's soul with a hammer. But 'Richard had scruples,' and because he knows Rachel prefers Charles to himself he decides instead to commit suicide by smashing the stone that is his own soul. A man cannot recognize his own soul, however, and, thinking it his own, he chooses Charles's stone. As the hammer smashes it, Charles, back in the house with Rachel, suddenly gibbers like a madman, and is captured by the police Inspector. Charged with the murder in Australia of two men and a woman, Charles is taken to the asylum. The score-keeper reveals that he is Charles. But then at times he is Richard also. A thunderstorm overtakes the cricket game, and in the thunder Charles/Richard recognizes a shout similar to his own. The erstwhile cricketers, hearing the thunder, relapse into lunatic fits. When Charles is ordered to his dormitory by the psychiatrist, he too loses control and threatens the doctor with his shout. 'His face was distorted in terror.' The visitor rushes out of the scoring-box, a sudden thunderclap at his heels. Lightning had struck the doctor and the madman dead together.

Here in a frightening knot are bound together all of Graves's problems, and his potential solutions. 'The Shout' does not resolve these terrible tensions objectively, as the White Goddess myth would do; it defines them in the clarity of a dream. Charles/Richard evidently is a man split against himself, both halves in love with the same woman. Richard is prudent, rational, and helpless; Charles is demonic, possessed by 'pure evil' learned from tribal magicians in Australia (where, by the way, Dr. Rivers had pursued ethnographic studies[1]) and is terrified by his own powers. Richard recognizes Charles's shout as the Druidic war cry of ancient Ireland, and as the shout of Pan that 'would infect men with a madness of fear.' The shout is both personal power, 'pure evil,' and thunder: a war cry that sounds like thunder would plausibly suggest, or be suggested by, artillery fire. And a soldier would know not only fright but also guilt at the thought that he had killed —and indeed Charles thinks himself a murderer. In fact he is one. The thunder that drives men mad crashes over a game of cricket: which is to say, in the synoptic imagery of

---

[1] It is only natural that the patient feel both gratitude toward and aggression against the psychiatrist who cures him by putting down part of his personality.

dreams, grown-up madmen are re-enacting the games of Charterhouse School under the clouds of the war god who would claim their lives.

Charles's first words in the story are an expression of doubt of an Easter sermon the premise of which was *'that the soul is continually resident in the body.'* Indeed, the soul is elsewhere, in a stone. Here Graves has used a belief of ancient Celtic provenience which Yeats had drawn on for his story, 'Hanrahan's Vision.' Not only does a stone appear among the Grail symbols, and as the sign of a king's descent from a god (as in the Stone of Scone), but until very recent times in the outer isles of Country Sligo, round stones were used for cursing, the stones of malediction.[1] Such a belief was known to Spenser (and in 1929, Graves wrote a sardonic ballad of the Blatant Beast). For Spenser says of Merlin (*F.Q.*, I, vii, 35), that

> Men into stones therewith he could transmew,
> And stones to dust, and dust to nought at all;
> And when him list the prouder lookes subdew,
> He would them gazing blind, or turne to other hewe.

Indeed the villagers recognize, from the effects of Charles's shout—the deaths of rabbits, birds, and men, the sudden stab in the hearts of passersby—that the Devil has passed.

Yet the shout is also a syllable uttered, a magic spell, a word. It is the ultimate concentration of primitive, poetic, and personal power. Its user is destroyed by his own power, which is inextricable from evil, murder, lost love, and the dislocation of the self, in a world where no reality can be believed in because none is fixed. Although the tale is prefaced by an epigraph from Apuleius ('Leave off now,

---

[1] See W. G. Wood-Martin, *History of Sligo . . . 1688 to the Present* (Dublin, 1892), p. 360, who describes such stones and quotes a verse about them by Sir Samuel Ferguson.

I pray you, and speak no more for I cannot abear to hear such incredible lies'), and although Charles admits he tells it differently every time, both Graves and his *persona* Charles insist that the story is true. This tale is the original version of the one story Graves would later tell in his books of myths and his poems.

The White Goddess would seem far to seek in 'The Shout,' but she is present there though as yet unrevealed. In his dedicatory epistle to Laura Riding in the first edition of *Good-Bye*, Graves compared himself to Lord Herbert of Cherbury (father of the founder of his regiment), who, like himself, 'fought in Northern France and wrote books; until at last his active life ended with a sudden clap of thunder from the blue sky' which made him resolve 'at this sign, to print his book *De Veritate*, concerning truth.' Graves also recalls his story 'which, though written two years ago, belongs here; blind and slow like all prophecies —it has left you out entirely.

The self divided into halves warring for the love of the Woman, the Woman as capricious bestower of her favor, the magical power of utterance, and the reiteration of a single truth under many forms—all these elements in 'The Shout' appear again in *The White Goddess*. But in that prodigious work the psychological tension is completely assimilated to mythic statement, which, because objective, redeems the relationship between these elements from the bewilderment and terror by which the lunatic narrator of 'The Shout' is so beset that his tale is a paradigm of murder and suicide. Even the epigraph from Apuleius, along with the Celtic cromlechs and Druid warrior-priests mentioned in 'The Shout,' will reappear in the total, liberating synthesis of *The White Goddess*.

We are now ready to pull together these disparate

strands of Graves's dispositions of feeling in the forest of erudition where he found the truths of his own soul displayed on every stone and tree.

III

We have already seen what were the circumstances of Graves's early life probably responsible for his ambivalent attitude toward love. In his childhood figured the love of his *gemütlich* mother and the undisguised sense of rejection by his preoccupied father, with whom he later feels in a relationship of rivalry both personal and literary. This relationship, or one imaginably like it, is mordantly externalized in a play, 'But It Still Goes On' (1930), in which the rivalry is posed in frankly Freudian terms, the father marrying the woman whom the son loves. From childhood on comes a fear of women, for during adolescence Graves was sequestered at a boys' school, and girls seemed remote and mysterious. His earliest conscious erotic attachment was for another boy, a direction of feeling he sternly repressed; perhaps so sternly that his conception of heterosexual love became endowed with a compensatory psychic intensity it might not otherwise have had.

Such an upbringing was, however, by no means unusual for members of his class at that time, and if his tensions are extreme in degree they are nonetheless not very different in kind from those of many of his readers. To this amatory conditioning by his family situation and schooling, we must add his conditioning by war: the shattering trauma of severe wounds and of being reported dead, the subsequent years of nightmarish disorientation, the sense of the unreality of life, and his discovery, with Dr. Rivers's help, of the

therapeutic powers that could be tapped from the unconscious and liberated in poetry.

It is a fundamental characteristic of the human mind that
two things or states of feeling that share something in common may be conceived of as being interchangeable with
each other. The operation of metaphor is of course based
on this principle. In Graves's mind it is apparent that the
thought of war produces a recrudescence of trauma, and
the fear of death is associated further with self-sacrifice,
with punishment, and with cosmic unreason. But a woman's love also evokes fear, and fear runs in the same chan-
nels however it is set loose: fear of death, fear of self-
sacrifice, imagined death as punishment, death as the stroke
of unreason.

But death, while feared, is also half a welcome liberator.
And love, while feared, is at the same time the giver of
ecstasy, the bringer of transcendence in 'that shivering
glory not to be despised.' Yet the loss of identity in the love
that is desired is all too exactly like the loss of self in the
death that is feared, so that even in the instant of love's
liberation fear strikes.

This poignant paradox is the emotional parallel of the intellectual paradox in which Graves's mind was caught: intelligence plays over a world of unreality, but instinct
reveals what is actual. Therefore, the world of his poems is
topsy-turvy, inside-out, as in 'The Bards,' the mirror poems
like 'Alice,' and the strangest of his love poems, 'The Terraced Valley.'

Yet a further set of conceptions which Graves in his
liberating myth made coalesce with those I have just mentioned are his views concerning the cool web of language
and the nature of poetry. Building his theory from the
bases provided by Dr. Rivers, Graves regards poetry as at

once a form of magic and a means of therapy. In it the
mind may solve the riddles of appearance, but the unwitting part of consciousness provides the real meaning, often
by an inversion of the work of intellect. The subject of
true poetry is therefore not even proposed by the poet's intellectual faculty, which, unaided by the unwitting, can at
best only create intricate word-games and is always enslaved to the poetic style or form in which he writes. Poetry's true subject is inescapable: it is the psychic problems
of the poet, who by stating them in his poems has already
achieved their clarification and hence their half-solution.
Edwin Muir, in *Transition*, objected long ago to this 'utili-
tarian' view of poetry that Graves expounds. But whether
or not we can accept this view as fully as Graves demands,
it is hard to deny the element of truth in it. Graves's distinction between Muse poetry and Gongorism, between
the poetry of inner life, of psychic necessity, and that of
conscious intellectuality, is an undeniably valid description
of two major conceptions of poetry. One might differ with
Muir's objection could it be shown that the poet's personal
problems offered also universal themes; where one would
be likely to differ with Graves is in his absolute condemnation of all poetry not conceived as a rite of worship of the
Muse.

For it is essentially his need to locate in the chaos of life
the source of what is numinous that compels Graves to
such an intense and indeed intolerant dedication to the
Muse and her exactions. And this sense of numinousness re-
sides in the closest human relationships he can experience or
envisage, fraught though they are with danger and fear. He
experiences the relations between son and mother, between
lover and beloved, as religious emotions, comparable to a
third numinous relation, that between man and death. It is

inevitable that in his conception of woman she plays in one person all three roles of mother, bride, and layer-out. Because consciousness in the sexual relationship is so besieged by guilt—no doubt the fear of incestuous relationship with the beloved in her aspect as mother—it is inevitable that she, in her role as layer-out, arrogates also the function of executioner. For in Graves's mythographic story, when the adept approaches his Muse she awaits him with an axe in her hand.

> All saints revile her, and all sober men
> Ruled by the God Apollo's golden mean—
> In scorn of which we sailed to find her
> In distant regions likeliest to hold her
> Whom we desired above all things to know,
> Sister of the mirage and echo.

Ensuing lines of this poem, first published as a dedication to *The White Goddess,* describe her white brow, her blue eyes and 'rowan-berry lips,' her 'hair curled honey-coloured to white hips.' As Douglas Day observes, this is a familiar portrait, probably influenced by 'the algolagnic heroines of Swinburne, the wan, hypnotic beauties of the Romantic poets, and the Fatal Women of Elizabethan tragedy; and [Graves's] vision of the Goddess corresponds so closely to these stereotypes that it is impossible to see her solely as the product of his personal experience.' [1] She is distinctively a Pre-Raphaelite goddess, perhaps directly inspired by Botticelli's Venus rising from the sea. She is, the poem continues, the embodiment of natural fecundity, 'the Mountain Mother,' praised by all song-birds;

> But we are gifted, even in November
> Rawest of seasons, with so huge a sense

---

[1] *Swifter than Reason* (Chapel Hill, N.C., 1963), p. 166.

> Of her nakedly worn magnificence
> We forget cruelty and past betrayal,
> Heedless of where the next bright bolt may fall.

If we are tempted to think of the White Goddess as an idiosyncratic figment of one poet's compulsions, or as a figure shaped by certain modern writers, the inaccuracy of such assumptions should be evident if only because we have met this woman before, bringing her gifts of ecstasy and doom. Yeats called her Aoife. Cuchulain, her mortal lover, took her body in a holy place on the mountain across the sea, in the land of spirits. When the theme has been played out we find that he too as been slain as punishment for the conflict with his son, which is itself a doubling of his prior conflict against his father. At the end of *The Death of Cuchulain* the hero is beset and besieged by female figures of fatality: his enemy in battle is Queen Maeve, his dying vision is of Aoife, his divine nemesis is The Morrigu, crow-headed goddess—of *war*—who 'arranged the dance.' Besides these there were his mortal women, his wife Emer and his mistress Eithne Inguba. The only other male character in *The Death of Cuchulain* is the Blind Man, the double of Cuchulain's anti-self, who ironically takes his life. And like the adept of the White Goddess, Cochulain is beheaded. The ritual sacrifice of a mortal lover to an immortal female figure is the theme also of other late plays of Yeats, *A Full Moon in March* and *The King of the Great Clock Tower*.

Not that Graves acknowledges the near-identity of this one among Yeats's themes with his own chief theme. Graves, whose work was virtually unread during the 1920's and 1930's when Yeats was receiving universal acclaim, has always been in a rather edgy relationship to the Irish poet. Perhaps Yeats was a successful image of himself, not to be abided; or a successful edition of the Irish man of letters his own father never really was. In *The Crowning Privilege* Graves attacks his elder with more ire than accuracy:

> Yeats had a new technique, but nothing to say, unless one counts the literary ballads written for the Irish War of Liberation—in which he took no active part. Instead of the Muse, he employs a ventriloquist's dummy called Crazy Jane. But still he had nothing to say.

This is a preposterous judgment of Yeats, yet when one reads Crazy Jane with Graves's necessities in mind it is obvious that such a poet would only scorn the beggar-woman's randy tongue and her seemingly guiltless delight in uncomplicated sexual ecstasy.

Yeats in his seventies could reconcile the divisions that Graves could but grimly endure. Yeats is not compelled to mix masochism and punishment with his imagination of delight. Or, rather, speaking through a daemonic *persona* presented as an outcast, Yeats can proclaim that the dichotomies we all endure are not only endurable but are the necessary conditions of delight.[1] He endows Crazy Jane with

---

[1] When Yeats, using other *personae*, does admit the impossibility of uniting man's divided nature in joy, he yet achieves a posthumous, Platonic resolution. In the series of poems in *Last Poems* commencing with 'The Three Bushes,' Yeats tells a ballad story of the lady, her lover, and the serving maid. The lady, a Platonic lover, sends the maid in darkness to her man's bed. Yeats follows an old ballad tradition in uniting the three after death: they are buried side by side and their spiritual union is symbolized by the intertwining of the roses planted on their graves. An analogous fulfillment after death appears in 'Baile and Aillinn' and in 'Ribh at the Tomb of Baile and Aillinn.'

Graves offers no such posthumous unions. Indeed he has a poem riddled with horrors which seems to be derived from an opposite folk tradition, the tale of ghostly lovers held apart by a curse even in death. There is the skeleton of such a blighted love story hidden beneath the Skeltonics of his late poem, 'The Devil at Berry Pomeroy' (1953), where 'the Devil snaps his chain / And renews his reign / To the little joy / Of Berry Pomeroy.' There witches, monsters, imps, and ghosts cavort and there

an heroic acceptance of the divided nature of man. Graves's heroism is in his not accepting man's divided nature; he therefore touches but the briefest 'shivering glory,' and walks willingly toward his numinous executioner. No Platonist he, yet was there not a time, of which we still inherit a dim remembrance, when love was not 'sick love'? This is the burden of his wry passion in 'Cry Faugh!' In this poem he rejects as lustful the philosophies of love espoused by Caria and Philistia; he spurns Socrates and Plato's 'homosexual ideology' and the 'chaste sodality' of 'Apocalyptic Israelites,' nor will he accept the ways that scientists, who study the animals, 'contrive to eliminate the sexual problem':

> Cry faugh! on science, ethics, metaphysics,
> On antonyms of sacred and profane—
> Come walk with me, love, in a golden rain
>
> Past toppling colonnades of glory,
> The moon alive on each uptilted face:
> Proud remnants of a visionary race.

It is no coincidence that in dramatizing their deepest tensions Graves and Yeats should have discovered patterns of symbolic action of such close resemblance. These patterns, which I have discussed in Graves thus far in terms of psy-

is 'Incest done / Between mother and son.' This is no love poem, but has anyone asked why all these catastrophes are heaped upon Berry Pomeroy? The likeliest reason is a local tradition peculiar to that place, Berry castle in Devonshire, where 'a son of the Pomeroys surprised his sister in an arbour with an enemy of their house' and slew the lovers. In 'a winding passage just within the castle entrance' one may yet see by night 'two shadowy figures, man and woman, parted by the width of this recess, pitifully struggling to reach and touch each other across the empty space, but held back by some power stronger than their love, still withholding from them . . . that satisfaction which the cruelty of Pomeroy denied them in their life'—A. H. Norway, *Highways and Byways in Devon and Cornwall* (London, 1930), pp. 83–4.

chological origins within an individual's experience, are in fact true to the experience also of many contemporary men. Once such patterns comprised the basis of man's religious life, for the White Goddess, like Yeats's version of the Cuchulain legends, is a modern adaptation and interpretation of a set of rituals and their accompanying myths from Bronze Age times. As was true of Yeats's myths, those used by Graves are taken from both Celtic and classical tradition. Having chosen the rocky acres of Wales as his imaginative home, Graves, with his curious and tenacious intelligence, made himself a master of Welsh romance. It was in the incomprehensible riddles of the poet Taliesin, supposed to have been a sixth-century contemporary of King Arthur and Merlin, that Graves found the thread that led him through a labyrinth toward the inescapable subject of all his meditations.

In discussing Graves's conception of the role of intellect I have hitherto stressed his view that 'the unwitting' by a truthful duplicity reveals the true meaning of what intelligence unsuccessfully struggled to understand. In the argument of *The White Goddess*, however, we find intellect granted a more positive role: it is much the same role that intellect enjoys in many of Graves's other discursive works, such as his 'restoration' of the true original texts of the story of creation in *Adam's Rib*, of *The Greek Myths*, *The Hebrew Myths*, and *The Nazarene Gospel Restored*. What fascinates Graves about these problematical texts is the challenge to solve puzzles nobody else has got right. What better demonstration of the acuity of one's intellectual processes? And particularly when the solutions are supraintellectual, available only to him who can bring not only brains and scholarship but poetic intuition into play. For Graves as mythographer and text-emender is very like

Poe's Monsieur Dupin, the detective who solved crimes the prefect of police (a rationalist) could not fathom because unlike the private detective, he was unable vicariously to commit them. The line between arch-detective and arch-criminal becomes very fine. In order to reassemble poetic texts, Graves must be able vicariously to have composed them. And how many of his texts are really holy books. Graves has rewritten the religious screeds of the Christians, the Jews, the Greeks, the Canaanites, and the Celts. They all prove to be variations on one story, for there is no other.

In the beginning, says a holy book, was the Word; and *The White Goddess* begins with the word in Wales. At the outset of this wild and wonderful book, Graves takes on himself the burden of rationalizing the scrambled text of *Câd Goddeu* (The Battle of the Trees), a poem ascribed to Taliesin in the romance translated by Lady Guest. Although Taliesin is supposed to have lived in the sixth century the romance was set down in the eleventh, and the world its characters inhabit, where men and marvels magically mingle, is clearly medieval in a culture that strongly conserved in its literature the attitudes toward the Otherworld of pagan antiquity. Further, in early medieval Wales poetry was the exclusive right and property of an arduously trained class of poet-priests, the Druids. This cult of word-wizards controlled the forces of the universe because they had secret, sacred knowledge. What they knew was the true names of things.

Remembering Graves's poem 'The Bards,' as well as his writings on the magical and therapeutic powers of poetry, we can see how attractive to him would be such a stage in the history of the art and of Wales. As had Yeats before him, Graves found compelling the conception of the Druids as poet-priests who actually wielded both spiritual

and temporal power. This role, like that which Pound discovered among the Provençal troubadours, could scarcely
be a more dramatic reversal of the minimal influence and
reverence given poetry today.

Graves's cultural primitivism is more than a cast of feeling, it becomes the method of his mind. Relentlessly he
pursues first things to their origins. To comprehend the
riddles of Taliesin it becomes necessary to discover the nature of language itself. Committed as he is to what one may
call a conspiratorial theory of cultural transmission, Graves
looks for cryptograms and cyphers to provide explanations
for the anagrammatic puzzles of the ancient texts. The
alphabet itself is a shorthand for divine meanings. The first
alphabet in Wales was the ogham script, in which each letter bore the name of a tree, each tree was sacred to a god,
and the combinations of tree-god-letters comprise acrostic
formulas for the invocation of divinities or the revelation of
the relations between them. (The ogham script, which survives in stone inscriptions found in every Celtic region
from the Hebrides to Brittany, is indeed given this arboreal
and invocatory character in the chief work of Victorian
scholarship about it.[1]) Not only is the alphabet, according
to Graves, a condensation of a sacred secret, but the texts
of Taliesin's songs contain further clandestine revelations.
Because their meanings are actually the invocations of a
heathen faith that were set down during the Christian era,
to escape persecution the poet-priests of Carridwen (the
Welsh name for the Muse) were obliged to pie or garble
the order of their incantations. Taliesin's songs are in fact a

[1] Richard Bolt Brash, *Ogam Inscribed Monuments of the Gaedhil in
the British Islands*, ed. G. M. Atkinson (London, 1879). The ogham
characters represented vertical stems and horizontal twigs in varying
positions. 'The letters of this alphabet are called *Feadha*, i.e., Trees'
(p. 58).

codex of the religious life of the Druids, and only by re-creating those texts in their original versions can the scrambled meanings that have come down to us be restored to intelligibility. The College of Druids was an academy of both poetic craft and pagan theology, so it may be inferred what qualities must be possessed by a modern man who would re-create the original texts in their true meanings.

Druidic religion, as it appears in *The White Goddess*, was the Celtic version of the fertility worship that spread all over Bronze Age Europe. The stations of the year in that religion were the seasons of growing and waning, the two-part year of the huntsman, later elaborated into the quarterly seasons of the agricultural year. Divinity is of course imminent in nature, and the alternation of summer and winter is likewise the war between grace and deprivation, growth and decay, life and death. The presiding power over the cycles of life and its forces is the deified image of maternity, the Great Mother whose womb is the source of life, whose will is the unifier, whose breast the nourisher, whose embrace all men desire, and whose fructifying power lasts forever although their lives last but for a day.

A prodigious learning is displayed in Graves's argument. A classical scholar since his school days, he had read widely over the years in the Greek and Roman historians and mythographers to track down things that intrigued him. Early on, he had come upon that book from the classical period which revealed to him the link between the Celtic fertility-worship to which he was now being drawn and the Graeco-Roman world whose myths had been over-layed, so it seemed, with sterile Virgilian stylization and so had lost all emotive power through their exhaustion by Apollonian poets (both Augustan and Neo-Augustan)

who used myth for decorative purposes rather than with
true understanding and piety. That book was *The Golden
Ass* of Apuleius (from which he had taken the epigraph to
'The Shout'). With characteristic thoroughness, Graves
eventually translated the whole thing. His translation is a
masterpiece, accurate, spare, a distinguished English prose
capable of satire, farce, gravity, and piety. Indeed, in
Apuleius Graves found the very mixture of the reverent
with the grotesque, the mixture of ecstatic emotion with
fateful foreordination, that corresponded to his own self-
knowledge. *The Golden Ass* is the book of divine transformations which served Graves in the way that d'Arbois's *Le
Cycle Mythologique Irlandais* and Madame Blavatsky's *Isis
Unveiled* served Yeats, that Ovid's *Metamorphoses* served
Pound, that Dante's *Divina Commedia* served T. S. Eliot.

The Golden Ass tells the story of Lucius, who would be
an adept of love, but by meddling with black magic because deflected from the true by his lust, becomes transformed not, as he had hoped, into a bird, but into an ass.
This is a perfect emblem for a human soul trapped in a
ludicrous and degrading animal's body. Lucius, as a donkey,
wanders all around the Grecian world, enduring the gibes
of the populace, overhearing the tale of Cupid and Psyche
(an allegory of the soul's progress in the pursuit of love),
and after many adventures at last he recognizes the way of
contrition and repentance by which he may be restored to
human form. This is Lucius's prayer to 'the supreme Goddess':

> 'Blessed Queen of Heaven, whether you are pleased to
> be known as Ceres, the original harvest mother . . . ; or
> whether as celestial Venus . . . who at the time of the
> first Creation coupled the sexes in mutual love . . . ; or
> whether as Artemis, . . . reliever of the birth pangs of

women . . . ; or whether as dread Proserpine to whom
the owl cries at night, whose triple face is potent against
the malice of ghosts . . . I beseech you . . . [to] have
mercy on me in my extreme distress . . .'

Falling asleep after this passionate, penitential outcry, before his eyes 'the apparition of a woman began to rise from
the middle of the sea.' He invokes the Goddess again to in-
spire his description, and tells how 'Her long thick hair fell
in tapering ringlets on her lovely neck.' She is crowned
with interwoven flowers, and wears a moon-shaped mirror
on her brow, supported by vipers and fringed with bris-
tling ears of corn. In the middle of her mantle 'beamed a
full and fiery moon.' Her right hand held a bronze rattle
curved like a swordbelt; from her left hung a boat-shaped
dish; while her feet were shod with 'slippers of palm leaves,
the emblem of victory.' Summoned by his prayers, the
Goddess in her merciful mood addressed him:

'I am Nature, the universal Mother, mistress of all the
elements, primordial child of time, sovereign of all things
spiritual, queen of the dead, queen also of the immortals,
the single manifestation of all gods and goddesses that
are. . . . Though I am worshipped in many aspects,
known by countless names, and propitiated with all manner of different rites, yet the whole round earth venerates
me.'

Then, after giving the donkey instructions to have faith
and to pluck the roses from the hand of the High Priest in
the morrow's procession, she adds,

I promise you that in the joy and laughter of the festival
nobody will either view your ugly shape with abhorrence
or dare to put a sinister interpretation on your sudden
return to human shape. Only remember, and keep these

words of mine locked tight in your heart, that from now onwards until the very last day of your life you are dedicated to my service. It is only right that you should devote your whole life to the Goddess who makes you a man again.[1]

Graves's synthesizing mind is Protean, and not surprisingly, critics of his theory less widely read than he have interpreted the construct in terms of their own knowledge rather than his. Thus Jarrell, an astute psychological critic, recognized *The White Goddess* as a personal myth, a projection on the universe of a poet's mother-fixation in one love affair, that with Laura Riding. Day, a literary scholar, recognized the Goddess as a familiar of Pre-Raphaelite, Romantic, and Elizabethan literature. Both of course are right, but only partly so. The Celtic myths are indeed analogous with those of the Graeco-Roman world in Apuleius, and Graves, with Germanic thoroughness has ferreted out every applicable parallel from the literatures of Sumer, Egypt, Melanesia, and the Orient to buttress the spire of his ancient but newly reconstructed religion.

Like the theologians of ancient Minos and the Druids, Graves conceives of wholeness as a property of woman, doubtless because of her biological role. Wholeness is opposed by dividedness, found in woman's opposite, man. This seems just, since, at least in ancient societies, woman played the one role of mother, bringer-into-being of life, while men played many parts as huntsman, warrior, sailor, scout, farmer, shepherd, potter, priest, physician, salesman, poet, lover. When man acknowledges the one among these roles which is his only really necessitous one, consort to

---

[1] *The Golden Ass*, translated by Robert Graves (New York, 1951), pp. 262–6. In *The White Goddess* Graves quotes this passage at length from Adlington's Renaissance translation, pp. 69–72.

woman in the begetting of life, he serves her until his potency fails and he is succeeded by a younger, stronger lover. In this way the fertility of the race, of the land, of the universe, is assured. The old worn-out lover, or fertility king, doesn't meekly abdicate when his time has come; he must render unto Latona that which is hers: his head. For it was man's head with its busy intellect that split him up into pieces and specialized functions, and his head is the lodgment of that intellect, his senses, his faculties. When in *The Mabinogion*, Pwyl exchanged blows on the neck with Arawn; when the Green Knight did the same with Sir Gawaine; when, in *The Green Helmet*, the Red Man from the sea exchanged beheading blows with the Champion of Ulster, it was the re-enactment of the succession of life by death and death by life that still has power to move us today.

But how can divinity belong exclusively to woman, who needs a partner in her fecundity? Graves modifies her claim and his devaluation of man to account for this, and so combines the broken images of divided man with the single image of the Muse: Man, he writes,

> is divine not in his single person, but only in his twin-hood. As Osiris, the Spirit of the Waxing Year he is always jealous of his weird, Set, the Spirit of the Waning Year, and vice versa; he cannot be both of them at once except by an intellectual effort that destroys his humanity, and this is a fundamental defect of the Apollonian or Jehovistic cult. Man is a demi-god: he always has either one foot or the other in the grave; woman is divine because she can keep both her feet always in the same place, whether in the sky, in the underworld, or on this earth.

Although woman, he adds, worships not her lover but her infant son, 'She is passionately interested in grown men

. . . because the love-hate that Osiris and Set feel for each other on her account is a tribute to her divinity. She tries to satisfy both, but can only do so by alternate murder.' [1]

Barbarous as it seems in summary, the great value of this mythic pattern to Graves is that it elevates to divine, eternal, and archetypal significance the experience of love as it may be known to the individual sensibility. The pattern embraces passion, fulfillment, and rejection. In the act of love the man performs the sacred and self-sacrificing ritual act of a priest in a fertility cult, his whole being intent upon the adoration of his beloved who represents to him the Goddess of Nature. Indeed she *is* the goddess, for by their re-enactment of the sacred mystery these individual participants assume the traditional roles attributed to the divinity and her high priest.

The tortuous ingenuity and startling comprehensiveness of Graves's theory have caused his books to astonish more readers than they have pleased, and in each of the eight or ten learned fields he has invaded Graves has stirred up far more controversy than endorsement. It is, I think, undeniable that he bends the evidence to conform to his needs, as seems evident, *inter alia,* in his discussion of the ballads, and as M. J. C. Hodgart and S. J. Papastravou rather testily demonstrate in their review of *The Greek Myths* in *Twentieth Century* (May 1955). But his methods and his main direction are not such idiosyncracies as might be supposed. The structure of *The White Goddess*—the labyrinthine trail through the mythologies of many countries followed to answer a religious question posed by pagan rites or texts—is closely modeled on that of Frazer's *Golden Bough*. In his use of iconography as a source of 'true readings' of myths (much of his evidence comes from bas-

[1] *The White Goddess*, p. 109.

reliefs, coins, etc.), Graves follows Goblet d'Alviella's *Migration of Symbols.* The matriarchal origin of religion had been fully proposed and expounded before him by Robert Briffault's magisterial study, *The Mothers;* it has been lately corroborated by the contemporary doyen of religious historians, E. O. James, in *Primitive Religions,* a book that does not mention Graves. His researches in Celtic pagandom are based on those of scholars older than his father's generation, including some whom Yeats consulted—Rhys, d'Arbois, P. W. Joyce—and of more recent scholars like Macalister and MacCulloch, and the Welsh researches of Lady Guest, Gwyn Jones, Ifor Williams, and others. He borrows much from Margaret Murray's *God of the Witches,* and his conception of myth derives from the work of Jane Harrison. Nonetheless, *The White Goddess* is one of the most extraordinary works of synthesis in our time. If it makes pretty free with the evidence and may not be certifiably accurate as a descriptive history of myth, it is yet invaluable for what it says it is: 'a historic grammar of poetic myth.'

I V

Because *The White Goddess* synthesizes not only all the scholarly works and disciplines I have mentioned but also unites the needs of a modern sensibility with the rituals of the ancient world, it makes possible a body of the most distinguished love poetry in the twentieth century. Whatever his shortcomings as a scholar—as the university considers scholarship—Graves discovered the identity of individual need with what was once the communal structure of myth and ritual devised to serve that need. He maintains, with some justice, that over the centuries the religious structures

based on the propitiation of fertility were repressed and replaced with more abstract and intellectualized conceptions
of the divine. Just as metaphysics is based upon physics, so
theology is based upon the structure of society; and its
main economic institutions—hunting, agriculture, or manu-
facture—are recognizable to anthropologists as the unmoved movers that determine the religious dispensations
under which the society operates. Yet the human creature
is biologically (and perhaps in important ways psychically)
unchanged by the five thousand years of cultural development since the worship of Isis, Latona, Caridwen. Graves is
grappling with latent dispositions of human character that
have been overlain by a few dozen centuries of social life.
Call his theory atavistic, yet none can deny that he restores
to an indestructible and necessary part of human experience its original mystery, spiritual energy, guilt, and wonder.

The conceptual system of *The White Goddess* might,
however, have made possible a wider range of poetry than
that which Graves has actually managed to write. Not all
the ingenuity and energy that went into his sometimes
devious proofs could be transformed into the poetry his
grammar of myth was designed to liberate. His mind ranges
further than his sensibility, caught within the circularities
of love. His principal application of his system is in the
analysis of love in all its aspects he can know. The identity
of the Muse changes in real life, as the poet offers his fealty
to various Muse-women in turn. But the conceptions which
each of these women embodies remain constant, perpetual,
while the poet is alternately the bringer of fruition and the
sacrificed victim in the fertility ritual they enact and re-
enact. It will be seen that these conceptions serve Graves
somewhat as the idea of chivalric love served the courtly

sonneteers and lyric-writers in the Petrarchan tradition. They too addressed their plaints to a beautiful, disdainful Muse, and the sequences of their sonnets became the spiritual autobiographies of such lovers as Astrophel. But, as is plain from 'Cry Faugh!,' Graves spurns their Platonic love as fruitless.

His love poems may be taken as mythical retellings of human love and as human re-enactments of myth. Of course these categories are interchangeable, in that mythical lovers are the archetypes or originals of the living poet and his Muse, whose present passion is the real subject of such reconstructed mythical poems as (to choose from among his recent examples), 'Liadan and Curither' or 'Anchises and Aphrodite' in *Collected Poems;* in *New Poems 1962*, 'The Ambrosia of Dionysus and Semele,' and, taking the transformations of love from the epic of *Gilgamesh*, 'Inkidoo and the Queen of Babel'; while his most recent collection, with the didactic title *Man Does, Woman Is* (1964), offers as mythic lovers Diarmuid and Grainne of Celtic tradition, Orpheus and Eurydice from the Greek, and now even 'Joseph and Mary' can be accommodated into the single theme. Each of these mythic poems concentrates upon a single state or paradox in the love relationship; but in the years during and immediately after the composition of *The White Goddess*, Graves wrote a number of poems which more fully draw upon the fantastic accumulation of lore and the complete pattern revealed in that work. I have already quoted his dedicatory poem, 'The White Goddess'; other such mythological love poems include those in section VIII of his *Collected Poems*, and 'The Young Cordwainer,' 'Darien,' and 'To Juan at the Winter Solstice.' This last is a poem which perhaps best exhibits Graves's special virtues, his incantatory rhythm, his primordial imagery, his embodiment of contemporary experience in a mold archaic, mysterious, and compelling:

> There is one story and one story only
> That will prove worth your telling,
> Whether as learned bard or gifted child;
> To it all lines or lesser gauds belong
> That startle with their shining
> Such common stories as they stray into.

Succeeding stanzas offer the imagery of 'such common stories'—all ancient, mythical variants of the one story as it is embodied among the trees, the beasts, the 'birds that croak at you the Triple will'; the tale is written in the Zodiac and on the waters of death and birth where the ark floats, as again in the circuits of the stars. It shines in the silvery Virgin-mermaid irresistibly beckoning the King who 'barters life for love'; and in the immortal snake hatching from chaos (an image from *Gilgamesh*) whom the King must battle in black water before he is cast up on the Muse's shore. The elements contend, the owl cries, and the heart cries fearfully, 'sorrow to sorrow,' yet the poet knows to

> Dwell on her graciousness, dwell on her smiling,
> Do not forget what flowers
> The great boar trampled down in ivy time.
> Her brow was creamy as the crested wave,
> Her sea-blue eyes were wild
> But nothing promised that is not performed.

In this poem the cruelty of beauty and the mystery of love are rendered in images at once mythologically appropriate, individually surprising, sensuously immediate. The associations we are likely to make—even if ignorant of the particular significance of these images in *The White Goddess*—

cannot help but place love at the center of a complex of feelings which ranges from the touch of two human beings to the farthest circuits of the outer stars. All the orders of creation, the natural, the supernatural, and man's heroic yet defeated effort to possess immortality, are embodied in the rippling stanzas of the poem. Like Gilgamesh, the lover plunges into chaos and tries to bring back to earth the serpent of immortality; here, more patently than in the ancient source, the plunge is susceptible of Freudian interpretation. Yet while 'To Juan at the Winter Solstice' is built of arcane materials the poem succeeds because its arcana are taken from the public domain. The main outlines of the single story are obvious to any careful and reasonably literate reader, who might begin by reflecting that the winter solstice is the turning of the year from waning to waxing, the obvious occasion for a poem praising fertility and its service.

An instance of the persuasive power of the poem occurs in its final stanza. There surely must be some supercharge of meaning in the injunction, 'Do not forget what flowers / The great boar trampled down in ivy time.' Without the aid of *The White Goddess* one might recall the great boar, so symbolic of bestial energy, which the Green Knight had to slay; or the fact that Circe turned her lovers into swine; or that pork was a favorite—originally a sacred —meat among the Celts; which might help explain why the sacrificed hero in Yeats's *King of the Great Clock Tower* was a swineherd trying to be transformed into a poet by the power of love. All of these reflections would strengthen one's apprehension of Graves's poem. Yet such is the compression of his poetic shorthand that he has in mind everything revealed of the boar in his deciphering of *Amerigin's Song*, a Druidic revelation from the mouth of God, as we see on page 209 of *The White Goddess:*

G, the ivy month, is also the month of the boar. Set, the Egyptian Sun-god, disguised as a boar, kills Osiris of the ivy, the lover of the Goddess Isis. Apollo, the Greek Sun-god, disguised as a boar, kills Adonis, or Tammuz, the Syrian, the lover of the Goddess Aphrodite. Finn Mac Cool, disguised as a boar, kills Diarmuid, the lover of the Irish Goddess Grainne (Greinne). . . . October was the boar-hunting season, as it was also the revelry season of the ivy-wreathed Bassarids. The boar is the beast of death and the 'fall' of the year begins in the month of the boar.

Although all readers of Eliot accept the notion that a poetry of allusion incorporates the original contexts into its own texture, Graves has not, so far as I know, been much read in this way. Yet like Yeats he does not really need to be monumentalized by a scaffolding of scholarship for the reader who is alert to his primary meanings and has enough empathy to imagine the elaborations they suggest. We are not all mythographers, but who cannot find in the imagery itself almost all that the gloss from *The White Goddess* provides? 'Do not forget what flowers / The great boar trampled down in ivy time': There are such strong suggestions of lust, death, strength, and helplessness in this swine-and-flower image that we might ask if mythic references are needed at all. If not, it is only because the myths can but offer us new names, or old ones, for what these figures from man's common dream portend. This poem, written for the birth of Graves's seventh child, concludes with the assurance that the Goddess will be true to her servant, who by then should know how short a date his summer's lease can have.

A seventh son may prove a solar hero, but it is hard even for lovers to live perpetually at the pitch of magic and enchantment invoked by 'To Juan at the Winter Solstice.' Yet, except for satirical pieces, Graves's poems have the evocation of such an ecstatic moment as their intention. In the twenty years since writing *The White Goddess,* he has continued to explore the ramifications of feeling in the several stages of his ritualized relationship. Occasionally, now, he is able to imagine his beloved in a more amiable guise, escaping for a moment even the reconciliation of lust and love foretold by his doctrine in 'End of Play': 'Yet love survives, the word carved on a sill / Under antique dread of the headsman's axe.' In a touching little poem, 'Like Snow,' his Muse appears without her avenging weapon, surrounded by images of a fertile world waking from its frozen sleep. Graves's wit, so metaphysical in ingenuity and cavalier in tone, is nowhere more delightful than in 'Beauty in Trouble,' a fanciful allegory in which Beauty first 'flees to the good angel / On whom she can rely' after her mistreatment by 'The fiend who beats, betrays and sponges on her.' But far from rewarding her suppliant benefactor with a constancy deserved by his own, as soon as recovered she deserts him for the fiend in 'the marriage of true minds.'

One of Graves's most persuasive statements of his doctrine of love occurs in what is doubtless the most unusual poem written on the crowning of Queen Elizabeth. In 'Coronation Address' he remembers his father's grief at the death of Victoria, and his father's outburst when his mother attempted the consolation that 'Our Queen was, after all, only a woman':

> 'To cry "God save the King" is honourable
> But to serve a Queen is lovely. Listen now:
> Could I have one wish for this son of mine . . .'

A wish fulfilled at last after long years.

And yet, in 'A Slice of Wedding Cake,' Graves is aware of the possibly excessive quality of his devotion, for he asks

'do I always over-value woman / At the expense of man?'
No doubt he does, since man he understands while woman
remains ever mysterious, as in 'The Visitation,' when,
'Drowsing in my chair of disbelief,' he watches the opening
door through which she comes, 'I quake for wonder at
your choice of me: / Why, why and why?'

I think these poems may fairly suggest Graves's range.
Few poets have dealt so constantly with love, or made this
theme so believable and human while at the same time so
magical and terrifying, as he. Yet much as one admires the
toughness and skill of Graves's poems, one is in the end
struck by the limitations of his treatment of his inescapable
theme. Intricate and complex as is the myth defined by *The
White Goddess*, that pattern proves at last a Procrustean
bed, and not the only bed upon which love may lie. If love
is ever not doomed, if constancy is possible between man
and woman, if Caridwen can love and live with the same
man for over a year without—in Millamont's phrase—
dwindling into a wife, if the fulfillment of love is an expan-
sion of feeling and the intellectual joy which other poets
from Shakespeare and Donne to Yeats have known, these
qualities of feeling are banished by 'the sceptre of Guess
Whom.' Indeed the worst of her exactions may be not that
her servant loses his head over her but that he is condemned
to perpetual repetition of the same wheel of feelings, an
Ixion-like determinism from which there is no escape.
Poems in Graves's recent volumes repeat not only the action but the very images and language of his earlier suc-
cesses in the *Collected Poems*. Yet Graves's style is still
capable of wresting out of the wry struggles between spirit
and body, mind and instinct, poems no one else could have
written. The best poems, as it seems to me, in *Man Does,
Woman Is* (his most recent book) are among those that do

not deal directly with the goddess theme: 'An East Wind,' 'Dance of Words,' and 'Consortium of Stones,' a strange poem recalling the fieldcrop of stony souls in 'The Shout.' The old tensions evoke an Apuleian image in 'The Green Castle': 'Mind is the prudent rider; body, the ass / Disciplined always by a harsh bit . . . / Holds converse with archangels.' But the fulfillment of desire elicits the diction of the Pre-Raphaelites—'a trance of love . . . ramparts of blue sea . . .'

Unlike Donne, who made images of cartography, astronomy, law courts, and chemical processes dramatize the emotions of love, Graves must resist the contemporary equivalents of these metaphysical conceits. Science, rational thought, materialism have made the topsy-turvy world he rejects in 'The Terraced Valley' and 'From the Embassy.' We have to live in the world of 'The Florist Rose,' where real blooms give place to plastic, and eagles to 'the robust male aeroplane . . . Who has no legend'; it may seem atavistic to write as though modern lovers were Diarmuid and Grainne, but the era of technology provides scant material to answer to the need. That need, of course, is a primordial part of our natures, as instinctual as our unwitting participation in the cycle of life. Graves has stripped away almost everything else as extrinsic to this first thing. Therefore Graves's poems deal with contemporary society only as a subject for occasional satire, a form which Graves identifies with the destructive power of the Druidic *rann*. Politics is a pointless game contrived by men who do not acknowledge the Muse; the true poet is not deflected from the one theme, choosing 'To be silent in Siloam' though the walls come toppling down. Serving the Muse is Graves's litmus test for true poets, and few pass it. It is sad that he has not had the magnanimity, now that honor and influence have caught up with him, to leave off berating his contemporaries for not writing as he does—would he praise them for doing so? But perhaps this polemical defiance of modern poets is necessary in his rejection of the world which they, in other ways than his, have tried to accept as the subject of poetry.

Graves, unlike Yeats, seems prevented from grappling with the world by the bonds of his own system. *A Vision* gave Yeats a means of accommodating the 'numb nightmare' of contemporary history: the history of the soul Yeats dramatized in the Cuchulain legend, refashioned to serve the needs of his theme. When we compare the poems made possible by *The White Goddess* with the treatment of love in Yeats's poems and the Cuchulain plays, it is evident that Graves's work is restricted to a much narrower emotional range. All is subsumed under his monomyth, which, despite the baroque extensiveness of reference and argument in *The White Goddess*, in the poems reduces all experience of love to the reiteration of the same pattern. Compared to the active force of Yeats's supernatural characters and superhuman forces, redolent as they are of Ireland's long-held traditions, Graves's goddess seems curiously bookish and remote from any historical or cultural particularity. For both poets the experience at the spiritual core of life gives a transfiguration we recognize as the equivalent of religious. But the ecstasy of religious possession is perilously attained in Graves's work, independently of history, of society, of everything in life save itself.

This isolation of spiritual grace from ethics, from the shared assumptions of behavior, and from our common participation in our time, is one consequence of a society in which the poet seemingly can function best by not belonging. A further result of this separation of ecstasy from the context of life is foretold by the structure of *The White Goddess*, in which the origin of truth is in the root nature of expression, of language. It may be suspected that the entire mythopoetic system is the last wild and quirky flowering of the Pre-Raphaelite aestheticism in which Graves grew up, yoked by violence to the Romantic primitivism of a unifying, ancient myth. As Graves says, praising astrology in a recent poem, his effort is 'to reinduce a pure, archaic vision' ('Non Cogunt Astra').

It may be that Graves's early poems of unreason will prove at least as durable as his mythological Muse poems. Certainly there are more of the gritty, tough, and frangible qualities of twentieth-century life in them. And they, too, culminate in the cool web of language. But this is inevitable. Graves is right: a poet's struggle to unify feeling is inextricable from the aesthetic that makes his expression possible. Who would say that this servant of the Muse has not earned the right to

> call that man a liar who says I wrote
> All that I wrote in love, for love of art.

Three: EDWIN MUIR

:8:

THE STORY AND THE FABLE

In the last poem before his death Edwin Muir wrote,

> I have been taught by dreams and fantasies
> Learned from the friendly and the darker phantoms
> And got great knowledge and courtesy from the dead . . .

Now that his poems are completed, his debts to fantasies and dreams and to the past are clear. His own past had itself the pattern of a quest that disclosed its direction only as it went, a pattern of continual revelation. And that direction seems a recapitulation in a single life of the fall of a society from pastoral innocence to the sufferings of modern man.

As Muir says in a poem he called 'The Myth,' 'My childhood all a myth / Enacted in a distant isle . . .' Edwin Muir is the only major poet in English in modern times to have grown up in a folk community where the farming economy and the literary culture were essentially what they had been five hundred years ago. Of his childhood on that Orkney farm he has written that 'there was no great distinction between the ordinary and the fabulous,' for there 'the lives of living men turned legend.' [1] Muir's sense

---

[1] *An Autobiography* (London, 1954), p. 14.

of archetypal action and of the continuity of the generations in their traditional pattern were conceptions which
this poet did not need to acquire by acts of will. They
seemed the given conditions of life itself in a close-knit
agrarian community, where men lived so that they might
be judged well by their neighbors with whom they took
part in all the yearly round of ritual in work and worship
and in play.

But this Adamic condition of life, this spare, islanded
Eden in the northern seas, was only the beginning for
Muir, the beginning toward which he spent the rest of his
life trying to return. His father was driven from the farm
by the exactions of harsh landlords, and the family moved
to Glasgow. There began Edwin Muir's sufferings as a
modern man. He knew a widely varied range of personal
involvements with the turmoil and revolutionary energies
of contemporary society; his family's tragic uprooting
from their feudal farm became a paradigm for him of the
Fall of man from the Garden. In the slums of industrial
Glasgow the Muirs knew only hopeless poverty, helpless
anonymity, and the deaths of father, mother, and two beloved brothers. As though this were not enough for a man
to bear, Edwin Muir next endured two years of spiritual
immolation in a landscape symbolic of the industrial waste-
land: innocently answering an advertisement for an office
job, he found himself working in a factory that turned rot-
ting animal bones into fertilizer. This nightmarish episode,
unforgettably described in his *Autobiography*, is haunt-
ingly like a tale by Kafka—whose work Muir later translated. Emerging from this desolation, Muir, a self-taught
intellectual, was caught up first in evangelical religion,
then, under Nietzsche's spell, in political millennialism. He
did not even begin to write poems until he was thirty-five;

starting with no formal training, he could but imitate what he already knew—Victorian narrative verse, religious allegories, and the Scottish ballads. To the end his verse never resembled the nondiscursive form and experimental diction of his younger contemporaries. Indeed, his work is so little like that of the modernist movement that for years he had no impact on American readers. In time he mastered his early defects of clumsy diction and too obvious allegory. His direct narrative, exploratory poems have at their best a purity of conception and the eloquence of the right word in the right place. His literary connections are partly with the Victorians (particularly Tennyson), but as he matured his work absorbed the influence of Continental symbolism rather than of contemporary English verse. He seems to fuse the self-transcendence of Hölderlin to the allegorized soulscape of Kafka. Muir plumbs the subconscious life; what rise in the nets of his language are archetypes and symbols.

As a poet who seeks his truths in 'dreams and fantasies' Edwin Muir summons the phantoms of his own unconscious life with the certainty that these are not merely the tormented or triumphant imaginings of one particular man, but take their forms and reveal their meanings as part of the inheritance of the race. In his *Autobiography* Muir has much to say about his dreams and their sources in childhood memories stirred up by later conflicts. It is quite clear that the images of animals, of struggles, of journeys, of recurrent visitations in certain landscapes attained to by great effort and endured with a sense of inevitability—all these materials are akin to those patterns of memory which Jung has proposed as the archetypes, residing not in exterior experience but inherently in the human mind. It is clear, too, that a workable correlation exists between such a theory of psychology and the Platonic conception of reality, a conception particularly attractive to a poet who inherits the intellectual attitudes of late Romanticism.

Platonism and Jungian archetype pass dramatically into one another in Muir's poem, 'Hölderlin's Journey' (1937). This is one of the many poems in which Muir sends his protagonist on a pilgrimage through life; in many of the others the destination is only partially revealed, but in this poem, based upon the life of a poet Muir much admired and translated, the journey ends in a perfect epiphany for despair:

> The evening brought a field, a wood.
>   I left behind the hills of lies,
> And watched beside a mouldering gate
>   A deer with its rock-crystal eyes.
>
> On either pillar of the gate
>   A deer's head watched within the stone.
> The living deer with quiet look
>   Seemed to be gazing on
>
> Its pictured death—and suddenly
>   I knew, Diotima was dead,
> As if a single thought had sprung
>   From the cold and the living head.

Like Socrates, like Hölderlin, Muir has learned from Diotima that we attain to knowledge of the Forms by passing from love of the beautiful to love of the idea of beauty. Her death then means the extinction of the Platonic possibility, 'a broken mind,' the end of the imagination's power to unite created things with uncreated perfection. Muir does not usually use philosophical terms or tropes in his verse, and Plato occurs rarely again—as in the very last lines of his *Collected Poems*

And now that time grows shorter, I perceive
That Plato's is the truest poetry,
And that these shadows
Are cast by the true.

If one conceives of life as the reiteration of archetypal patterns, it is necessary to devise a way of making the accidents of a particular existence conformable to the necessities of a preordinate pattern. The title of the first version of Muir's *Autobiography* indicates his terms for doing this. He called the account of his life until the age of thirty-five *The Story and the Fable*. What he means by 'fable' and 'story' is explained in this passage from the *Autobiography:* he is speaking of the correspondences between his dreams of animals and his childhood experience in a farming community.

If I were recreating my life in an autobiographical novel I could bring out these correspondences freely and show how our first intuition of the world expands into vaster and vaster images, creating a myth which we act almost without knowing it, while our outward life goes on its ordinary routine of eating, drinking, sleeping, working, and making money in order to beget sons and daughters who will do the same. . . .

It is clear that no autobiography can begin with a man's birth, that we extend far beyond any boundary line which we can set for ourselves in the past or the future, and that the life of every man is an endlessly repeated performance of the life of man. It is clear for the same reason that no autobiography can confine itself to conscious life, and that sleep, in which we pass a third of our existence, is a mode of experience, and our dreams a part of reality. In themselves our conscious lives may not be particularly interesting. But what we are not and can never be, our fable, seems to me inconceivably interesting. I should like to write that fable, but I cannot even live it; and all I could do if I related the outward course of my life would be to show how I deviated from it; though even that is impossible, since I do not know the fable or anybody who knows it. One or two stages in it I can recognize: the age of innocence and the Fall and all the dramatic consequences which issue from the Fall. But these lie behind experience, not on its surface; they are not historical events, they are stages in the fable.[1]

What is this myth, this fable, which we try to live but cannot even fully know? Muir conceives of it in partly Christian, partly Platonic terms. He speaks of a Fall from the age of innocence, and we think at once of Adam's fall —Muir's last book of verse was titled *One Foot in Eden*— and of Wordsworth's 'Intimations of Immortality' in childhood. If one is tempted to see Muir as a religious poet, and rightly so, we must be warned by his assertion, 'I do not know the fable or anybody who knows it'; for Edwin Muir, though a deeply religious spirit, remained to the end a seeker of this fable, not a receptor of the revelations of others. He is as free, and in his patient and gentle way indeed as bold, with Christian theology as he is in adapting to his own needs the patterns of mythology received from the ancient world.

As he tells us, his dreams are rooted in childhood memories, and he has not only learned from 'dreams and fantasies' but 'got great knowledge and courtesy from the dead . . . from two mainly / Who gave me birth.' We would therefore do well to look first at the life Edwin Muir knew as a child, to see 'how our first intuition of the world expands into vaster and vaster images, creating a myth which we act almost without knowing it.'

[1] *An Autobiography*, pp. 48–9.

II

His childhood on farms in the Orkney Isles, to the north of Scotland, give Muir a sense of fulfillment and perfection outside of time:

> Over the sound a ship so slow would pass
> That in the black hill's gloom it seemed to lie.
> The evening sound was smooth like sunken glass,
> And time seemed finished ere the ship passed by.

Yet even in this idyllic tranquillity there were menacing natural shapes and forces, the exactions of the weather and the frightening energy of animals:

> Those lumbering horses in the steady plough
> On the bare field—I wonder why, just now,
> They seemed terrible, so wild and strange,
> Like magic power on the stony grange.
>
> Perhaps some childish hour has come again,
> When I watched fearful, through the blackening rain
> Their hooves like pistons in an ancient mill
> Move up and down, yet seem as standing still . . .

'Our first childhood is the only time in our lives when we exist within immortality,' Muir has written, 'and perhaps all our ideas of immortality are influenced by it.' This orthodox Romantic sentiment runs strong in Muir, and strong is the memory of that time within time that was beyond time. In his poem about the horses, though, even that remembered Eden is menaced by 'conquering hooves' that 'Were ritual that turned the field to brown.' Threatened though that Eden was by those huge mechanistic beasts imposing change upon a changeless landscape, he still longs to recapture it—

> Ah, now it fades! it fades! and I must pine
> Again for that dread country crystalline,
> Where the blank field and the still-standing tree
> Were bright and fearful presences to me.

His childhood was clustered with 'bright and fearful presences.' His father was a good man, patient and loving but luckless; he would have made a fine informant had there been a Lady Gregory or a Campbell of Islay to take down his tales:

> My father's stories were mostly drawn from an earlier age, and I think must have been handed on to him by his own father. They went back to the Napoleonic wars, the press-gang, and keelhauling, which still left a memory of terror in Orkney. But in his own time he had known several witches, who had 'taken the profit of the corn,' turned the milk sour, and wrecked ships by raising storms. . . . The devil himself, as Auld Nick, sometimes came into these tales. . . . My father had also a great number of stories about the Book of Black Arts. This book could be bought only for a silver coin, and sold only for a smaller silver one. It ended in the possession of a foolish servant-girl who paid a threepenny-piece for it. It was very valuable, for it gave you all sorts of worldly power; but it had the drawback that if you could not sell it to some one before you died you would be damned. . . . My father also knew the horseman's word—that is, the word which will make a horse do anything you desire if you whisper it into its ear. . . . From what my father said I imagine that the word was a shocking one.[1]

His mother's memory too was filled with old tales of shipwrecks, phantom vessels sailing past the cliffs, nocturnal appearances of spectral Danes. The Orkneys, like Ireland or

---

[1] *An Autobiography*, pp. 12–14.

Wales, have an ancient culture, partly Gaelic but more dominantly Viking in its heritage. Had Yeats been an Orcadian, or had Muir pursued in the Orkneys such interests as Yeats followed in Ireland, there were materials aplenty in the still available traditions of those northern islands for a recreated literature of ancient myth and epic action. As late as in his father's generation one could hear in oral tradition versions of the ancient *Norse Tales* translated by Dasent, the folktale analogues of the Norse and Danish epics. The islands are honeycombed with burial mounds, Pictish barrows in which live a subterranean race of supernatural beings. There are circles of standing stones inscribed in ogham characters, and among the farmer folk, marriages and crops are controlled by the growing of the fruitful, or waning of the fruitless, moon, while fishermen are loath to start a voyage if their boat has been turned widdershins. And again, a poet with the haunted imagination of Robert Graves would have reveled in the fact that the largest island of the Orkneys is named Pomona, for the Roman goddess of fruit trees; or in memories of the witch at Stromness 'who sold favorable winds to mariners at the low charge of sixpence'; or in the knowledge that the drowned dead are turned into seals, and that sea-fairies inhabit the waters, and that fishermen can show you near Stronsay the Mermaid's Chair in which She sings, enchanting the waters. And, at New Year's Eve, Orcadians were used to troop from house to house, one dressed as the scapegoat Hobby Horse, and sing,

> Here we hae brocht our carrying-horse—
> We're a' Queen Mary's men;
> A mony a curse licht on his corse;
> He'll eat mair meat than we can get;

He'll drink mair drink than we can swink,
And that's before our Lady.

These details of Orkney folklore may well have been available to Muir: I take them from a local history published in 1868.[1] The hobby horse and his companions, who symbolize the intercourse of the dead with the living at the stroke of the New Year and whose begging of meat and drink initiates a rhyming contest with the master of the house, is in fact the subject of a fine contemporary poem, *Ballad of the Mari Lwyd* by the Welsh poet Vernon Watkins. But Muir makes none of these myths or folktales part of his own myth, as Graves or Yeats assuredly would have done. He could not assimilate naturally a heritage he felt history had denied him; differing with C. M. Grieve ('Hugh MacDiarmid') on the possibility of Scotland's contemporary writers using dialect, Muir has pointed out that the Scot habitually thinks in English but feels in Gaelic; Scottish life does not provide an organic community on which a national literature can be based.[2] These conditions account for the strange fact that 'Scotland is a country whose past has been moulded by poetry but which has produced very few poets.'[3] Unlike Yeats, who believed it his mission to create in the Irish a sense of nationality, or Graves, who had no need to concern himself with politics to discern an eternal truth, Muir feels debarred from much of his Celtic and Viking background, although his need for a unifying mythical interpretation of life is no less great than theirs.

In his poem 'Merlin,' Muir tries to summon Druidic

[1] Daniel Gorrie, *Summers and Winters in the Orkneys* (London and Edinburgh, n.d. [1868]), ch. VIII.
[2] *Scott and Scotland* (London, 1936), pp. 21–2, 14–15.
[3] *Scottish Journey* (London, 1935), p. 93.

spells such as those that worked for Yeats and Graves—
belief in the Celtic Otherworld, in the power of magic—as
an alternative to Christian responsibility for sin in a world
of change:

> O Merlin in your crystal cave
> Deep in the diamond of the day,
> Will there ever be a singer
> Whose music will smooth away
> The furrow drawn by Adam's finger
> Across the meadow and the wave?
>
> .   .   .   .
>
> Will your magic ever show
> The sleeping bride shut in her bower,
> The day wreathed in its mound of snow
> And Time locked in his tower?

Although this poem has an incantatory rhythm, the questions it asks are asked because considered impossible of fulfillment. For Muir there is no escape from time through
magic. He finds his freedom from time not in Merlin's outworn spells but through re-experiencing the Fable, as we
shall see. Muir speaks of pagan antiquity in another poem,
'The Old Gods,' which makes an interesting comparison to
Yeats's long search for what the beggar found at Windy
Gap, or to those old gods who swooped from Graves's
Rocky Acres, 'Terror for fat burghers on the plains below.' Auden, too, in 'A New Age,' conceived of the old
gods as taking violent revenge upon the reasonable era that
succeeded their reign. But in his calm sonnet Muir sees
neither the self-obliterating ecstasy of Yeats, nor the primordial avengers of Graves and Auden. Characteristically,
his view is more humane than theirs. He sees the undying
conflict between eternity and time, between perfection and

change, as having been somehow reconciled in the reign of the old gods, and this reconciliation of the opposites that make our life difficult to bear compels his wonder. Muir does not call his 'old gods and goddesses' by their names, and in the context of his other work it seems most probable that they answer not to the names of Celtic or Norse pagandom but to the same names Homer invoked. Despite his experience at first hand of Orkney folk life, when Muir thinks of antiquity it is to Troy and Greece that his mind turns.

III

We may identify his three most important themes as the Matter of Scotland, The Matter of Troy, and the Matter of the Fable. The first two are landscapes in which the protagonist's journey in the third takes place; in these real or imagined places are revealed the origin, destination, and meaning of his fabulous journey.

The Matter of Scotland is a double *donnée* for Muir. It comprises his remembered rural childhood, with its special qualities, and his adult consciousness of Scottish culture.

Muir's memories of his first ten years on the islands of Pomona and Wyre center on infantine intuitions of immortality, and on the ritualistic quality of the communal life there. His earliest memory is one of timeless tranquillity and escape from change or pain:

> I was lying in some room watching a beam of slanting light in which dusty, bright motes slowly danced and turned, while a low murmuring went on somewhere, possibly the humming of flies. My mother was in the room, but where I do not know; I was merely conscious of her as a vague, environing presence. . . . The quiet

murmuring, the slow, unending dance of the motes, the sense of deep and solid peace, have come back to me since only in dreams. This memory has a different quality from any other memory in my life. It was as if, while I lay watching that beam of light, time had not yet begun.[1]

This moment may seem, from the viewpoint of our day-life, to be a mere infantile regression, a flight from reality similar in feeling to Yeats's poems of retreat into an island hermitage and a 'bee-loud glade.' From a position of greater sympathy to Muir's view of life we may recognize a more positive significance in his timeless moment, as he himself does in 'The Myth,' a poem from his 1946 volume, *The Voyage*

> My childhood all a myth
> Enacted in a distant isle;
> Time with his hourglass and his scythe
> Stood dreaming on the dial,
> And did not move the whole day long
> That immobility might save
> Continually the dying song,
> The flower, the falling wave.

Childhood meant not only the dreamlike trance when 'time seemed finished ere the ship passed by,' but also a cycle of violence as the environing world went through its seasonal changes of begetting and slaughter:

A child could not grow up in a better place than a farm; for at the heart of human civilization is the byre, the barn, and the midden. When my father led out the bull to serve a cow brought by one of our neighbours it was a ritual act of the tradition in which we have lived for thousands of years, possessing the obviousness of a long dream from which there is no awaking. When a neighbour came

[1] *An Autobiography*, p. 18.

to stick the pig it was a ceremony as objective as the rising and setting of the sun; and though the thought never entered his mind that without that act civilization, with its fabric of customs and ideas and faiths, could not exist —the church, the school, the council chamber, the drawing-room, the library, the city—he did it as a thing that had always been done, and done in a certain way. There was a necessity in the copulation and the killing which took away the sin, or at least, by the ritual act, transformed it into a sad, sanctioned duty.[1]

It is thus the transformation through ritual of necessary action into sanctioned duty that redeems life from chaos. Such repetitions create the unchanging forms which extend through time and give us the grace of merging our individual existences with an eternal existence.

> Nothing yet was ever done
> Till it was done again,
> And no man was ever one
> Except through dead men,

for, as Muir adds in the same poem, 'Even a story to be true / Must repeat itself.' The idea of discovering freedom through participation in our underlying fable is itself frequently repeated in Muir's poems:

> We meet ourselves at every turn
> In the long country of the past.
> There the fallen are up again
> In mortality's second day,
> There the indisputable dead
> Rise in flesh more fine than clay
> And the dead selves we cast away
> In imperfection are perfected. . . .

[1] *An Autobiography*, p. 36.

There is still another way in which 'the long country of the past' had a special implication for Edwin Muir. As a Scot the past of his country meant not only his own memories but the time when Scotland was a nation; as a poet, the Scottish past suggested to him the era when the greatest Scottish poetry had flourished. And as the son of an Orcadian farmer, Muir looked not to the courtly poetry of Dunbar and Allen Ramsay, nor to the sentimental songs of Burns, but to the Scottish ballads. In a 'Complaint of the Dying Peasantry' he recalls the glory of those ballads, and now laments:

> The singing and the harping fled
> Into the silent library;
> But we are with Helen dead
> And with Sir Patrick lost at sea.

Although Muir wrote but few ballads, the tragic view of fate found in the best Scottish balladry is central to his own understanding of life. His two essays on balladry in *Latitudes* (1924) and *The Estate of Poetry* (1955, published 1962) are among the best of his critical writings. His understanding of the intensity with which passion in the ballads appears simplified because pure, came from some analogy within himself to the character of the ballad writers, and from his comprehension of the life that made the ballads possible. No one who has written about ballads has known their poetic qualities or the conditions of their origin with like authority.

By 'the estate of poetry' Muir means 'the actual response of a community to the poetry that is written for it: the effective range and influence of poetry. . . ." In his discussion of the relation of poetry to society in our own day he looks back to the ballad community, extending in time unchanged to the heroic age, as a condition when that relation was most intimate, far-reaching, and fruitful. Now, however, we no longer have, or are, a true community, an audience. Instead we have to deal with a new thing: a public. 'It seems to be an impersonal thing, a collectivity which, if you break it up, does not reduce itself to a single human being, but at best into chunks of itself, sections, percentages.' It speaks in clichés, slogans, 'the language of the third party and the onlooker.' But poetry is the instrument of the imagination, 'that power by which we apprehend living beings in their individuality, as they live and move, not as ideas or categories. . . . The public seems designed for one purpose and the poet for another.'

The ballad community on the other hand appears as analogous for society to the unfallen state of childhood for the man. Muir does not sentimentalize or falsify the primitive life of such a community. Yet here was an audience that participated in the dramatic action and cherished an art that was traditional, not 'popular' or condescending. Here poetry presents a tragic acceptance of the life of reality and its surrounding mysteries where the natural and the supernatural (whether Heaven, Hell, or pagandom) were intermingled. Here great themes were handled, at their best, with brevity, strength, and passion. To such a community poetry is 'a natural thing, an exercise of the heart and the imagination,' expressing 'an ancestral vision simplified to the last degree.' Muir bids the contemporary poet ignore the modern public, that abstraction, and write for his true audience, which he creates by assuming that it exists. Somehow, among the statistical fractions of the public, live the individual readers whose humanity he can reach only by being true to his own. The growing reputation of Muir's poems is a validation of his hope, and a testament to his heroic conception of the poet's privileged obligation.

When Muir began to write poems—he was thirty-eight years old when his *First Poems* appeared in 1925—he began by taking over to his own needs such traditional usages as the lyric soliloquy and the ballad. In fact, the major attempts in *First Poems* were three ballads, two of which he later omitted from his work; fortunately they have been restored in the posthumous *Collected Poems*. Although by no means among his faultless poems, they tell us much about the sensibility that was later refined in other poems (not ballads). One of these early efforts is a rare excursion of Muir's into writing in Scots dialect. It is called 'Ballad of the Flood':

> 'Last night I dreamed a ghastly dream,
>   Before the dirl o' day.
> A twining worm cam out the wast,
>   Its back was like the slae.
>
> 'It ganted wide as deid men gant,
>   Turned three times on its tail,
> And wrapped itsel the warld around
>   Till ilka rock did wail.

This strong opening with the supernatural serpent's sudden appearance is clearly modeled on 'The Laily Warm and the Mackrel of the Sea.' But Muir's 'twining worm' is no enchanted princess, it is an apocalyptic dragon, portending the destruction of the world. In thirty-nine stanzas Muir tells the tale of the unrepenting folk sunk in sin, and Noah's building of the Ark. With the deluge and the sailing forth his ballad successively echoes 'Sir Patrick Spens' and 'The Daemon Lover':

The first day that auld Noah sailed
  The green trees floated by.
The second day that auld Noah sailed
  He heard a woman's cry.

And tables set wi' meats were there,
  Gowd beakers set wi' wine,
And twa lovers in a silken barge
  A-sailing on the brine.

They soomed upon the lanely sea
  And sad, sad were their een.
'O tak me in thy ship, auld man,
  And I'll please thee, I ween.'

'Haud off, haud off,' auld Noah cried,
  'Ye comena in to me!
Drown deep, drown deep, ye harlot fause,
  Ye wadna list to me.'

She wrang her hands, she kissed her make,
  She lap into the sea,
But Noah turned and laughed fu' loud:
  'To hell, I wat, gang ye!

This vindictive condemnation of the sinner is the dominant tone of the ballad, not wholly ameliorated by the later echoes of 'The Ancient Mariner,' or the concluding promise of a rebirth of mankind.

'Ballad of the Flood' is what the Scots call a dour poem. It is the first of Muir's poems to retell part of the Matter of the Bible as the Matter of the Fable; most of these are, like that ballad, drawn from the Old Testament. The stories of Adam and Abraham reveal stages in Muir's fable. But more significantly, I think, 'Ballad of the Flood' shows directly the repressive and vengeful Calvinism that repelled Muir in the Scottish character. In a poem called 'Scotland 1941'—a polemical poem unusual for Muir—he writes,

We were a tribe, a family, a people.
Wallace and Bruce guard now a painted field,
And all may read the folio of our fable,
Peruse the sword, the sceptre and the shield.
A simple sky roofed in that rustic day,
The busy corn-fields and the haunted holms,   [hills]
The green road winding up the ferny brae.
But Knox and Melville clapped their preaching palms
And bundled all the harvesters away,
Hoodicrow Peden in the blighted corn
Hacked with his rusty beak the starving haulms.   [stalks]
Out of that desolation we were born.

Thus we pass from the Matter of the Fable to the Matter of Scotland. If on the one hand the Matter of Scotland gave Muir images of the unfallen purity of childhood, menaced by terrible animal powers and the turning of time, on another his fate as a Scot made Muir poignantly aware of disinheritance, of the fall from glory, as a cultural, not only a personal, theme. With scathing irony in 'Scotland 1941' he puts the Reformers Knox, Melville, and Peden at the head of his list of those who have robbed his land of the unity of culture enjoyed when 'We were a tribe, a family, a people.' Later in the poem he attacks the mean materialism by which the Scots completed their own spiritual disfranchisement: We, he writes, who

> crush the poet with an iron text,
> How could we read our souls and learn to be?

> .   .   .   .

> Now smoke and dearth and money everywhere,
> Mean heirlooms of each fainter generation,
> And mummied housegods in their musty niches,
> Burns and Scott, sham bards of a sham nation,
> And spiritual defeat wrapped warm in riches,
> No pride but pride of pelf.

To the theme of the Fall (whether of man or of a nation) we shall return, but first let us follow the consequences of the Calvinism that Muir exhibits in 'Ballad of the Flood' but spurns in 'Scotland 1941.' This theme recurs in one of his most memorable poems. Characteristically for Muir, there the power of the statement derives from the transformation of the theme into a complex of images which came to him in dreams and seem to have nothing to do with the circumstances in his actual life that drove them into his unconscious. The poem is 'The Combat,' recounting a horrible nightmare of defenselessness in unmitigated battle with aggressive power, yet all but victorious in its capacity for eternal suffering. These abstract qualities are imagined as beasts, one an allegorical gryphon, the other a soft and furry slug. The stanza is a five-line two-rhyme unit, in merry octosyllabics, jigging along as unadapted to its grim tale as is the ballad meter to its. There is something indefinably terrifying in this vision of struggle without end between the unappeasably destructive element and the undefeatable passivity of pure suffering:

> It was not meant for human eyes,
> That combat on the shabby patch
> Of clods and trampled turf that lies
> Somewhere beneath the sodden skies
> For eye of toad or adder to catch.
>
> And having seen it I accuse
> The crested animal in his pride,
> Arrayed in all the royal hues
> Which hide the claws he well can use
> To tear the heart out of the side.

'The Combat' seems in fact to be the crystallization in verse of several memories and dreams, the memories dreamlike, the dreams long remembered. One is of two animals in endlessly recurrent battle. This seems the direct source of the poem, but its real source lies behind the dream. Later in his *Autobiography* he recalls two sordid incidents in Glasgow. A large, muscular woman is pummeling a 'little, shrinking man,' cursing him for having seduced her and started her ruin; 'I do not know how it ended,' he writes, 'for the thud of the big, red-haired fist on the man's face sickened me. The crowd looked on without interfering.' And in another crowd he came on a young man systematically punching another who made no effort to defend himself. When queried by a bystander 'Why dinna you let the chap alane? He hasna hurt you?' the assailant replied, 'I ken he hasna hurt me, but I'm gaun tae hurt him!' and continued to strike his unresisting enemy.

These dismal scenes struck Muir 'as if they were an answer to some question which, without my knowing it, had been troubling me.' What is behind these dreams and memories is the merciless suffering which his brother Johnnie had endured in a protracted death from a brain tumor.

> In both these memories there was the quality of Scottish Calvinism: the serious young man's reply had the unanswerable, arbitrary logic of predestination; and the encounter of the red-haired woman with her seducer, when both were so greatly changed that their original sin might have been committed in another world, and yet lived on, there in that slum, was a sordid image of fate as Calvin saw it. Somewhere in these two incidents there was a virtue of a dreary kind, behind the flaunted depravity: a recognition of logic and reality.[1]

In the poem the inexorable fight goes on, but the victor cannot win, the victim slips away, until once more they meet,

[1] *An Autobiography*, p. 107.

And all began. The stealthy paw
Slashed out and in. Could nothing save
These rags and tatters from the claw?
Nothing. And yet I never saw
A beast so helpless and so brave.

And now, while the trees stand watching, still
The unequal battle rages there.
The killing beast that cannot kill
Swells and swells in his fury till
You'd almost think it was despair.

It seems an impertinence to extract significances beyond
those given by the poem itself, and they are the more compelling for growing not out of causes but out of being.
There is no motive attributed to either beast, they simply
act out their natures. While the context of Calvinist predes-
tination is suggested by Muir's *Autobiography*, in his book
The Labyrinth this poem is closely followed by one called
'The Interrogation.' There, at the border of a country (it is
surely Czechoslovakia after the Communist *coup d'état*),
when 'We could have crossed the road but hesitated, / And
then came the patrol'. . . .

We have stood and answered through the standing day
And watched across the road beyond the hedge
The careless lovers in pairs go by,
Hand linked in hand, wandering another star,
So near we could shout to them. We cannot choose
Answer or action here,
Though still the careless lovers saunter by
And the thoughtless field is near.
We are on the very edge,
Endurance almost done,
And still the interrogation is going on.

Between the 'careless lovers' in 'the thoughtless field' and the unwitting victims of suspicion and hatred there is no speech. Muir's compassion is moved by impersonal vengefulness menacing the dignity of the individual, whether its source be an authoritarian religion or a police state. Man's individuality is precious to Muir, for it is as individuals, if only as victims, that we can retrace the outlines of the fable, and so be delivered from chaos and suffering into the knowledge of grace.

I V

A second early ballad is among his most successful poems. The origin of his 'Ballad of Hector in Hades' was the memory of a childhood fight with another boy. In a period of childish aggressiveness, Muir had had an earlier fight with Freddie Sinclair over possession of a knife, which he had won. But their second encounter was a debacle.

> What I was so afraid of I did not know; it was not Freddie, but something else; yet I could no more have turned and faced him than I could have stopped the sun revolving. As I ran I was conscious only of a few huge things, monstrously simplified and enlarged: Wyre, which I felt under my feet, the other islands lying round, the sun in the sky, and the sky itself, which was quite empty. For almost thirty years afterwards I was so ashamed of that moment of panic that I did not dare to speak of it to anyone, and drove it out of my mind. I was seven at the time, and in the middle of my guilty fears. On that summer afternoon they took the shape of Freddie Sinclair, and turned him into a terrifying figure of vengeance.[1]

Muir exorcised that fear thirty years later 'in a poem describing Achilles chasing Hector round Troy,' where Hec-

[1] *An Autobiography*, p. 42.

tor returns 'after his death to run the deadly race over again.' Their encounter is described with that scrupulous attention to the minutest tactile details ('The grasses puff a little dust / Where my footsteps fall') that obsess the combatants in the tales of Stephen Crane and Hemingway, or in Robert Graves's *Good-Bye to All That*. At the reenactment of the fatal blow,

> The sky with all its clustered eyes
>   Grows still with watching me,
> The flowers, the mounds, the flaunting weeds
>   Wheel slowly round to see.
>
> Two shadows racing on the grass,
>   Silent and so near,
> Until his shadow falls on mine.
>   And I am rid of fear.
>
> The race is ended. Far away
>   I hang and do not care,
> While round bright Troy Achilles whirls
>   A corpse with streaming hair.

'I could at last see the incident whole by seeing it as happening, on a great and tragic scale, to someone else.' This is the transforming and therapeutic power of the imagination, dependent upon unconscious 'solutions of the past projected into the present, deliberately announced as if they were a sibylline declaration that life has a meaning . . . depending on a different system of connected relations from that by which we consciously live.' Not that Muir accepts the proposition Graves was expounding at about the time this poem was written, that such therapeutic power is the purpose of poetry for both poet and reader.[1] Yet this

---

[1] *Transition* (London and New York, 1926), p. 166.

curative imaginative power to come to terms with fears and repossess the wholeness of life by a transcendent conception of destiny makes available to Muir the most precious material from which poetry may be made. When, as in this ballad, the material and the means of its expression coalesce, he writes his most valuable poems.

'Ballad of Hector in Hades' is the earliest use Muir makes of the Matter of Troy. His use of this Homeric material is markedly different from Yeats's. The conception of Helen by Jove upon Leda does not, in Muir's mind, mark the supersession of an epoch; nor is he drawn to Helen as a heraldic representation of mortal beauty in immortal dress. It is the destruction of Troy and the return of Odysseus to the faithful Penelope which fascinate Muir, the themes of mortal defeat and predestined journey. Neither does Muir think of himself as a modern Homer, as did Yeats. A modest poet, as he was a modest man, Muir aims only to capture or recapture intimations of life's meaning from what 'sibylline declarations' come to him. Although his imagination is seemingly passive, awaiting the revelation of its materials, he is in fact boldly synoptic in the expression of his themes once they announce themselves.

In his scrupulous study of Muir, R. P. Blackmur has likened the poet to Virgil.[1] The analogy, though at first surprising, bears out well our perception that Muir is among the last—indeed perhaps *the* last—of poets who can conceive of history as a continuous reiteration of human destiny. The Rome of which Muir is chronicler is not an empire but a faith—I do not mean the Roman Church, but faith in the continuity of Christendom as a mode of feeling, as a civilization. Blackmur takes courage for his thesis from

---

[1] 'Edwin Muir: Between the Tiger's Paws,' in D. C. Allen, ed., *Four Poets on Poetry* (Baltimore, 1959).

Muir's assertion, at the end of the *Autobiography*, that he 'discovered in Italy that Christ had walked on earth, and also that things truly made preserve themselves through time in the first freshness of their nature.' So the northern child of Calvinism was in middle age awakened to a sensuous as well as a spiritual perception of what the Mediterranean world might take for granted.

I would modify our view of Muir as Virgil's heir by acknowledging his sympathy, or his bias, in using the Tale of Troy. It is true that Aeneas was a Trojan, but *The Aeneid* is, of course, more concerned with the hero's triumphs in Latium than with the destruction of his first homeland. Blackmur, commenting on the 'Ballad of Hector in Hades,' observes that 'within our psyches we all run in great heat around that wall, and it makes little difference whether the other fellow is Hector or Achilles.' Yet Muir distinctly sees himself not as Achilles. As the now-vanquished former champion he is Hector, and in other poems he is a Trojan slave serving the victorious Greeks, or a mad old man left behind by the conquering Argives to live in the sewers of ruined Ilium until tortured to death by wandering brigands. I think that as a Scotsman Muir found his sympathy not with the triumphant imperialist Greeks who dominated the ancient world, but with the futile heroism of the defeated people. Allowing for stylistic alternation in these two passages between the Eliotic and rhetorical, a similar tone of lamentation appears in each:

> The rat-hordes,
> Moving, were grey dust shifting in grey dust.
> Proud history has such sackends.

> Such wasted bravery idle as a song,
> Such hard-won ill might prove Time's verdict wrong,
> And melt to pity the annalist's iron tongue.

The first is from 'Troy,' the second from 'Scotland 1941.'
As Muir interpreted her fate, Troy offered images of a
fallen city, a society destroyed despite its valor as much by
its own natural laws as by the power of its enemies. His
sense of Scotland's history as well as his own experiences
made Muir acutely aware of social inequities and of individual responsibility for them. His *Scottish Journey*, a
book describing Scotland in the depression, should rank
with Orwell's chronicles of that decade. Like attitudes toward society and history inform Muir's poems on Troy.
The soliloquist of 'A Trojan Slave' tells us that history itself is a reduplication of fate, just as Hector relives his
dying. The speaker, now enslaved to Greeks, was formerly
enslaved by the Trojans, who may well have fallen because
'they would not arm us, and preferred / Troy's ruin lest a
slave should snatch a sword.' This poem (published in
1937) clearly speaks with the same sense of injustice that
runs through *Scottish Journey* and the early chapters of
Muir's *Autobiography*. In his imagination Scotland's fate
has been endured before, on the Trojan plains.

V

In Muir's thought both the Matter of Scotland and the
Matter of Troy are subordinate to his most insistent theme,
the Matter of the Fable, which indeed the lesser themes exemplify. In poems in which he tried to discover the fable
independently of the concrete situations these lesser themes
provided, however, Muir often wrote gropingly or ab-
stractly. He felt early the compulsion toward an intuitive
understanding of destiny, but what full course of action
the fable required was not revealed to him until the end of
his life. Thus its first treatment, in the early 'Ballad of the
Soul,' is, as Kathleen Raine observes,

halting and obscure; the archetypal images come so thick
and fast that they fail by reason of their too great purity,
their insufficiently incarnated quality. Yet few poets can
ever have started to write from an inspiration more au-
thentically imaginative.[1]

In this early ballad Muir imagines the world's destruction
by fire and flood, then in journeys reminiscent of 'The Ancient Mariner' he sees or takes part in apocalyptic struggles
(similar to that later in 'The Combat'). The phantasmagora
dissolves in a promised rebirth, but when the protagonist
questions its meaning 'then the fading dream / Had nothing
more to say.'

Life itself is the journey Muir's imagination records, and
its destination is hidden in winding corridors and narrow
places, though hinted at in recurrent glimpses of a perfection and a peace independent of the changes wrought by
time. The pilgrimage is rendered larger than reality in 'The
Mythical Journey' (1937); now the episodes, though as
'archetypal' as any in 'Ballad of the Soul,' are more effective because drawn from recognizable mythologies rather
than the private symbolization of dreams.

'The Mythical Journey' takes mankind from its origin
'First in the North,' amidst malevolent nature and bitter
spirits—'Tall women against the sky with heads covered, /
The witch's house. . . .' Escaping from 'The twice-dead
castle on the swamp-green mound,' we enter a natural
world of plenitude and freedom.

> But the ship hastened on and brought him to
> The towering walls of life and the great kingdom
> Where long he wandered seeking that which sought him. . . .

Now we seem poised for the revelation of who it is we
seek. Once that were known, man's intellect could come

---

[1] 'The Journey from Eden,' *New Statesman* (23 April 1960), p. 595.

into conscious activity and construct a philosophy of life and a theology of supernatural reality which can be transmitted from one to another generation. Without such certainty we are each individual seekers, retracing in our aloneness the archetypal processes that can only be intuitively apprehended, not consciously understood. The one who is both sought and seeker, this poem tells us, remains

> Beyond all knowledge. Only the little hills
> Head-high, and the winding valleys,
> Turning, returning, till there grew a pattern,
> And it was held. And there stood both in their stations
> With the hills between them. And that was the meaning.

As a poetry of revelation these lines are sadly wanting in intensity; the abstractness of the situation makes nearly impossible the expression of the thought in images of tactile reality, and the verse rhythms are accordingly slack. Introduction of the traditional image of the Tree of Knowledge in an unexpected way makes for a livelier if inconclusive ending:

> That which he had sought, that which had sought him,
> Glittering in death. And all the dead scattered
> Like fallen stars, clustered like leaves hanging
> From the sad boughs of the mountainous tree of Adam
> Planted far down in Eden. And on the hills
> The gods reclined and conversed with each other
> From summit to summit.
> Conclusion
> Without fulfilment. . . .
> Beneath its branches
> He builds in faith and doubt his shaking house.

'The Mythical Journey' begins before legend and concludes 'Without fulfilment' before history has begun. What made possible Muir's success in his later poems was

the slowly nurtured encompassing of actuality by his imagination so fully committed to the archetypal rather than to
the accidental. The poems in *One Foot in Eden* accept
reality—'This is a difficult country, and our home.' The
title poem of that book welcomes it, for 'Strange blessings
never in Paradise / Fall from these beclouded skies.' The
Fortunate Fall places man in the grip of time, of history, of
change, but also makes possible 'hope and faith and pity
and love.' Muir's *donnée* is to see life as unified and history
as continuous in the great clarification of the journey of the
soul. We each fall anew from Eden and retrace the long
voyage through the narrow place and the perilous place in
search of the sufficient place. The journey may be through
the life-long labyrinth, or through the adventurous seas
that detained Odysseus on his homeward way; when all is
done and sung we return to the sacred place from which
our life began. These themes, frequently reiterated, are not,
however, in themselves the guarantees of successful poems,
whatever their validity psychologically. For the fable needs
at every point the story, to dramatize its incarnation and
make its action relevant to human life. The story must redeem the fable from abstraction. When there is no historical reality in which the fable is both concealed and revealed, no tactile world, no solid landscape, no living characters nor believable chimaeras, in short no story, there is
only the fable. And as the fate of the word itself suggests,
fables are illusory and not to be believed but for the sake of
the moral—which is to say, we have an imaginative action
inferior to the incarnation of truth in life. But when Muir
fuses his fable with his stories, whether of his own remembered childhood on the farm above the bay, or of Hector
and Priam and the crazed survivor of the fallen city, or of
Odysseus re-entering the hall where time has been woven

and unwound, or of Old Testament patriarchs or the dreamed combat of beasts, the shape of life and the meaning become clear together.

Muir's fable resembles the Christian story—without the Redeemer. Perhaps it is his unexorcised Calvinism (as well as Romantic longing) which makes the Fall, rather than Christ's rising, the moment of greatest psychological power in the pattern. But if Muir is a recusant Calvinist he is so in his own fashion; he cannot believe in a redemption through another's sacrifice—it must be won by his own sufferings, whose meaning he must seek himself. Each man is his own Adam, and Second Adam. In Muir we find religious feeling, religious conviction unsupported by religious dogma. Repelled by the inexorable and unforgiving logic of Calvinism, and distrusting equally the facile emotionalism of evangelical Christianity, Muir, with the aid of psychoanalysis, discovered a secular myth of divine things. This he held with piety and hope, evoked by painful processes of self-knowledge and patient receptivity to transcendent truths which come not from the exercise of will or reason but from the submerged treasuries of mankind's common dream.

Though indeed a gentle and forgiving man, Muir is neither a theological thinker nor a programmatic ethical poet. He tells us neither what we should believe nor how we should behave. His poetry has no intellectual platform, his myth requires no revision of history, as do those of Yeats and Graves. It is partly a matter of temperament; Muir is a patient extractor of meaning from event, not an imposer of willed unity upon experienced chaos. If his result is seemingly more tenuous than Yeat's intellectual suit of mail or than Graves's all-absorbing psychomachia, Muir does not require of us such self-surrender, such undeviating

acquiescence to his own particular view of reality. He tells
us his fable and his story, and when in his poems the two
coalesce

> you shall know
> Before you Troy goes up in fire,
> And you shall walk the Trojan streets
> When home are sailed the murdering fleets,
> Priam shall be a little boy,
> Time shall cancel time's deceits,
> And you shall weep for grief and joy
> To see the whole world perishing
> Into everlasting spring.

He compels our assent not by the force of an argument but
by the clarity with which he has illuminated a part of the
deepest truth our culture can give us.

INDEX